Adolf Hitler

A Portrait

ADOLF HITLER

A PORTRAIT

Michael FitzGerald

SPELLMOUNT

British Library Cataloguing in Publication Data:
A catalogue record for this book is available
from the British Library

Copyright © Michael FitzGerald 2006

ISBN 1-86227-322-7

Published in the UK in 2006 by
Spellmount Limited
The Mill, Brimscombe Port
Stroud, Gloucestershire GL5 2QG

Tel: 01453 883300
Fax: 01453 883233
E-mail: enquiries@spellmount.com
Website: www.spellmount.com

1 3 5 7 9 8 6 4 2

The right of Michael FitzGerald to be identified
as the author of this work has been asserted by him
in accordance with the Copyright, Designs
and Patents Act 1988

Printed in Great Britain by
Oaklands Book Services
Stonehouse, Gloucestershire GL10 3RQ

Contents

Introduction

The career of Adolf Hitler was one of the most extraordinary in world history. He rose from abject poverty to the very summit of political power. Within a few months of his appointment as Chancellor of Germany in 1933 he showed a ruthlessness and determination that astonished the world. He destroyed the existing democratic institutions and forced the giants of German capitalism to submit to state control. In spite of coming to power as the head of a coalition government containing only three Nazis, his political skill completely outmanoeuvred his opponents. At first they were stunned into a shocked silence, then into resigned obedience to his will, and finally to something like the enthusiasm shown by the masses. Even hardened generals and aristocrats sure of their own superiority fell victim to the belief that somehow Hitler would find a solution to every problem.

Few people have been so hated and so loved. Millions of people saw him as their saviour, and National Socialism became for a time a new religion. No other political leader of this century still provokes such a violent response, not even Stalin. Although Marxism – the other major new religion of the last 200 years – still has millions of followers, it was never so bound up with one person, except under Stalin's and Mao's rule. Nazi ideology was associated with Hitler to such an extent that the movement was often described as Hitlerism. While Stalin also had the same dubious distinction, it was and is possible for people to believe in Marxism while rejecting Stalin. Though this is partly because Communism survived in Russia from 1917 to 1991, whereas National Socialism flourished for twelve brief years, it is also the result of Hitler's mistakes. His own personal defects are largely to blame for the collapse of National Socialism. On his death, his movement – which had held the allegiance of millions – died with him. Marxism and even Fascism are still 'live' ideologies in a way that National Socialism is not. The contemporary racist parties, even in Europe, owe almost nothing to the Nazis.

Though National Socialism left no legacy behind it, and few who truly mourned its passing or wished for its return, the figure of Hitler remains, and continues to fascinate new generations. This is not simply the result of his military success, although that is unparalleled in modern European history. Somehow this shabby, bohemian character of unquestionable mental instability still manages to grip the imagination of people. Hitler's vision was a powerful one, but its dark side was so appalling that it was bound to fail. Like Genghis Khan or Attila the Hun, Hitler left a trail of corpses across the lands he occupied. Like theirs, his name lives on, but only as an almost cartoon-like universal destroyer. Only through the eternal fascination which evil exerts on the human race does Hitler's 'fame' survive. He saw himself as another Charlemagne or Barbarossa, yet it is as Bluebeard or Jack the Ripper that he is widely remembered.

Whatever else may be said of him, Hitler had the power to move people and win their loyalty and trust. Such a surprising fact cannot be explained away simply by fear. However hard it may be for us to believe it today, Hitler was unquestionably loved and admired by millions. How was it that so many came to love him? Even though the full scale of the genocide programme against the Jews and gypsies was probably not known to them, that violence was rampant they certainly *did* know. Yet the astonishing loyalty and love which Hitler commanded lasted almost to the very last days of the war. How could a mass murderer command such genuine and extraordinary affection and trust? To answer this question above all is the primary purpose of this book.

CHAPTER I

The Mind of Adolf Hitler

There have been many tyrants in the course of world history, but there has only been one Adolf Hitler. No one before or since has gone from park bench to master of Europe. How was it that a semi-literate down and out from a small town in Austria came to be the leader of Germany and, for a time, ruler of a vast empire? People have pointed to Germany's defeat in the First World War, to the economic troubles which handicapped the German nation for most of the 1920s and the early 1930s, even to sinister plots by capitalists, aristocrats and Communists.

There is some truth in all these explanations. However, one of the most important factors lies in the political skill of Hitler himself. Without that, even though the Nazis might still have been a force in Germany, they could never have climbed to the very top of the tree. It is not easy to imagine any other German politician of the time threatening war and then, when his bluff was finally called, persevering with it as successfully as Hitler. Not even Napoleon enjoyed the enormous military success that Hitler did until 1942.

It is hardly surprising that myths and legends have grown up around such an extraordinary man as Hitler. The simple facts are remarkable enough, and often more bizarre than the inventions. Some of the stories about Hitler were of course fabricated deliberately, both by the Nazis and their opponents.

The historian who wants to establish the truth about Hitler faces many problems. There is a genuine shortage of research material in some areas. Archives and witnesses were also lost during the Second World War. Most of all, even now many completely untrue ideas about Hitler are still believed by people. For example, many people believe that his name was Schicklgrueber. In fact, the family name was changed to Hitler some years before his birth. In the same way, the completely false idea that he was a house painter, or even a paperhanger, is still widely believed. The fact is that Hitler was an artist, and one of the subjects that he painted was houses.

One of the most curious problems for the historian concerns the question of Hitler's 'racial' origins. In spite of the enormous importance that he attached to an Aryan family tree, Hitler's own bloodline is altogether obscure. The two main theories are those put forward by Hans Frank, the governor-general of Poland under the Nazis, and the historian Werner Maser. Frank, who was actually asked by Hitler to investigate the matter of the Fuehrer's racial origins, stated firmly that his grandfather was Jewish. [1]

There is no doubt that Hitler's father was illegitimate. The name of his mother, Maria, is known, but the identity of his father is quite uncertain. Maria worked at Graz as a cook for a family by the name of Frankenberger. She became pregnant and was paid a paternity allowance by the Frankenbergers. Correspondence between the family and Hitler's grandmother also survived, the tone of which implied that her child had been conceived 'in circumstances which rendered the Frankenbergers liable to pay a paternity allowance,' as Frank put it. He believed that the family's son was the father of Maria's child, and therefore Hitler's grandfather.[2]

Franz Jetzinger, one of the leading authorities on the early life of Hitler, disputes Frank's story. He also points out that, even if it was true, Frankenberger is not necessarily a Jewish name. Frank (and Hitler?) may have simply assumed that it was.[3] Maser, another historian who has researched this subject extensively, believes that the real secret of the Hitler family origins was not a racial one but the existence of an incestuous relationship. Hitler's father, he claims, was his own wife's uncle, and Hitler's mother his own cousin.[4]

There are certainly difficulties to be faced with both theories. The very hint of an incestuous liaison in his family would certainly have damaged Hitler's prospects during his pursuit of power, especially in his own power base of Catholic Bavaria. On the other hand, Maser can produce no evidence in support of his claims. The strongest point in his favour is that when Maria married a miller's apprentice called Hiedler, her husband's brother, Maser's candidate for the father of her child, fostered her illegitimate son.

However, the fanatical nature of Hitler's anti-Semitism, which exceeded the ravings of the racists with whom he associated and by whom he was influenced, was unique even among Nazi leaders. The extent to which he links Jewishness with sexual pollution of Aryan females is also striking, as is the vivid and intensely excitable way in which he spoke and wrote about it. It seems hard not to believe that some personal motive must have been involved. The image of the Jewish male as wanton seducer of Nordic womanhood is one that haunted Hitler all his life. However ridiculous and obscene these fantasies rightly seem to us now, they must have come from somewhere. It is also quite remarkable that, in spite of the emphasis which he placed upon clear documentary proof of 'Aryan blood' he was completely unable to produce any such evidence in his own case. Indeed, the event that led Hitler to commission an investigation into his origins by Frank was the receipt of a blackmail letter sent to him in 1930 by the son of a half-brother. This threatened to reveal 'very definite facts concerning our family history.' This could have been about the alleged incest, of course. In view of the emphasis on anti-Semitism in his campaigns, though, Hitler might well have seen the hint of Jewish ancestry as a more devastating threat. Hitler certainly knew of, or at least suspected, some dark secret concerning his own origins. In a conversation with his nephew William Hitler, he said nervously: 'These people must not know who I am. They must not know from where and from what family I come.'[5]

There is, then, some pretty strong circumstantial and also psychological evidence in favour of the theory that Hitler either knew or at least believed that his grandfather was Jewish. It is also clear that the paternity payments from the Frankenberger family to their servant would not have been made without a reason. It is, of course, possible that Maria tricked her employers into believing that their son was the father of her child. They would hardly have paid up, though, unless they were in no position to make a credible denial. On balance, then, Frank's account, which he had absolutely no reason to invent and which seems quite plausible psychologically, is the more likely interpretation of the curious mystery of the origins of the Hitler family. [6]

Whoever his real grandfather may have been, Hitler's father changed his name to that of his foster father in 1877. Owing to a clerical error, his name was now recorded, not as Hiedler, but Hitler. Hitler himself later remarked that it had been a fortunate mistake, as Hiedler did not have the strong sound of Hitler. Whatever the truth about the origins of his family, there is no doubt that Adolf Hitler hated his father with a more than common hatred. After he had conquered Austria in 1938 he turned the village of Döllersheim into an army training camp. The tanks of the Wehrmacht destroyed his father's birthplace and his grandmother's grave.[7] However irrational the nature of Hitler's resentment against his family, hatred as deep as that is clearly rooted in something deeper than simple personal dislike.

When Hitler started to become a national figure from 1923 onwards, he set out to create a largely fictitious account of his childhood and youth. According to the legends, he was a leader of men, physically strong, and academically the best pupil in the schools that he attended. The truth is that he was a lonely, moody, unpopular boy, lazy and undisciplined. His school record ranged from the average to the abysmal. Even in German he was regarded as a poor pupil. His best subjects were gymnastics and history. [8]

By the time Hitler left school, his father had died. Only his mother remained, and she tried hard but vainly to impose some discipline upon her son. He was already determined to become an artist. The 16-year-old

3

Hitler was full of romantic notions about the art world. He had a vision of a free and easy bohemian life, together with the seductive promise of fame and fortune as a great painter and architect. His mother fought him at first, but gradually stopped even trying to get her son to look at the world in a more realistic manner. She had troubles enough of her own as it was. Two years later she was to die of cancer. In the end, Hitler won. He went to Vienna in 1907, at the age of 19, to enrol for the painting course at the Academy of Fine Arts. However, he failed the entrance examination. His mother's death followed soon after, the effort of controlling a wilful and headstrong son on top of her illness having become too much for her.

Hitler was alone in the world now, living on his father's legacy, his mother's estate, social security payments obtained fraudulently and financial support from his aunt. The combined total of all these sums amounted to some £50 a month, a very good income for those days. In spite of this Hitler could not manage money at all. Within two years he had squandered his inheritance.

His childhood friend August Kubizek relates how Hitler used to stay in bed until midday, then go for a walk in the park and sit up till late at night devising ambitious architectural designs. He also visited the opera frequently, Wagner's music being his first love. On one occasion Kubizek and Hitler attended a performance of Wagner's early opera *Rienzi*, the story of which concerns a medieval Roman citizen from a humble background who became for a time the leader of the city of Rome. As Kubizek relates, Hitler was electrified by the opera. 'Like a dammed-up flood bursting through the embankment, the words came rushing out of him. In grandiose, stirring images he painted for me his future and the future of his people.'[9] Years later Kubizek reminded Hitler of this moment in his early life. The Fuehrer remarked excitedly 'At that hour it all began!'[10] The effect of *Rienzi* was twofold. In the first place, it led to Hitler's attempt to compose an opera of his own, on a subject once considered but rejected by Wagner himself. He also tried to write dramas based on the old German sagas. [11]

The most fundamental effect that *Rienzi* had upon Hitler was to spur him into thinking about politics, a subject he had taken little interest in previously. Hitler began sounding off to Kubizek and anyone else who would listen. He attacked landlords, civil servants, the educational system, the Habsburg monarchy and the Austrian aristocracy. His political prejudices in those days were in the direction of socialism. It was at this time that he began watching the massed street processions of the Viennese Social Democrats, and he observed how effectively large crowds could both intimidate opposition and attract support for the cause being promoted. This insight was certainly one that stayed with him and led him to set up the SA as a kind of street army when he finally decided to make the Nazi Party his full-time career.

However, Hitler's political dreams had to be put on ice for some considerable time, as a result of his sudden descent into poverty. Having finally spent the whole of his inheritance, he found himself reduced to sleeping on park benches in Vienna. When winter came he managed to be accepted by a charity ward at Meidling.[12] Hitler later claimed that during this period of his life he had been working on building sites, and that his encounters there with Communists had first led to his political awakening. Extensive research on this aspect of his career has demonstrated that this was, quite simply, a lie. Hitler never did a day's work in his life, in the ordinary sense of the word. He was of course an artist, though rarely sold any of his work. His only other jobs were as a soldier during the First World War, an agent for German military intelligence after it and then a full-time politician.[13]

Historians have consistently underrated the extent to which Hitler's vision of himself as a great artist influenced every aspect of his life. Their attitudes have ranged from the dismissive comment that Hitler should have stuck to art as a hobby, to completely omitting any reference to it when they write about his life, or even tired repetition of the long-discredited myth that he was a housepainter or paperhanger. When he finally took control of Germany, art and architecture were high on Hitler's list of priorities. He designed plans for the buildings and cultural centres that he intended to create once he had won the war. To fail to see that Hitler's conception of himself was as an artist first and foremost is to miss one of the most basic and important aspects of his psychological make-up. Hitler saw himself, not as a politician or even a military genius, but as partly a priest and partly an artist whose job was to renew the German people. Hitler's vision of himself as an artist dominated his whole approach to both politics and life.

At this moment in his life, however, Hitler was an artist who had fallen on very hard times. The charity ward was a step up from the park bench, but only just. He lost touch with his childhood friend Kubizek, feeling too ashamed of his present situation to face him. The puzzled Kubizek searched for him for a while, but then gave up. He had no idea of his friend's dramatic descent into the world of the dosshouse. [14]

Hitler's only source of income now was his fraudulently obtained orphan's pension, given to him on the understanding that he was an art student. He simply lied about it to the authorities, pretending that he had been accepted and was still studying. To supplement the meagre sum he received, he went out on to the streets and begged passers-by for money. At this desperate time in his fortunes, he made two friends in the charity ward. One was a tramp by the name of Reinhold Hanisch and the other a Hungarian Jew named Neumann. Hanisch describes Hitler as wearing a frock coat that reached down below his knees, given to him by Neumann.

As for his general appearance, Hanisch tells us, 'From under a greasy black derby hat, his hair hung over his coat collar and a thick ruff of fluffy beard encircled his chin.'[15] Hanisch, who did casual work from time to time, tried to persuade Hitler to find some form of employment. The future Fuehrer refused violently, declaring that he would never take what he described as 'a bread-and-butter job.' Instead, he just drifted aimlessly.

'There were days,' Hanisch wrote, 'when he simply refused to work. He would hang around night shelters, living on the bread and soup he got there, and discussing politics, often getting into heated arguments.'[16] We shall have a closer look at these political discussions shortly. In the meantime we will examine the way in which Hanisch's influence on Hitler started to improve his present situation. To begin with, Hanisch persuaded him to move into a hostel for men. This was a marginal improvement on the charity ward. The money to make this move possible came from Hitler's aunt. Hanisch, who was quite enterprising for a tramp, had also discovered that Hitler was an artist. While he painted his views, Hanisch went out on to the streets and sold them, while taking a percentage of the profits.

By this time Hanisch was Hitler's only friend. Always introverted and difficult, Hitler's continuous association with down and outs was now becoming very hard for him to accept. He tried to get through this period of his life by seeing himself as an artistic genius who had been forced by poverty to live in the gutter and among the dregs of society. From this period his tendency to snobbery began. In the men's hostel, Hitler had only his dreams for the future and memories of the past to console him.

In *Mein Kampf* Hitler declared, for once entirely truthfully: 'During those years, a view of life and a definite outlook on the world took shape in my mind. These became the granite basis of my conduct at that time. Since then I have extended that foundation only very little, and I have changed nothing in it.'[17] This passage has often been challenged by commentators, both on the grounds that Hitler did in fact change his mind occasionally and, more importantly, that National Socialism did not spring up overnight fully-fledged from his brain. However, these objections miss the point. Hitler is not writing about ideas as such; he is referring to a way of life, an attitude of mind. From that attitude he most certainly never deviated. Of course his intellectual development was influenced by a large number of people. Even Hitler never denied that. His attitude towards life, however, as a struggle for survival in which only the strong stayed alive, never left him at any time. That is what Hitler meant by the passage quoted above.

As the historian Francis King pointed out, he also meant anti-Semitism. Once he had adopted that as his principal platform, he never once deviated from it under any circumstances. He showed none of the hesitancy about the policy that Himmler displayed towards it, the concealed contempt for it manifested by Goebbels and the open derision that Goering occasionally ventured to show for it. If there was one 'principle' in his life from which Hitler never wavered, it was his hatred of the Jews.[18]

In many ways this is surprising. We have already seen that Neumann the Hungarian Jew was one of his few close friends. Hitler himself also recorded, obviously truthfully, that his parents were politically liberal and that he never once heard the word Jew mentioned in their home. He even admitted that at first he did not know what a Jew was. It was in Vienna that he first met Orthodox Jews, an event which astonished him.

One day I suddenly encountered a phenomenon in a long caftan and wearing black sidelocks. My first thought was: Is this a Jew? I watched the man stealthily, but the longer I looked upon this curious countenance the more the question shaped itself in my mind: Is this a German? As always in such cases I turned to books to help me resolve the question.[19]

He began by reading some anti-Semitic pamphlets written by the notorious Adolf Lanz, who liked to be known as Baron Lanz von Liebenfels, though he was in no way entitled to style himself thus. Lanz's broadsheets were issued under the title *Ostarat Briefbucherei der blonden Mannesrechtler*, which means 'newsletters of the blonde fighters for the rights of man.' The views of Lanz struck Hitler as a revelation. Instead of wondering gloomily why he was hungry, lonely and unrecognised, he could now provide a 'rationale' for his own failure. It was obvious that he was an Aryan, and as such, the natural enemy of the Jews. This not only immediately elevated him in his own eyes, since he was at least an aristocrat by race as an Aryan rather than a Jew, but it also led him straight down the path of the conspiracy theory. Hitler saw himself as an artistic genius, yet he was not only unknown, but also poor and despised by the very middle classes to which he aspired and to which he was convinced that he belonged. Now, for the first time, everything became suddenly clear to him. He was the victim of a Jewish conspiracy.

I have dealt with Lanz and his decisive influence upon Hitler in a previous book. Here it is only necessary to add that the type of racism that Lanz preached was not simply the normal anti-Semitism of the gutters. It was based through and through on a mish-mash of occult fantasies. For a more comprehensive account of Lanz's bizarre delusions, and the extent to which he influenced Hitler, the reader is advised to consult my earlier work.[20] The relevant features here are that he believed that Jews were literally not human beings, but the offspring of human relations with apes. From an early period Lanz advocated outlawing sexual relations between Jews and Aryans, forced labour in concentration camps for 'impure' breeds, and the ultimate goal of the complete extermination of the Jews on earth as a people. Even from this brief summary, Lanz's influence on Hitler is obvious. It was altogether deeper than has been realised. One of his ventures was an occult order known as the Order of the New

Templars. After reading Lanz's pamphlets, Hitler met him in Vienna and received personal occult instruction. Later, the writer and editor of *Ostara* said proudly: 'Hitler is one of our pupils. You will one day experience that he, and through him we, will one day be victorious and develop a movement that will make the world tremble.'[21]

Through Lanz, he came to know the equally bizarre occultist Guido von List. It was von List who first introduced Hitler to the occult symbolism of the swastika. The Guido von List Society was formed in 1908 and worked hard to promote his 'Arminian ideology.'[22] Through this group, he went on to discover and sample a whole range of occult societies and bizarre religious sects. All of them added their own extraordinary racial fantasies to the combustible pile of notions he had already discovered during his time in Vienna. [23]

Hitler also discovered another pseudo-scientific doctrine that was to obsess him for years, *die Welteislehre*, the World Ice Theory. In essence this stated that our present Moon was not native to the Solar System, but a planet from outside which had been captured by the Earth's orbit. There is some evidence that Hoerbiger, the inventor of the World Ice Theory, may have been right about this. However, he was not content with this claim, but also went on to claim that there had been previous moons in the Solar System – for which, again, there is a certain amount of evidence – and that the history of the universe was the story of the struggle between fire and ice, for which there is no evidence at all. The Moon, he believed, was made of ice and the interaction between this cosmic ice and heat was responsible for all the catastrophes in human history.

Hitler remarked, with regard to this particular notion, at his own headquarters during the war: 'I'm quite inclined to accept the cosmic theories of Hoerbiger.'[24] I have already written at length about the nature and extent of the involvement by both Hitler and Himmler with regard to Hoerbiger's theory in my earlier work.[25]

In spite of the fact that Hoerbiger's cosmology was completely unscientific and contrary to the scientific evidence about the Moon available to the scientists of his time, it still dominated the thinking of two of the most powerful men in Germany. From 1933 onwards both Hitler and Himmler wasted incredible amounts of money in a vain attempt to prove its truth. In the end it was partly responsible for their losing the war against Russia.[26]

Other friends and acquaintances of Hitler have also spoken of his deep involvement with occultism. Kubizek tells us that Hitler was interested in astrology, hypnotism, yoga, oriental religion and various occult pursuits.[27] Joseph Greiner, one of Hitler's acquaintances from his time as a dosser, speaks of his habit of placing his hand in the burning flame of a gas jet to prove the supremacy of 'will over matter.'[28] Hermann Rauschning's conversations with Hitler, of course, reveal an exceptionally detailed knowledge of even quite obscure aspects of occultism, knowledge which is also referred to by Greiner and another of Hitler's acquaintances from his Vienna years, Walter Stein.[29] All this occult training was later put to use following the First World War.

Between about 1909 and 1913 – certainly until 1912 – Lanz and others of his circle were still training Hitler. I have written in more detail about the range of occult and magical activities in which Hitler was involved in my earlier book.[30] As with the extent to which Hitler's vision of himself as an artist dominated his life until the very end, so too the extent to which he was influenced by various occult doctrines and practices has also been either ignored completely or else dismissed derisively. Among the acknowledged experts on the period, only Hugh Trevor-Roper seems to have grasped the fundamental importance of occult ideas to Hitler and many of his closest associates.[31] The fact is that Hitler remained obsessed by them right up to the very end. In some ways, their influence upon him was greatest during the last days in the Berlin bunker.[32]

Art, anti-Semitism and the occult were three of the decisive forces responsible for moulding Hitler's mind. As we have already seen, the taint of his father's illegitimacy – especially with the possibility that it had involved him in bringing Jewish blood into the family – was another. His poverty and sense of degradation during the years he spent as a dosser were also crucial factors in moulding his attitude to life. Another decisive event in the creation of Adolf Hitler into the force that he became now took place. The outbreak of the First World War gave him his first chance to feel a valued member of society.

When war was declared, Hitler volunteered for service with the German army. He was 25 years old, and sick of drifting. For the first time he had a purpose in life. Hitler himself admitted the decisive impact of the conflict upon his life: 'The war caused me to think deeply on all things human. Four years of war give a man more than thirty years at a university in the way of education in the problems of life.'[33] He brought with him a philosophy of life that the experience of war could only reinforce. It was probably at this time that he began to study the history and principles of war, a subject on which many German writers had commented.

Hitler took with him into the trenches the peculiarly vicious form of Social Darwinism – the idea that all life was a struggle for existence in which only the strong survive and the weak are to be despised and crushed – which he had picked up in Vienna. Although his experiences in the dosshouses of the city had led him to think along those lines already, it was through two of the leading politicians of Vienna that the more 'intellectual' form of the doctrine became known to him. These two individuals were Karl Lueger, mayor of Vienna, and Freiherr Georg von Schönerer, leader of an extreme nationalist and anti-Semitic party. Lueger's charisma made a big impression on Hitler. In *Mein Kampf* he was described as 'the mightiest German burgomaster of all time.' A typical example of the wit and wisdom of Lueger was his notorious statement 'when I see a book I want to puke.' Though Hitler was to criticise both these repulsive individuals, his debt to them was enormous.[34]

The war also led Hitler to discover a new interest, which was to become a lifelong obsession. During his four years on the Western Front, even so fanatical a nationalist as Hitler could not help noticing the shortcomings of the German propaganda effort. The Kaiser's 'PR team' had neither the humour and lightness of touch nor the ability to touch the heartstrings which their Allied counterparts possessed. Hitler decided that he would try and improve German propaganda. When he spoke about his ideas to other soldiers, they only laughed at him, but from 1919 onwards Hitler was to demonstrate that he did indeed have a genius for propaganda.

Hitler claimed that the British scandal sheet *John Bull* was the biggest influence on his ideas for propaganda warfare. This seems quite probable. This lurid rag, whose own proprietor was to be eventually imprisoned for corruption, dealt for the most part in sordid tales of sex and drugs. It was aimed at the lowest possible denominator of reader. During the wartime period it also added to its repertoire of smut with highly coloured accounts of German atrocities, ranging from salacious stories of helpless maidens ravaged by Prussian troops to vivid descriptions of torture and massacre by German soldiers. These fabrications, which sprang from the fevered imagination of the paper's proprietor, were completely untrue. For tactical reasons the British government did not correct the lies which *John Bull* spread so eagerly. This was a mistake that they were later to regret, as its fantasies had gripped the British people and led them to insist on the harshest possible peace terms at Versailles. Later, when the first accounts of Hitler's concentration camps began to leak out of Germany, the not unnatural reaction of the British people was to assume that once again they were being lied to for political reasons. It also inspired one of Hitler's most audacious propaganda techniques, which he referred to contemptuously as 'the big lie.'

The extent to which Hitler conducted his foreign policy on the same kind of basis as *John Bull* is quite remarkable. A chorus of faked stories of anti-Nazi atrocities allegedly carried out by the Austrian Government accompanied both his campaigns against Austria. Similar fabrications were also dragged out for use against the Czechs and finally, the Poles. As he remarked to his generals a few days before the outbreak of the Second World War: 'I shall give a propagandist reason for starting the war, no matter whether it is plausible or not. The victor will not be asked afterwards whether he told the truth or not. When starting and waging war it is not right that matters, but victory.'[35]

During the last series of German offensives on the Western Front, Hitler was gassed and sent to a military hospital to recover. He went there with high hopes, convinced that the Germans were winning the war at last.

It was in fact a very near thing. Four years of trench warfare had seen only inches change hands and then change back again. Suddenly the German armies were rolling back miles before them. The French Army wobbled badly and came close to cracking under the strain. Even the British, though their morale was higher, were forced to retreat. The great poet Wilfred Owen, a serving officer in the British Army who was soon to be killed himself, thought that the Germans would win the war now. To Hitler, still in hospital, it must have looked a certainty. However, the Allied armies did not break. Before long, the Germans were in full retreat.

By the time Hitler was discharged from hospital, Germany had been defeated and was left facing two years of virtual civil war. The news of the German defeat stunned Hitler. Having been invalided out during the final series of offensives, he had last seen the army on the brink of winning the war. When he heard that it had all been in vain he hid his face in his hands. He simply could not understand how his adopted country had lost. In addition to his astonishment about the fate of the nation, he was also indulging in one of his frequent bouts of self-pity. At least during the war his country had required his services. How could he bear to return to his former life as a civilian, perhaps even going back to spend the rest of his days in squalid dosshouses? Still shaken by the enormity of events, Hitler wept.

It is, of course, impossible to say how many of his tears were shed for his adopted country and how many for himself. He recorded his feelings in *Mein Kampf*: 'I had not cried since the day I stood beside my mother's grave. But now I could not help it. During those nights my hatred increased – hatred for the originators of this dastardly crime.'[36]

This statement by Hitler, years after the event, is unquestionably false. That he shed tears is quite possible. However, his own behaviour immediately after the end of the war is completely inconsistent with his later claim that he knew at once that the Jews were responsible, and grew hardened in his hatred of them. The fact is, rather, that for the last time in his life Hitler flirted with Communism. There is no doubt that Hitler had despised the old ruling classes of Germany and Austria, the monarchists and aristocracy ever since his days in Vienna. His contempt for them and their attitudes was the only principle that he maintained as fanatically as his anti-Semitism. It seems probable that at this moment in time he blamed them rather than the Jews and Marxists for the dramatic collapse of German arms. Certainly this was the almost universal reaction in Germany, where the sight of an officer's uniform enraged crowds into spitting on the streets and for a brief time even the middle classes swung violently to the left, giving power for the first time in German history to the Social Democrats.

Hitler joined the short-lived Soviet Republic of Bavaria, ironically under the leadership of the Jewish Marxist, Kurt Eisner. Eisner was a man who was so charismatic that he even enjoyed some surprising support in unlikely places, such as among senior generals and leading conservatives. It is perhaps not too fanciful to suggest that Eisner's combination of charisma and the ability to win the support of both working-class and conservative people was another of the influences on Hitler – one which, for obvious reasons, he could not declare. That this is not just plausible speculation is suggested by one of the many extraordinary actions that Hitler took later when he had been appointed Chancellor.

Count Arco-Valley was a young army officer with strong monarchist and conservative views. On 21 February 1919 he shot and killed Eisner. When he became Chancellor in 1933, one of Hitler's first acts was to have Arco-Valley arrested and imprisoned. Why would Hitler have wanted to imprison a man whose deed had made him a national hero in conservative circles? Only two plausible reasons suggest themselves. One is that Hitler had never quite got over his youthful hero-worship of Eisner and wanted to see his murderer punished. The other, and probably the more plausible, is that he wanted to remove a dangerous witness to his own political activities during the time of the Red Republic in Munich.

A moderate socialist, Hoffmann, succeeded Eisner. His policy was one of reconciliation with all elements in Bavarian political life, and he worked hard to secure the backing of conservative forces, with some success. This moderation infuriated the more left-wing elements in Munich, who seized control of the government and drove Hoffmann out of the city. The leader of this new Soviet Republic was the Jewish author Ernst Toller. It was a mixture of impractical and visionary intellectuals and at least one madman. It lasted for only a week before hardline Communists, acting on instructions from Russia, seized power in their turn.

Throughout these various changes of administration Hitler remained in Munich as a member of the Soviet militia. He even managed to get himself elected as a representative on one of the workers' councils in the city. When a mixture of federal troops and irregular forces finally succeeded in fighting their way into Munich and suppressing the revolution, Hitler was actually arrested for shooting at them during their entry into the city. With the extraordinary luck that accompanied him for so much of his life, though, he was actually recognised by some of his former comrades from the war. This period in Hitler's life has never been satisfactorily explained. Indeed, it is hardly ever mentioned by historians. The curious fact is that he was a willing and enthusiastic supporter of a regime that was not only Marxist but also contained more than a few Jews among its leading lights.

In my own opinion it seems that only the suggestion that the socialist side of Hitler's nature was dominating him at this time makes sense. His hatred of the monarchy, the aristocracy and the middle classes had, at least at that time, outweighed his obsession with the Jews. Hitler's own excuse was to lie about his role and pretend that he had been an undercover agent working in secret for the downfall of the Red Republic. There is no doubt that this was completely untrue. For one thing, disciples of von List were working within the city organising anti-republican activity. While Munich was being stormed by anti-Soviet forces, they even opened a recruiting centre in a hotel. Yet Hitler, who had met von List and knew that his supporters were recruiting soldiers, stayed away from their group. Instead he served as a soldier for the Munich Soviet, now totally dominated by Communists and whose main leaders were Jewish. He preferred to fire upon federal troops in defence of the Soviet Republic than join the conservative forces within the city.

Maybe Hitler realised how shaky his claim to have been a hostile agent was and looked. Certainly he tried to back it up by quickly betraying as many of his former comrades as possible. He also made a rambling and inflammatory speech. Giving him the benefit of the doubt, the soldiers took no action against him. More than that, before long he had impressed the army authorities enough for them to appoint him as an agent for military intelligence. They soon noticed his abilities at propaganda and public speaking.

On the face of it, Hitler's first peacetime job was not very exciting. His role was to influence demobilised soldiers away from socialist and Communist ideas and towards nationalist ones. At the time the army had every reason to worry. Numerous units of dissatisfied soldiers had found the propaganda of the extreme left highly attractive. As for the army leadership, made up as it was almost exclusively of the aristocracy with a tiny sprinkling of rich middle-class officers, it found itself completely unable to understand the men's disaffection, still less to talk to them on their own level. Solemn speeches about duty and patriotism were not producing the desired result. Discipline among the soldiers continued to break down at an alarming rate.

Hitler, of course, who had sunk to the very bottom of the pile of society before the war, knew exactly how the troops felt. After four years of struggle and death they had returned to a country they hardly recognised. Not only had the Kaiser gone and been replaced as head of the country by a former saddler of horses, but soldiers had become so unpopular that they hardly dared to show themselves in the streets for fear of being attacked by hostile crowds. Only those troops who had joined forces with the far-left elements enjoyed any popularity with the people. This culture shock came as a devastating blow to the returning soldiers. These men had left their homes and families, risked their own lives in the service of their country, and yet now found themselves unwelcome in their native land. They had come back to a Germany in defeat, which had barely avoided a Communist revolution, and had now crashed overnight from one of the richest countries of the world to a land in the grip of hunger, poverty, homelessness and civil war.

To these brave but bewildered men, who were shocked and angry at this astonishing turn of events in Germany, Hitler opened his heart. He denounced clear and identifiable enemies for their military and political disasters, and told the soldiers that they carried no blame for the defeat of their country. Although his range of subjects was narrow, the passion with which he spoke rekindled hope in the hearts of the soldiers who heard him. Before long he was being asked to answer letters of enquiry from puzzled servicemen.

It was on the orders of his superiors that Hitler attended a meeting of the German Workers' Party on 12 September 1919. This encounter was to lead to the most decisive development in Hitler's life. Before long he had taken over the party and renamed it the National Socialist German Workers' Party – nicknamed the Nazis for short by its political opponents. For the next four years Hitler, who never felt anything but contempt for the democratic process, worked hard to turn his party into a movement which would be capable of seizing power by force in Germany.

It was only the fiasco of his attempted *putsch* at the Munich beer hall in 1923 that forced him reluctantly to change his tactics. From now on he would use the parliamentary process which he despised to come to power. Sentenced to five years in prison after the coup, of which he only served one year, Hitler spent his time there reading. Before long he had discovered new influences upon his thinking which reinforced his existing philosophy of life. The result of all this massive but ill-digested reading was, of course, *Mein Kampf.* In this work Hitler poured out a torrent of abuse, hatred, and downright lies in a bitter and stiflingly obscene mixture. In spite of attempts by the publisher to tidy it up, the grammar and style are also quite atrocious. At the time Hitler was convinced that he would always be a failure. So deeply was he depressed that he considered suicide.

Some years later even Hitler came to regret his authorship of the book, dismissing it as 'fantasies behind bars.' He remarked later to Frank: 'If I had had any inkling in 1924 that I should become Reich Chancellor, I should never have written the book.'[37] Imprisonment changed Hitler temperamentally as well as politically. Before the *putsch* he had been quite approachable. On his release from prison he adopted the remote, haughty image of the Fuehrer. It soon became quite difficult to talk to him at all.[38] As well as his new remoteness, over the previous three years his snobbish tendencies had become worse. He now preferred to mix with the higher social circles to which he had now been introduced than with his old comrades. Hitler's first *entrée* into Bavarian society was brought about through the agency of the poet and occultist Dietrich Eckhart, one of the leading lights in the Thule Society. Of Eckhart and the Thulists, and their involvement with Hitler and the Nazis, I have written elsewhere.[39]

14

In 1932 Hitler decided to become a German citizen. This was because, as a foreigner, he could not otherwise run in the presidential elections due that year. In a frenzied campaign Hitler polled thirteen and a half million votes. The almost senile Hindenburg was narrowly re-elected, however. Fresh elections for the Reichstag followed, in which for the first time the Nazis became the largest party, but Hindenburg still refused to deal with 'that Austrian corporal.' Yet another election at last led to a dramatic drop in support for the Nazis. It was as if the German people, trembling on the brink of the abyss, had recovered their sanity at the critical moment.

The result of the election devastated Hitler. His party was now demoralised and nearly bankrupt, and he wondered in his depression if he would ever win power. Yet again his response to the crisis was to talk of committing suicide. If only the nonentities who controlled the German government had had the sense to either do nothing or else to call fresh elections, the Nazi bubble would almost certainly have burst. Instead, they took one of the most insane and irresponsible decisions in history, persuading Hindenburg to appoint Hitler the new Chancellor.

The transformation in the man and his fortunes was immediate and unmistakable. There were only three Nazis in his first Cabinet, but that did not matter to Hitler. At last he had control of the machinery of power, and he used it to the full in pursuit of the realisation of his 'vision.' Once he had won power, of course, the remainder of the National Socialist programmes – racism, rearmament and eventually war and even mass murder – seemed to take on the depressing inevitability of a Greek tragedy. The worse things got, the more Hitler lost touch with reality. Even with the Russians at the door, he gave priority to the extermination programme over everything else. His murderous tendencies also became concentrated on everyone. If he had had the means, he would gladly have destroyed the whole world in his own overthrow.

Was Hitler mad, then? Or was he evil? Or neither? His military ambitions, though they lost touch with reality as time went on, were certainly achievable. With just a little more luck, and, of course, some better judgement, they could have succeeded. In the same way his totalitarian rule was not necessarily irrational in itself. What made it become so was his obsession with anti-Semitism, which came to dominate every decision he made until it robbed him of clear judgement. On the charge of actual insanity, though, he should probably be acquitted.

Was Hitler evil, perhaps? By all generally accepted standards of Western civilisation at that time, yes. The problem is that Hitler rejected those standards completely. In fact, to him it was his own values that were good and those of his opponents that represented the real evil. If we start from his own premises it then becomes almost impossible even to ask the question in those terms.

The real truth seems to be that Hitler was a gifted but completely inadequate individual. He was a talented painter whose work has been undervalued. Perhaps if he had been able to achieve recognition for his art he might never have turned to politics and, ultimately, mass murder. There is also no doubt that his years as a dosser embittered him profoundly. He was never really a fully human person. Hitler remained emotionally a child all his life. He was able to live out his infantile fantasies on a larger scale than perhaps anyone else of his type since Nero.

One cannot imagine men like Genghis Khan behaving as Hitler did in the face of defeat. Napoleon certainly did not do so. For his type one has to look at such inadequates as Caligula, Nero and Domitian, all of them spoilt children given matches to play with and completely unable to resist starting fires with them. Though Stalin murdered more people in cold blood than Hitler, in comparison the Soviet leader was almost rational. The sad fact is that Hitler never grew up and other people had to pay the price for his infantile tendencies.

Notes

1. Having a Jewish grandfather, according to Orthodox Jewish law, would not have made Hitler Jewish, as the bloodline is traced through the female. It is, though, a curious fact, probably more the concern of a psychiatrist than a historian, that numerous people who are Jewish or partly Jewish have been passionate anti-Semites, including a number of senior members of the Nazi Party.
2. Hans Frank, *Im Angesicht des Galgens*, Beck, 1953. It is also worth remembering that one of the first pieces of anti-Jewish legislation to be introduced by Hitler was one forbidding Jewish families to employ 'Aryan' women as servants unless they were past child-bearing age.
3. Franz Jetzinger, *Hitler's Youth*, Hutchinson, 1953
4. Werner Maser, *Hitler*, Allan Lane, 1973
5. *Der Spiegel*, No. 31, 1957
6. It is also curious that the only Nazi who shared something even close to Hitler's obsessive preoccupation with the sexual 'pollution' of 'Aryan maidens' by Jewish males was the notorious pervert Streicher. Again and again Hitler protected this incompetent and repulsive thug until at last, after sustained pressure from the Gestapo, the SS and the civil police, he reluctantly removed him from office. By then he had spent years as a constant embarrassment to the party, and only Hitler's hand had protected him. It is difficult to explain this except by the known fact that Hitler shared Streicher's pornographic tastes. It is also worth remembering that Hitler's definition of Jewish ancestry included anyone with Jewish grandparents. If

Frank's account is true – and it seems probable that it is – this would have made Hitler feel Jewish in his own eyes.

7. Jetzinger, op cit. It is only fair to add that Schuschnigg, the Chancellor of Austria at the time of the Nazi takeover, disputes Jetzinger's claim. He blames the Russian invaders in 1945 for the destruction of Döllersheim. Nonetheless, it is a fact that the village was turned into an army camp and artillery range in 1941.

8. One of the more curious aspects of Hitler's youth is that his history teacher was a fanatical racist. Yet there is not one shred of evidence, in spite of a number of claims to the contrary which have been disproved, that Hitler displayed *any* racist attitudes before he had been living in Vienna for some considerable time. It seems to have been his discovery of the Jews who had come to Vienna from the less Westernised communities of Russia and Eastern Europe that first turned his thoughts in the direction of anti-Semitism. It is highly doubtful if he had met a single Jew in his birthplace, Braunau, or the small town of Linz where he grew up. Even in Vienna, the overwhelming majority of Jews were almost wholly Germanised. In fact, the whole question of Hitler's anti-Semitism is riddled with contradictions. In Vienna, he mixed with racists such as Lanz and von List, yet he loved Mendelssohn and Mahler and was even friendly with several Jews, particularly Neumann. He admired Kurt Eisner and took part in the largely Jewish-led Soviet Bavaria in Munich, as a soldier fighting for the regime. Nor is there any recollection by his comrades of anti-Semitic utterances by him when he was a soldier in the trenches. Something happened around 1919 that fundamentally changed his whole attitude towards the Jews. To this day, what motivated his sudden fanaticism is quite unclear. It is also quite extraordinary that not only did numerous people with Jewish and partly Jewish blood join the Nazi party, but they were allowed to stay in it and even helped to implement the Final Solution.

9. August Kubizek, *The Young Hitler I Knew*, Allen Wingate, 1954

10. Ibid

11. Ibid

12. Konrad Heiden, *Hitler, A Biography*, Constable, 1936

13. Jetzinger, op cit

14. Kubizek, op cit

15. Hanisch's observations are largely to be found in Heiden, op cit., and in the *New Republic*, 1939

16. Heiden, op cit

17. Adolf Hitler, *Mein Kampf*, Hurst & Blackett, 1939

18. Francis King, *Satan and Swastika*, Mayflower, 1976

19. Hitler, op cit

20. Michael FitzGerald, *Storm Troopers of Satan: An Occult History of the Second World War*, Robert Hale, 1990

21. Lanz, in a private letter to a New Templar student 1932. For more on Lanz

see: a) FitzGerald, op cit. b) Wilfried Darré, *Der Mann, der Hitler die Ideen gab,* Isar, 1958

22. For more on von List, see: FitzGerald, op cit

23. Trevor Ravenscroft, *The Spear of Destiny,* Corgi, 1974

24. Adolf Hitler, *Hitler's Table-Talk,* Phoenix, 2000

25. FitzGerald, op cit

26. Ibid

27. Kubizek, op cit

28. Joseph Greiner, *Das Ende des Hitler-Mythos,* Amalthea, 1947. Greiner is highly controversial as a source. Not only does he make some careless errors, as do Hanisch, Kubizek and some others who knew Hitler, but his emphasis on the occult aspects of Hitler's interests has led many historians to dismiss him out of hand. However some writers have used Greiner's account without citing him as a source. It is also worth remembering that the historian James Webb, clearly with extreme reluctance, concluded, after much research, that the credibility of Greiner's testimony has been dismissed altogether too hastily and too completely. As Webb put it, 'there may be more to Greiner's account than has been admitted hitherto.'

29. Hermann Rauschning, a) *Hitler Speaks,* Thornton Butterworth, 1939; b) *Germany's Revolution of Destruction,* Heinemann, 1939. Stein's testimony is to be found in Ravenscroft, op cit. It is fashionable nowadays to ignore or even dismiss Rauschning's testimony. However, not only is it intrinsically plausible, it also agrees with what is known of Hitler's interests in these areas from other sources and has never been successfully contradicted on any point. All in all, the decision by historians to ignore Rauschning is a most curious one, which seems to fly in the face of all the evidence. One can only speculate as to their motives, which are, quite clearly, not the dispassionate pursuit of truth.

30. FitzGerald, op cit

31. Hugh Trevor-Roper, *The Last Days of Hitler,* Pan, 1962. Trevor-Roper's awareness may reflect the fact that, unlike most historians of the period, he actually knows something about the paranormal, as his writing on witchcraft demonstrates.

32. FitzGerald, op cit

33. Hitler, *Mein Kampf*

34. J P Stern is one of the few historians to have understood properly the full extent of the debt owed by Hitler to these men. See J P Stern, *Hitler: The Führer and the People,* Fontana, 1975

35. Hitler delivered this speech to the Wehrmacht High Command on 22 August 1939. A record of it can be found in *Trials of the Major War Criminals before the International Military Tribunal,* Nuremberg 1947–49, Vol. xxvi, 1014-Ps

36. Hitler, *Mein Kampf*

37. Frank, op cit

38. Hitler seems to have adopted the Fuehrer pose largely as a result of the

influence of two men. One was the German philosopher Count Herman Keyserling, whose work enjoyed an enormous vogue between 1920 and 1940, not only in Germany. Hitler took two ideas from Keyserling, one being the notion that each race and nation had its own 'group soul.' This meant that each nation was an organic whole rather than a collection of individuals who spoke a common language. The other notion was that of the leadership principle. According to this, it was the job of gifted individuals to rule; and they were born to do so. The ordinary people had to obey the leader since he was the only authentic incarnation of the group soul of the nation. The other influence on Hitler at this time was Karl Haushofer, an occultist of exceptional power. Hess introduced the two men to each other and Haushofer was responsible both for the emphasis on *lebensraum* – living space – found in *Mein Kampf* and also for encouraging Hitler to become a more remote, consciously messianic individual.

39. FitzGerald, op cit

CHAPTER II

Hitler the Soldier

On 1 August 1914 Germany declared war on Russia. A photograph of a large and enthusiastic crowd outside the Hall of Field Marshals in Munich on that day includes the unknown Hitler, near the front of the crowd, dressed neatly but without his hat. The face shows his lips parted with excitement, his eyes ablaze with enthusiasm. Two days later Germany was also at war with France. Hitler at once enlisted in the Bavarian army and reported to his regiment on 16 August. For the time being all his problems were solved. He had no need to worry about food or shelter, no need to concern himself about the necessity to earn a living. He had a simple purpose in life, to serve as a soldier and help his adopted country to win the war.

Hitler's training as an infantryman now began. He drilled, went on route marches and practised using his bayonet. According to one of his comrades, when he first received his rifle he 'looked at it with the delight that a woman looks at her jewellery.'[1] On 7 October Hitler said goodbye to his landlord and landlady. Next day his unit left Munich for more arduous training. It took them three days' hard marching in the teeth of driving rain before they reached the new training camp. Nine days of mock combat, night marches, basic training and field manoeuvres followed. Hitler's lieutenant watched the new recruits leaving for the front with a distinct lack of confidence in their ability to perform under fire. A professional soldier himself, he noted sourly that the commanding officer was a man who had not seen any real fighting for years. Most of the officers in charge were inexperienced and he doubted if the men had received anywhere near enough training for the hardships of real war. The troops had almost no machine guns and no iron helmets. Instead they marched bravely off to battle in cloth caps. Even the telephone equipment had been made for the British Army. He had deep misgivings about their ability to deal with the realities of modern war. Events were to show that his fears were only too justified.[2]

Hitler and his comrades first saw action at the bloody battlefield of Ypres. Four days of heavy fighting saw the commander of the regiment killed and his deputy wounded. Hitler and a medical orderly dragged the wounded man back to safety, under heavy fire. The battle of Ypres had been a disaster for the Germans. Not only had they been defeated, but they had also lost most of the officers and eighty per cent of the men. In spite of this spectacular proof of what Wiedemann, Hitler's lieutenant, had feared, the new commander simply gave orders that the attack must be resumed. He took Hitler and another man with him to observe the enemy positions. During this rash reconnaissance they were seen and a volley of machine-gun fire swept the area. Hitler leapt up and saved his commander's life, pushing him into a ditch. Next day the rash commander was wounded at last and the battle for Ypres now settled down into trench warfare. All attempts to capture it were abandoned for the time being.

The new experience of trench warfare quite suited Hitler. It was, of course, almost as dangerous as the waves of frontal attacks which had been tried and failed, but it gave him more time. He used this time to return to his beloved art. He painted a number of watercolours, which demonstrated considerable coolness of mind in the face of conditions in the trenches. He also found himself, for the first and last time in his life, called upon to perform the only thing which ever came close to the myth of the housepainter. Lieutenant Wiedemann asked him to repaint a room in the officers' mess. Apparently Hitler decided on the colour – blue – and then, fetching a ladder and the necessary tools, chatted with the officer as he worked.[3]

Meanwhile Hitler's exploit in saving the life of his commanding officer had earned him a recommendation for the award of an Iron Cross, 1st Class. However, with the snobbery rife in the German army at that time, it was felt that an enlisted private could not possibly deserve such a high honour. Instead, he was awarded the Iron Cross, 2nd Class. To compensate for this snub he was also promoted to corporal. Though Hitler was honoured to receive the award, he was also sad. As he wrote sourly to his former landlord: 'Unfortunately, my comrades who also earned it are mostly all dead.'[4]

Hitler by now had become a respected member of the regiment. The other soldiers still found it hard to understand why he was with them rather than with the Austrian army. As one of his fellow-messengers remarked to Mend: 'He is just an odd character and lives in his own world but otherwise he's a nice fellow.'[5] Hitler was respected for his bravery, his cool head when trouble came and his loyalty to his comrades. His art also made him friends. He would draw cartoons for the amusement of his comrades as well as his more ambitious watercolours. His lack of family meant that Hitler missed out on the packages from home which the other soldiers received. He refused to share his comrades' rations, however, and indignantly refused an offer of ten marks as a Christmas present from Lieutenant Wiedemann. Instead, he spent his pay on buying extra food from the kitchens, earning himself the nickname of 'glutton.'

During his time in the trenches Hitler captured and domesticated a white terrier which had belonged to an English infantryman. This gave him not only company – they became inseparable in the trenches – but also diversion. He spent hours teaching the dog tricks and it refused to leave him. It even slept by his side at night, however fierce the bombardment became. Hitler also had many conversations with his fellow-soldiers. They noticed his natural gift for speaking and listened spellbound as he held forth on painting, poetry, architecture and opera. He became known as an intellectual who was always reading. His pack always contained a number of books, one of them a selection from his favourite philosopher, Arthur Schopenhauer. So often did he read Schopenhauer that his copy eventually became completely worn out.

As a messenger he had now become indispensable to his chiefs. Not only was he brave, but also unorthodox. As a child he had been held spellbound by tales of the 'Wild West' and often adopted techniques to get through enemy lines which he had come across from the American Indians. He was also undoubtedly helped by his frequent flashes of extra-sensory perception, no doubt finely developed during his years as a student of occultism in Vienna and Munich. As he later told the English reporter Ward Price:

> I was eating my dinner in a trench ... Suddenly a voice seemed to be saying to me 'Get up and go over there.' I rose at once to my feet and walked ... along the trench, carrying my dinner. Then I sat down to go on eating ... Hardly had I done so when a flash and deafening report came from the part of the trench I had just left. A stray shell had burst ... and every member of it was killed.[6]

He also wrote poetry in the trenches, though it was far below the quality of his work as an artist. Nonetheless, it does testify to his continuing preoccupation with the occult and is at times almost reminiscent of Coleridge's mystical poems. Its use of language at times shows signs of anticipating devices later used by the Surrealist poets of the thirties.[7]

It was over two years before Hitler was finally wounded. This was certainly not due to any lack of bravery on his part. However, as he remarked later, for most of the war it was as if he led a charmed life. His reaction to the wound, an exploding shell that hit his tunnel and fragmented into his thigh, was to plead with his lieutenant to be allowed to remain at the front. This was, of course, impossible. After two months spent in a military hospital near Berlin he returned to his regiment, following a brief spell in barracks at Munich. He found the mood in both Berlin and Munich not at all to his taste. Shortages and the seemingly endless attrition in the trenches had led to the beginnings of a mood of war-weariness at home. Worst of all, it was not confined to the civilian population. He found the mood in the barracks in Munich one of resentment, hatred of the Kaiser and the upper classes, and a general desire not to fight at all if it could be avoided. Used to the loyalty and comradeship of the men on the front-line, Hitler was appalled and disgusted. He longed to be back with his regiment.

As a result of a personal appeal by Hitler to Lieutenant Wiedemann, he was recalled to the colours. On his return they welcomed him cheerfully, even making a special meal in his honour. He was happy again at last, back with his friends and away from the spirit of defeat which was beginning to affect morale in Germany itself. Hitler continued to paint his watercolours and even a light-hearted Easter present. He surprised his commander by painting some eggshells with the greeting 'Happy Easter 1917.'

After five months of war, this time compounded by having to face the new British secret weapon, tanks, Hitler's regiment was relieved. At their quarters in Alsace he experienced two unpleasant shocks. A worker on the railways tried to buy Hitler's dog from him and when he refused, simply stole the dog from the helpless corporal, whose unit was on the move again and could not go back to reclaim his pet. Hitler was quite devastated by this loss. He remarked later: 'I was desperate. The swine who stole my dog doesn't realise what he did to me.'[8]

The second loss suffered by Hitler at this time was when one of the new recruits stole a leather case that contained numerous paintings, drawings and sketches. Infuriated and disheartened by this latest blow, Hitler laid aside art for a long time to come. It was not until the war had ended that he took up his paints and brushes again. Even then, as politics became a more pressing calling, he reluctantly abandoned his art altogether. Years later the stolen paintings were recovered and presented to Hitler as a gift.

It was October 1917 before Hitler took his first leave. Until that time he had always refused, but now a comrade persuaded him to spend eighteen days with him in Germany. He visited museums and art galleries, and would have gone to the opera except that Wagner was not being performed when he was there. He loved Berlin and Leipzig.

By the time the winter of 1917 arrived, the food situation had become desperate. Not only civilians but also even front-line troops were reduced to eating cats and dogs. Hitler tried to avoid both if he could but apparently preferred the taste of cat meat. This may, of course, have been partly because of his affection for his own lost dog. Meanwhile the end of January 1918 saw the situation on the home front become so desperate that, in spite of the fact that Germany had now became a military dictatorship, a General Strike swept the country. In Berlin almost half a million workers went on strike. The numbers in the rest of Germany were far less impressive. All the same, though the strike failed, it set alarm bells ringing in the minds of the German Government.

The front-line soldiers were not on the whole sympathetic to the strikers. Some of the newer recruits shared the feeling of war-weariness, but the battle-hardened veterans like Hitler saw the strike as a betrayal of the nation. Hitler referred to it scornfully in *Mein Kampf* as 'the biggest piece of chicanery in the whole war.' However, the surrender of the Russians at last brought a glimmer of hope to the exhausted troops. Hitler now became convinced that, with the Russians out of the war, Germany could and would win. The mood across the whole army became positive again. For the next four months Ludendorff, with fresh troops now available from the Russian front, launched his massive campaign of offensives. At first the Germans carried everything before them, but in the end they ground to a halt.

During this period Hitler was finally awarded the Iron Cross, 1st Class. The inscription on it read 'For personal bravery and general merit.' The Jewish Lieutenant Gutmann presented it to him, ironically, in the light of his later career. This highest of all awards came on top of five previous military honours. Hitler's relationship with Gutmann has been the subject of some controversy. Mend, who is not the trustworthiest of witnesses to Hitler's military career, claims that Hitler refused to salute Gutmann, claiming: 'I'll only acknowledge this Jew on the battlefield.' Another of Hitler's comrades not only denied the story but also added that Gutmann was an unpopular officer, not because of his Jewishness but his general character. This second comrade, Westenkirchner, claimed that Hitler did refer to Gutmann as 'an arse-crawler and a coward.' Other comrades from this period have no recollection of *any* anti-Semitic utterances by Hitler, except for a humorous reference to a Jewish telephone operator. Whatever his own relations with Hitler may have been, Gutmann not only presented Hitler with his medal but had actually been the one who recommended him for it. All in all, the story told by Mend shows all the signs of having been made up after the event in an attempt to read history backwards.

Four days later the Allies counter-attacked at Amiens. The German lines buckled but held. Fresh troops were moved up to reinforce them but it was the end of any chance of German victory in the war. Even the Kaiser commented sadly: 'The war must be ended.' In spite of this rare moment of realism, the war dragged on for nearly four more months before the Germans, now in revolution and virtual civil war, gave up at last.

Defeatism continued to spread among the army, especially with the arrival of new troops from the home front. Hitler got into a furious argument with one of the newcomers who complained that there was no point in continuing to fight an already lost war. Hitler and the soldier then came to blows and, after taking a terrific beating himself, Hitler overcame his opponent. He despised these newcomers who had never seen service as cowards. If men like himself, who had seen four years of war, still wanted to carry on fighting, why should the shirkers who had not give up so easily?

Finally Hitler was gassed and sent back to hospital. This spared him from witnessing the actual surrender of the German forces some three weeks later. During his convalescence he saw visions and heard voices, which he later claimed were the beginnings of his awakening to the real extent of 'Jewish-Bolshevist' conspiracies. In the light of his actions almost immediately after his discharge from hospital, however, it seems certain that this was yet another piece of myth making by Hitler. Even his discharge from hospital was handled ineptly. Not only did he still have a burning sensation in his membrane, but his sight was still sufficiently bad for him to worry if he would ever be able to read again. As a supreme touch he was actually sent out of the hospital without his soldier's pay book.

Near Berlin, he first went to the city and saw the Spartacists virtually running the place.[9] As ordered, he made his way back to barracks at Munich, observing the flames of revolution burning brightly all across Germany as he went. Wherever he passed on his journey, all law and order seemed to have broken down completely. The Spartacists and their sympathisers had abolished drill and saluting officers, and Hitler saw how the discipline that had held the troops together seemed to have evaporated almost overnight.

Hitler was still technically a soldier at this time. His actions now have been virtually ignored by historians. Of those who *have* dealt with them, only one seems to have realised the truth. Some have swallowed Hitler's later excuses totally (a very dangerous thing to do). One or two blinkered people have taken the view that the events demonstrate that Hitler was never really a Nazi at all, but only a tool of the Jews and Communists (a transparently absurd idea). The most common reaction, other than simply ignoring the events completely, is to try and paint Hitler as standing aside from the whole struggle until he knew which way the proverbial cat would jump.[10] It seems difficult for any impartial historian to read the facts in any other way than that, for a time, Hitler himself was caught up in the sudden and massive drift to the left in German politics. Of course when the situation changed, Hitler altered his position for tactical reasons. In the course of time he even became so fanatical in his beliefs that he actually appears to have been convinced of the truth of his own patently false account of his actions. All the same, that Hitler was a willing and enthusiastic soldier of 'Soviet Bavaria' has been demonstrated beyond any reasonable doubt. Only his extraordinary later career, with its constant emphasis on anti-Semitism and anti-Communism, have led otherwise objective historians to lose sight of the obvious truth.

What kind of a soldier was Hitler? Brave, obviously. To have been decorated so many times testifies to it. Unorthodox, too; we have the word of a number of comrades on that account. His personal oddity was also remarked upon by a number of them, though. It was partly the fact that his officers doubted that he could command the respect of the men that led to their decision not to promote him to sergeant. However, he was so good at his job of messenger that this also held him back, since such a role could not have been given to a sergeant, who had a wider range of responsibilities. Exactly how odd Hitler's behaviour during the war was is still a matter of some dispute. Lieutenant Wiedemann, perhaps the most reliable of all witnesses to the Nazi leader's wartime career, specifically stated that Hitler would not have been able to command the respect of his men if he had been promoted to sergeant.

According to accounts received by Rudolf Olden, he was 'a dreamer, who had no friends, and spent his time lost in thought, and none of us was able to coax him out of his apathy.'[11] Otto Dietrich also claimed that when Hitler revisited Lille in 1915, several members of his former company showed him a garden where Hitler used to hold forth about his political opinions.[12]

Both Olden and Dietrich need to be treated with some caution as sources. They suffer from the common failing of projecting events from the future back into the past, as well as the all-too-common tendency to demonise Hitler. It seems as if some people are incapable of recognising that he was not always what he became in the course of time. The general picture that emerges from the majority of accounts by Hitler's comrades is of an intellectual but popular soldier with a quiet sense of humour. A certain oddity was occasionally remarked upon but not in general considered either important or even all that noticeable. Once again we see the dangers of reading history backwards.

Notes

1. Hans Mend, *Adolf Hitler im Felde,* Eher, 1931
2. Fritz Wiedemann, *Der Mann, der Feldherr werden wollte,* Velbert, 1964
3. Ibid
4. Letter from Hitler to Herr Popp. Quoted in Maser, *Hitler,* Allan Lane, 1973
5. Mend, op cit. Mend needs to be treated with considerable caution as a source. His book, written years after the events he describes, has a tendency to read history backwards and to describe behaviour by Hitler that is contradicted by all other sources. He also later contradicted some of his own testimony. In addition, and something that cannot be brushed aside, he was a man with a string of criminal convictions, mainly for fraud and embezzlement. Where his account can be corroborated, however, or at least seems plausible, I have made use of his memoirs.
6. C Ward Price, *I Knew these Dictators,* Harrap, 1937
7. An example, written during the autumn of 1915, is the following:

'I often go on chilly nights
To the oak of Woden in the quiet woods,
Weaving a union by the use of dark powers –
The Moon shapes runic letters with its magic spell,
And all who are full of pride in daylight's hours
Are humbled by its magic formula!
They draw their swords of shining steel – but instead of fighting
They freeze into solid stalagmites.
So are the false parted from the true souls –
I reach into a nest of words
And hand out gifts to the good and just
And my formula brings them blessings and riches.'

8. Adolf Hitler, *Hitler's Secret Conversations*, Signet, 1961

9. The Spartacists were an extreme left-wing movement considerably more radical even than the German Communist Party. Their principal leaders were Rosa Luxemburg and Karl Liebknecht, and their political philosophy might be described as 'libertarian Trotskyism.'

10. For the various theories, see: a) Colin Cross, *Hitler*, Hodder, 1973; b) Alan Bullock, *Hitler and Stalin: Parallel Lives*, Fontana, 1993; c) Douglas Reed, *Lest we Regret*, Jonathan Cape, 1943; d) C H Douglas, *The Big Idea*, Bloomfield, 1983. Cross's account seems to me to explain the facts most adequately.

11. Rudolf Olden, *Hitler the Pawn*, Left Book Club, 1936

12. Otto Dietrich, *The Hitler I Knew*, Harper Torchbooks, 1967

CHAPTER III

Hitler the Artist

It has already been pointed out how Hitler's conception of himself as an artist dominated every aspect of his life, even after he came to power and even as the Russian tanks were closing in on Berlin. From the moment he first began to draw, Hitler displayed more than average ability. Before long it was to become an obsession with him. He often spent time drawing when he should have been paying attention to his lessons. During the Boer War of 1899–1902 he kept his classmates amused and impressed with his sketches of 'heroic Boers' defending their land from 'British imperialists.' More interesting than these early propaganda efforts is his drawing from memory, at the age of 11, of a large castle. It was perfectly executed in the correct architectural proportions.

These fairly happy times came to an abrupt end with the death of his father when Hitler was 13 years old. He moved into lodgings in the town of Linz, where he got into the habit of staying up half the night, drawing by candlelight. During the summer of that year his mother took him to stay with her brother-in-law, Anton Schmidt. Hitler made them a kite 'with a long coloured tail from different coloured paper,' as well as reading and drawing. He was especially prone to draw or paint when it was raining outside, and hated being disturbed while he was working.[1]

At the age of 15, having just scraped through his examinations, he was forced to change schools. He lived with another family in Steyr, where he soon lost all interest in schoolwork. Again he spent his time in reading, drawing and painting. He also wrote a bizarre poem, which reads like a cross between Aleister Crowley and Christian Morgenstern's verse. This poem was illustrated by an even more bizarre drawing of a buxom woman beating a man.[2]

At 16 years old, school finally behind him, he drifted. Reading, going to museums, drawing and listening to music dominated his life. Then he met Kubizek, who wanted to be a musician. Soon they became friends, going to the opera together and talking eagerly about art, music and literature. Finally Hitler plucked up the courage to show Kubizek one of his poems. Soon, even more shyly, he produced some sketches for his approval.

In 1906 Hitler spent a month in Vienna. Contrary to the slanders he later wrote in *Mein Kampf*, Hitler loved the city. He spent day after day at the opera, discovering in the process a new ambition. Now he wanted to be a composer and musician as well as an artist. Soon these ambitions took yet another turn, as he decided to become an architect. He drew plans, detailed and impressive, for remodelling the town of Linz and some of its key buildings. Soon his ideas moved on to an even grander scale, that of town planning. He redesigned and relocated the railway line and station, extending the park on to the old site. A new hotel and a large tower were also planned, looking down over a new bridge across the river.

In 1907 Hitler returned to Vienna to take the examinations for the Academy of Fine Arts. He entered the test with high hopes. To his utter astonishment he was rejected. Before he had time to recover from that shock he was forced to return to Linz, where his mother was dying. He drew her, on her deathbed, in his sketchbook. To the postmaster and his wife, who had helped him to nurse his mother in her last illness, he gave one of his paintings as a token of gratitude.

In his absence, the distinguished Professor Alfred Roller, in charge of the scenery at the Viennese Royal Opera, was persuaded to examine Hitler's portfolio with a view to his possible employment with the opera. Encouraged by this news, Hitler returned to Vienna. Five days later Kubizek, now registered as a music student, followed him. Hitler showed his friend the sights of the city and took him to a performance at the opera. Meanwhile Hitler kept on going to see Roller but whenever he actually arrived at the professor's studio he lost his nerve. Too shy and nervous to introduce himself to this notable, each visit became more of an ordeal than the previous one. In the end he tore up his letter of introduction in a frenzy and the whole project faded away. Even when he was leader of his country, Hitler often lacked self-confidence. As a shy provincial boy of 19, this side of his nature was even more pronounced.

Wagner was, and remained all his life, Hitler's first love in music. Again and again he attended every performance of the composer's work he could find in Vienna, even if the production was a mediocre one. Kubizek, who was an admirer of Verdi, did get Hitler to come to his operas too, but *Aida* was the only one he genuinely liked. His musical tastes were also somewhat extended as a result of Kubizek's ability as a music student to get free tickets for concerts. Beethoven, Schubert, Schumann, Bruckner, Grieg and, ironically, in view of his later prejudices, Mendelssohn and Mahler all appealed greatly to Hitler. Schubert, Beethoven and Mendelssohn became particular favourites.

At this time Hitler also began writing a play. It was heavily symbolic, written in language reminiscent of James Macpherson's *Ossian* poems, and based on the clash between Teutonic paganism and Christianity. Even at this early stage of his life, the play sided with the pagans. Hitler also wrote several other plays in the same vein. At last he decided to write an opera, *Wieland the Smith*, which had been considered as a subject by Wagner. Hitler played the music on the piano in their flat, and then Kubizek wrote the score. Hitler's friend thought that the work was a pastiche of Wagner, but that it still showed a surprising ability for musical composition. While Kubizek was writing out the score from Hitler's playing, Hitler was also busy designing the costumes, the props and even drawing Wieland. After a month or so of this frenzied activity, however, Hitler lost interest in the project, probably to the great relief of his friend.

Now Hitler made a second attempt to be admitted to the Academy of Fine Arts. During the year that had passed, he had done countless drawings, sketches and paintings. Surely this time they would recognise his ability? However, his second attempt turned out even worse than his first. This time, after a brief glance at his portfolio, they refused even to let him take the examination. This second rejection both crushed and embittered him. He spoke wildly about blowing up the building with the academicians inside it. So full of anger was he that Kubizek grew concerned. However, when Kubizek asked him what his plans were now, Hitler calmed down. He told his friend not to worry about him and simply began reading.

Meanwhile Hitler returned to his interest in town planning, which he now combined with a new interest in poverty. He went out to the poor areas of the city and studied the housing and living conditions of the workers. On his return he drew up vast new plans for Vienna, including a new village for the city's workers. Later in life he was able to put these visions into practice, when he became the leader of Germany.

Soon after this, Kubizek returned home for the summer holidays. Hitler had no means of support other than his orphan's pension and what little was left of his father's estate. He moved out, first to one and then another cheaper lodging-house. By late summer he was sleeping on park benches and in the doorways of shops.[3] When he moved into the dosshouse it was Hanisch who reawakened his artistic career. To find the money to eat, Hitler had sold his clothes, books, and all his paints and brushes. Hanisch persuaded him to write to his aunt to borrow money. She sent him a fifty Kronen note. Having bought himself a winter coat, he first moved to a new hostel for homeless men. Hanisch got the apathetic Hitler to work at his paintings. Before long he was turning them out at the rate of one a day. Hanisch went out on to the streets and the bars of Vienna, selling Hitler's sketches and water-colours so successfully that both men managed to drag themselves up from poverty. Hitler was still unable to afford a change of clothing, but at least he was no longer cold and hungry.

Hitler would often hold forth on political and artistic topics during his time in the men's hostel. According to Hanisch, most of Hitler's favourite singers and actors were Jewish. Indeed, most of his friends at the hostel were also Jews. One of them was the Hungarian art dealer, Josef Neumann. Not only did he like Hitler well enough to give him a coat, but through Neumann he was also able to sell his work to three other Jewish art dealers. Hitler actually told Hanisch that he preferred dealing with the Jews because 'they were willing to take chances.'[4]

Later that year Hitler made his final attempt to be accepted by the Academy. He took a large portfolio of his paintings for the attention of a professor at the Hofmuseum. The professor acknowledged the technical merit of Hitler's work but criticised his inability to depict the human form. He now finally admitted to himself that he would never be able to gain admission to the Academy. Sunk in depression, he carried on painting in his room at the hostel. Hanisch had left the hostel now, and he was less able to sell his work in the absence of his regular agent.

At this critical time of his life, another new friend came into the hostel. Josef Greiner was attracted to the quiet artist who worked away quietly at his desk. Both men shared common interests in art, the occult and economics. Hitler and Greiner struck up a close friendship and under the influence of his new friend, Hitler's painting actually improved. Even those few hostile critics who have taken the trouble actually to examine his work have been forced to admit that his pictures displayed excellent technique of the kind that might have been expected from a professional painter. Yet Hitler had no formal art training at any time in his life. What he did have was a natural ability that, if only it had been guided by an artistic academy, might have seen him winning recognition as an artist rather than as the infamous mass murderer he eventually became. He was fluent as a drawer in charcoal and pencil, excellent as a water colourist and quite outstanding when he painted in oils.[5] Again it was to his network of Jewish art dealers that he sold most of his work. However, for a variety of reasons, Hitler was to leave Vienna soon, not to return until his days as the conqueror of Austria.

Making progress in Munich was much harder than it had been in Vienna. He had managed to build up a network of friends and art dealers there. Now, alone in Munich, he had to start all over again. For all that, Hitler fell in love with the city as soon as he got off the train. Taking a room with the Popp family, he worked hard at his painting. As in Vienna, he tried to gain admittance to art school, but once again he was disappointed. Even marketing his work was more difficult. In Vienna he had been able to deal directly with art dealers. Here, he was reduced to hawking his paintings round bars and even trying to sell them by knocking on doors.

Nevertheless, Hitler came to Munich at the right time. With the possible exception of Paris, Munich was probably the most exciting city in Europe for art and culture at this period. Wagner had lived here in his time and written three of his finest works while staying in the city. Stefan George, widely thought of as Germany's finest living poet, and Rilke, who as time showed was the real holder of that title, also chose to live in Munich. On a lighter note, the cabaret in Schwabing allowed the controversial Frank Wedekind to hold court. Wedekind, a man of extraordinary if undisciplined talent, was a poet of real power, a playwright of interest, and a songwriter of genius. Although Hitler found his work 'decadent,' he was nevertheless an admirer of Wedekind. In this heady bohemian atmosphere, Hitler felt entirely at home.

In time he was able to make a living from designing advertising posters as well as selling some of his paintings. It was the war which brought an end to this phase of his career. As we have seen already, Hitler continued to paint and draw throughout most of the war. Only the theft of his paints and artwork made him put aside his art in disgust. After the war he went back to painting for a while, but the rapid rise of his political career compelled him reluctantly to put his dreams of art away for ever. He did still find time to write the odd poem during the early years of the Nazi movement, however.

In 1922 he made a new friend, Ernst Hanfstaengl, a man from a quite different social class from himself. Hanfstaengl had been to Harvard and was partly of American descent. He was also, unlike Hitler, able to enter freely the highest circles of Bavarian society. Hanfstaengl gave an extraordinary description of Hitler's living conditions in Munich at this time. He lived in a dark and dilapidated building, in a room with hardly any furniture. All that was in the room was a bed and a bookcase. The walls, however, were covered with prints and drawings. From time to time he went out into the hall, where he played his favourite Wagner melodies on the house piano. According to Hanfstaengl, this old instrument was badly in need of the attention of a piano tuner.

Nevertheless, at Hitler's request he played a few pieces for him. He began with a Bach fugue, which Hitler listened to absent-mindedly. Bach was never one of his favourite composers. When he moved on to Wagner, however, Hitler became tremendously excited. 'This music affected him physically and by the time I had crashed through the finale he was in splendid spirits.'[6]

Apparently Hitler knew Wagner's opera *Die Meistersinger* by heart, and could even whistle the entire work in tune. He loved music, though he did have his blind spots. Hanfstaengl claimed that Hitler never had any ability to appreciate the genius of Bach and Mozart. Next to his beloved Wagner, Beethoven and Chopin were his favourites. Presumably by now Hitler's old admiration for Mendelssohn would have been politically embarrassing for an anti-Semitic politician and so had probably been dropped quietly.

Hanfstaengl, in fact, had completely captivated Hitler. He found himself being dragged around to Hitler's social gatherings and compelled to play the piano to the assembled guests. One of Hanfstaengl's musical excursions had more lasting consequences than all this transient show-manship, however. At the home of Hoffmann, Hitler's photographer, he began to play some of the Harvard marches for their games of American football. His account of the system of cheerleaders and bands, and how they got the crowd behind their team, fascinated Hitler. Hanfstaengl then played a few German marches in an American style. Hitler was ecstatic, and immediately ordered his friend to write some for the SA band. His most famous composition was *Sieg Heil*, based on a Harvard song.

Hitler felt at ease with the family and began to do impressions of his Nazi followers for their benefit. He was a natural mimic and Hanfstaengl and his wife and son were genuinely fond of him at this time. They went out together, often to the cinema. On a visit by Hitler and Hanfstaengl to Berlin, Hitler insisted on visiting the War Museum and the National Gallery. He particularly admired Rembrandt. Returning by a roundabout route – Saxony was under Communist control at that time – Hitler livened up the long drive home with his mimicry and habit of whistling Wagner. At Bayreuth, they had to make the pilgrimage to see Wagner's theatre.

Now he began to add artistic and theatrical touches to party rallies. Even his speeches started to acquire the form of a symphony in three movements. His flags and banners, martial music, and pageantry made them more exciting as spectacles than anything offered by the other politi-cal parties in Germany. Hitler certainly repelled some of his listeners, but he did not bore them.

During his visit to Bayreuth, Hitler visited Wagner's widow, his son and daughter-in-law. The son had nothing but contempt for Hitler, but his daughter-in-law Winifred became a disciple. After the failure of the Munich *putsch*, Winifred sent him a Christmas parcel, together with a book of poetry. In the Schwabing quarter of Munich, the artists' area, a group of artists held a Christmas celebration for Hitler.[7] This astonish-ing display of support for the Nazis by the artistic community was to become more pronounced as time went on. Nor was it was only the more conservative artists, writers, composers and musicians who supported them. Many conservative artists were opposed to the Party and even had the courage to say so. In the same way, many of the avant-garde artists were enthusiastic Nazis. Of all the artists who backed National Socialism, the most outstanding were Emil Nolde and Georg Kolbe. Nolde was the leading German Expressionist painter, and his support for the Nazis has been a constant embarrassment to the art world ever since. The general response from art historians has been to either downplay or even ignore his involvement with National Socialism.

Unfortunately, this is simply at variance with all the facts. Nolde joined the party in 1920, only a year after its foundation, and at a time when the very name of Hitler was almost completely unknown in Germany. He remained a member throughout the next twenty-five years.[8] Kolbe was the finest sculptor of his day in Germany. What is more, unlike Nolde, who simply carried on painting in the same style throughout the regime, Kolbe was the one artist whose work actually improved under the Nazis. For this the art establishment has never forgiven him. Nolde's activities have been fictionalised into the image of a non-political painter. Because Kolbe had the audacity to show that a great artist can produce masterpieces even if his political views are repulsive to most people, his fate has been much worse. Historians of German art in this period prefer to go straight from the Weimar period to post-war art, with perhaps a brief glance at the somewhat pretentious – but surprisingly impressive for all that – sculptures of Breker and Thorak. Kolbe is, quite simply, written out of the art history books.[9]

Probably the most notable name in music to give support, however qualified and reluctant, was the composer Richard Strauss. This support was more on the level of a hope that Hitler might bring about the regeneration of Germany than on the basis of any significant support for Nazi policies. Certainly Strauss did not share the regime's anti-Semitism. In fact, he was soon to fall out of favour with the Nazis after he commissioned the Jewish writer Stefan Zweig to write the libretto for his new opera.[10] Among writers, the most notable names to support the Nazis were the poet Gottfried Benn, the dramatist Gerhard Hauptmann, the philosophers Heidegger and Keyserling, and the jurist Carl Schmitt. But there were many, many more, some as obscure then as they are today.

In 1933 Hitler made another pilgrimage to Bayreuth. As well as enjoying the festival he also met the Wagner family. To Winifred Wagner he expressed his sadness that he had not come to power ten years earlier. He felt that he was getting old and time was not on his side. There was a long history of early death in his family and he had to press ahead quickly with his plans for Germany's regeneration.

In 1934 Hitler turned to a young architect, Albert Speer. Speer was ordered to stage manage the Nuremberg rally of the party that year. He built a massive stone stadium topped with the figure of a flying eagle. Almost the entire store of anti-aircraft searchlights was also borrowed to create an awesome visual effect.[11] Hitler himself turned to the young director Leni Riefenstahl and asked her to film the event. At first she refused, but his powers of persuasion eventually prevailed upon her. Riefenstahl set up shots from many unusual angles, including fire engines and even roller skates. Thirty thousand spectators saw Hitler and his close colleagues come on to the platform. Martial music played, and speeches were made to the enthusiastic crowd. By the seventh day there were nearly a quarter of a million people present, carrying banners. Speer's searchlights gave an almost mystical air to the whole proceedings.

Riefenstahl went away and edited the thousands of feet of film that she had shot into the famous movie *Triumph of the Will*. This did not at first impress the Nazi leadership but when Goebbels, who had tried to hinder her throughout the film's making, realised that it was actually quite effective as propaganda he changed his mind. It was awarded the prize for best film of the year in German. In spite of its tendency to glorify Hitler and the Nazis, the film is an outstanding work of art, a fact that was duly recognised by the award of a gold medal at the 1937 Paris World Exhibition.[12] Riefenstahl also made a film of the 1936 Berlin Olympics, which again showed that a great artist could function even under the restrictions placed upon filmmakers in the Third Reich.[13] Until 1937, in fact, there was something of a continuing debate within the party about art and culture in general. There was a very strong lobby, headed by Goebbels and supported to some extent by Goering, in favour of the encouragement of the modernist trend. Men like Nolde were held up by those Nazis who took this view as showing that not all experimentalists were anti-patriotic or Communist sympathisers.[14]

These four years of relative freedom, except for the disgraceful episode of the mass burning of books in 1933, came to an abrupt end in 1937. Hitler decided to make a definitive pronouncement and declared that all the modernists represented degenerate art. An exhibition of 'degenerate art' was organised and toured the country, drawing enormous crowds. Even Nolde was included in the condemnation, to his complete bafflement. Henceforth the conservatives dominated art under the Nazis. Some gallant souls, most notably Schmitt-Rottluff, tried to work within the new restrictions as well as they could. It was as late as 1941 before he was finally declared to be incapable of adapting himself enough to the new standards and was forbidden to paint.[15] On the other hand, the ardently Communist artist Käthe Kollwitz applied for membership of the Reich Chamber of Culture, and was admitted. She also furnished a family tree showing no Jewish ancestry. Not only was she allowed to continue to paint and sell her work throughout the Third Reich, but during the war Kollwitz was actually allowed to hold a public exhibition of her work. The fact that the Nazis allowed an openly Communist artist, who was also considered avant-garde, to exhibit in Germany at a time when the Germans were at war with the Soviet Union shows that when it suited the authorities, even the official policy of the regime could be disregarded.[16]

Architecture and town planning are also aspects of Hitler's policy to which historians have not paid sufficient attention. There is a general and fairly justified consensus that his favourite architects, Troost and Speer, are exaggeratedly monumental in their approach. It is only fair to add that both men complained that this was more the result of Hitler's taste than their own. All the same, some of Hitler's ventures, particularly his plans for workers' villages, are remarkable achievements. His interest in ecological and human scale considerations were completely against the general trend of architecture at that time, and were not to attract widespread support again until the 1980s.

In the end, Hitler's vision of himself as a great artist was one of the few convictions that he never abandoned. The extent to which it came to dominate his life has already been amply demonstrated. Perhaps the most telling sign of this was that, even when he knew objectively that the war was lost and that the Russians were only miles from Berlin, he still spent hours discussing his plans for the glorious future renaissance of art and architecture which he expected to come about under his regime.

Notes

1. Maria and Johann Schmidt. Hauptarchiv der NSDAP file 17, Reel 1
2. Bundesarchiv Koblenz, R43 II/957 p. 71. Parts of the poem are indecipherable.
   A translation of what can be identified follows:
   'The people sit there in a ventilated house,
   Filling themselves with beer and wine,
   Eating and drinking ecstatically,
   (-) out then on all fours.
   There they climb high mountain peaks,
   (-) with faces full of pride,
   And fall down like acrobats somersaulting,
   And cannot find balance.
   Then, sad, they return home,
   And quite forget the time
   Then he sees (-) his wife, poor man,
   Who cures his injuries with a good hiding.'
3. Most of the above from August Kubizek, *The Young Hitler I Knew*
4. Hanisch, *The New Republic*
5. Greiner, *Das Ende des Hitler-Mythos*
6. Ernst Hanfstaengl, *Hitler: The Missing Years,* Eyre and Spottiswoode, 1957
7. Ibid
8. Richard Grünberger, *A Social History of the Third Reich,* Penguin, 1971
9. Ibid
10. *Die Schweigsame Frau.* Zweig's libretto led to a formal Nazi boycott of the opera on its public performance.
11. Albert Speer, *Inside the Third Reich,* Macmillan, 1970
12. David Hull, *Film in the Third Reich,* University of California, 1969
13. Richard D Mandell, *The Nazi Olympics,* Macmillan, 1971
14. Grünberger, op cit
15. Letter from Ziegler to Schmitt-Rottluff, 1941. In: Walther Hofer, *Der Nationalsocialismus. Dokument 1933−1945.* Frankfurt, 1957
16. Grünberger, op cit

CHAPTER IV

Hitler and Women

The first woman in Adolf Hitler's life was his own mother. He adored her and she thoroughly spoilt him. Although he was attracted to girls, his shyness held him back. Then, at the age of 17, he fell in love for the first time. The girl in question lived in the same suburb of Linz as Hitler and his mother. Her name was Stephanie Jansten, and Hitler told Kubizek in great excitement that he was in love with her. She was tall and blonde, the type that Hitler found attractive throughout his life. The young Hitler wrote a string of poems to her and the long-suffering Kubizek had to listen to them all. Hitler admitted that he had never dared to speak to Stephanie, who was always accompanied by her mother. The practical Kubizek suggested that he should simply introduce himself.

This idea plunged Hitler into a deep depression. Partly he was afraid that reality would shatter the dream he had built around the girl, but he was also frightened of her mother. On top of his own painful shyness, he could not bear to tell her that he had no occupation at present. Then he started fantasising about kidnapping Stephanie while Kubizek talked to her mother, an idea that his friend hastily persuaded him to give up. Hitler's gloom grew greater still when she took no notice of him in spite of his constant surveillance of her. He decided that she must be angry with him and that his only way out was suicide. At once he announced that he planned to jump into the Danube river, but only if Stephanie joined him in a suicide pact.

Fortunately for Kubizek's peace of mind, Hitler suddenly lost interest in girls and became obsessed with architecture. Unknown to the two friends, Stephanie herself had just become engaged to a lieutenant in the Austrian army. It was not until the publication of Kubizek's book years later that she realised that she had been the object of an unrequited passion on the part of Adolf Hitler.[1]

When Hitler and Kubizek went to Vienna together, it was the future dictator's friend who who began by attracting the women to him. On the occasion of a young woman's visit to their home to see Kubizek, the jealous Hitler flew into a rage and his worried friend thought 'Adolf had become unbalanced.'[2] Although the cheerful Kubizek was successful with women, he noticed that they were more attracted to his shy friend than to himself. Hitler, however, still lacked the confidence to approach them. Although he told his friend that pre-marital sex was sinful, he was tormented and fascinated by thoughts of the many prostitutes who lived in Vienna. On one occasion he insisted on taking Kubizek on a tour of the red-light district.

Although no definite proof exists, it seems virtually certain that, at some time during his years in Vienna, Hitler frequented prostitutes. It also seems probable that he caught syphilis from these contacts. The chapter on syphilis in *Mein Kampf* is perhaps the most repulsive in the book. It is also curious that Hitler spoke of it not only with a sense of anguish so deep that it must surely have been rooted in personal experience, but also that he associates it with racial degeneracy. This at least gives some plausibility to the idea – often suggested by other writers – that Hitler may have caught syphilis from a Jewish girl.[3]

During the four years he spent as a soldier the only women Hitler saw were the nurses he met when he was in hospital. Possibly this experience of an all-male society at the front may have been responsible for Hitler's remarkable tolerance of homosexuality among his political disciples. Perhaps, though, his bohemian life in Munich before the war or his experiences in the dosshouses of Vienna may have played a part in this extraordinarily untypical attitude towards the subject. Not unnaturally, some psychologists have suggested that possibly Hitler was at least a latent homosexual himself. Such evidence as there is suggests that, however bizarre Hitler's sexuality may have been, he was not a practising homosexual.

After Hitler began his political career he soon discovered that he was attractive to women and played on this sexual element at his party meetings. Before long he had decided that, even though he was now receiving the attentions of many attractive women who wanted to marry him, it would harm his political career to get married. Eckart, one of his closest friends at this period of his life, insisted that he must remain a bachelor in order to attract the support of women to the party. There were now millions of women who after the war had won the vote in Germany for the first time. Hitler realised that a skilful campaign could win wide support among them for his own party.

It was Eckart who introduced Hitler to Hélène Bechstein, whose husband was the famous maker of pianos. Through the Bechsteins he began to meet women from a higher social class than those he had been able to mix with until that time. Though few of these were influential to any degree, it helped him to persuade at least a section of the German middle and upper middle classes that he was not simply a rabble-rouser, but a politician to be taken seriously.

Even aristocratic women found the gauche and socially inept Hitler irresistible. He had to be shown by them how to use a knife and fork, how to dress correctly in society, and how to behave in general. None of their efforts were able to cure him of his embarrassing problem with wind, which continued to dog him throughout his life.

When Hitler became friendly with Hanfstaengl, he was immediately attracted to his wife Helene. She was an American woman, tall, brunette and strikingly beautiful. He used to spend hours round the Hanfstaengl house and one of the main attractions there was Helene herself. Hitler never made any sort of pass at his friend's wife, but she sensed that he was attracted to her. On the other hand, although she liked him, she did not find him attractive. In fact, she was convinced that Hitler had no interest in sex at all.[4]

Hitler's principal chauffeur at this time, Emil Maurice, told a quite different story. As well as being his driver, Maurice was also for many years one of Hitler's closest friends. He told of how the two of them would not only visit life classes to gaze at the naked women posing for artists but would also visit nightclubs and even try to pick up girls on the streets. From time to time Hitler would bring a woman back to his room. He always made the woman a present of flowers.[5]

There was also a persistent rumour at around this time that he had made the sister of one of his drivers his mistress. Certainly the woman, Jenny Haug, was in love with Hitler. She always carried a gun with her and saw herself as being an extra bodyguard, willing to give her life for the man she loved.

Hanfstaengl gave accounts of some less normal behaviour on the part of Hitler. He described how the bottom shelf of his bookcase held a collection of pornography, most of it written by a Jewish author. He also mentioned that Hitler was fascinated by the women boxers he saw in Berlin.[6]

When Hitler was put on trial after his failed *putsch* in Munich, the courtroom was filled with female admirers. On the day that he was due to be sentenced, large numbers of women turned up, bearing bouquets of flowers for him. Even though the prosecutor ordered them removed, the women remained, gazing at the defendant in a state of near delirium. Some of the women actually asked to be allowed to take a bath in the tub which Hitler had used. This even more bizarre request was also refused.

Even when he was in prison, Hitler received one of his favourite delicacies from a group of Nazi women who came every Friday. In fact, he enjoyed a constant stream of women visitors throughout his time in prison. On his release his circle of female admirers was greater than before. He was now a national figure and at a New Year's Eve party a crowd of new women fans besieged him. One of them had the audacity to give him a kiss under a sprig of mistletoe. The furious Hitler sulked briefly before storming out of the party altogether.[7]

Hitler was beginning to lose interest in Helene Hanfstaengl. Although there had never been any sexual involvement between them, he had adored her quietly. Now he was beginning to look elsewhere. Matters came to a head when Hitler plucked up the courage to ask Helene to share her life with him. She was taken completely by surprise and told him that she could never be his mistress. Instead she suggested that he ought to get married. With a sad face he told her that he could never marry as he had to dedicate his life to his country.[8]

Now Hitler began an affair with a 16-year-old girl called Mitzi Reiter. She ran a boutique with her elder sister and Hitler was violently attracted to her. Before long she had become his mistress. While she was filled with dreams of marrying the man she loved, he tried constantly to dissuade her from the idea.[9]

In 1923 Hitler became involved in the most tempestuous and disastrous love affair of his life. His half-sister Angela was persuaded to come to his new house at Berchtesgaden. With her came her two daughters, Friedl and Geli. Geli was a 20-year-old whose charm and personality captivated her uncle completely. Opinions on Geli among Hitler's entourage varied widely. Hanfstaengl described her as 'an empty-headed little slut,' but his wife thought that she was 'a nice girl.' Hitler's photographer Hoffmann said that she 'captivated everybody,' though his daughter Henriette called her 'coarse' and 'provocative.' Rudolf Hess's wife Ilse thought that 'she had the famous Vienna charm.'

Hitler should have been warned by the behaviour of Mitzi the previous year. Desperate at his continuing refusal to marry her, and filled with jealousy as she realised that he was also having relations with other women, the unfortunate woman tried to hang herself. Although she did succeed in losing consciousness, her brother-in-law saved her life. Far from bringing Hitler back to her arms, it drove him away from Mitzi altogether.

Meanwhile the relationship between Geli and her uncle had begun to deepen. He set her up in an apartment which she shared with him. From time to time they were seen together in public. He even went shopping with her, in spite of the fact that he loathed going to the shops. He told his friend Hoffmann outright that 'I love Geli, and I could marry her.'

This did not stop him from an unsuccessful attempt to seduce the 17-year-old Henriette Hoffmann. When she rejected him he went away in a foul mood. However, in Hoffmann's photographic shop he was to meet another young girl who played a lasting part in his life. Her name was Eva Braun and she was soon to captivate Hitler completely. Eva too became obsessed with Hitler and was soon boasting that she had become his mistress. At the time she made this claim, it was untrue.

Meanwhile the relationship with his niece Geli had taken a sudden and surprising turn. She had become engaged in secret to his chauffeur, Maurice. As soon as Hitler found out he went into a berserk rage, sacked Maurice from his job, and told him that he wanted nothing more to do with him.

Although Maurice was now out of the picture, before long Geli had taken up with another admirer, an impoverished artist from Vienna. Again Hitler forced her to break off the liaison as soon as it came to his notice. At this point Geli decided to escape from her uncle altogether. She set out to go to Vienna, presumably in pursuit of the artist, but an urgent telephone call from Hitler summoned her back to Munich. On her arrival they had a blazing row and finally Geli went to her room in a huff. She remained there until her uncle was due to leave, when she came to the door to say goodbye.

As Hitler drove off towards Nuremberg, he was seized with one of his precognitive flashes. 'I have a most uneasy feeling,' he told Hoffmann. The photographer told him not to worry, and reluctantly he agreed to go on with their journey. Hoffmann noticed, however, that he was brooding silently the whole time.

Next morning the housekeeper became alarmed when Geli did not answer her door. A locksmith was called to the scene and when the door was forced open Geli was lying dead on the floor, a pistol by her side. Her suicide had apparently been sparked off by the discovery of a letter from Eva Braun to Hitler thanking him for his invitation to the theatre. Hitler was informed of the news by Hess and drove back to Munich in great haste. Hitler was in a state of shock and spent the entire journey in complete silence. To make matters worse, in addition to the genuine grief that he felt at his niece's death, there was also the enormous political scandal that it created. Already ugly rumours of incest had been circulating about their relationship. Now the anti-Nazi press was hinting pretty broadly that Geli had been murdered by her own uncle to put an end to the scandal. It was even alleged that she had been the victim of frequent beatings from Hitler.

Stunned by the scale of the disaster, Hitler fled with Hoffmann to a country retreat. He was so depressed that, in spite of the recent triumph which the party had scored in the German elections, Hitler was seriously thinking of quitting politics altogether. For three whole days he refused to eat anything.

Hitler was *not* guilty of murdering his niece. He could not have done it physically as he was in Nuremberg when it happened. Nor is it likely that Goebbels or Himmler carried out the killing. Apart from the inherent improbability that either would have risked an unauthorised murder of Hitler's own niece, both men would have covered their tracks. The *last* place that Geli would have been killed would have been Hitler's own home. All the attempts that were made then and have been made since to paint the death as anything other than suicide are completely incredible. The account of the housekeeper, that Geli shot herself during the night, is the most logical and consistent way of interpreting all the facts.

There remains only the question of why she killed herself. Perhaps she had found her relationship with her notorious uncle stifling. This was an idea which both Ilse Hess and Henriette Hoffmann considered the most likely reason for her suicide. It is also significant that the letter to

Hitler from Eva Braun had been torn up by Geli and was pieced together afterwards by the housekeeper. Perhaps, then, it was a sudden outburst of jealousy which led her to kill herself. Brigid Hitler, estranged wife of Hitler's half-brother Alois, had her own theory on the subject. She told Hanfstaengl that Geli killed herself because 'she was pregnant by a Jewish art teacher in Linz.' Not only have other members of the Hitler family denied this, but Brigid Hitler is an unreliable source at the best of times. In particular her opinion on this matter is almost valueless, as she was not even in Germany at the time and had only met Hitler very briefly. On balance the most probable cause was the combination of Geli's dissatisfaction with her relationship with Hitler combined with the jealousy aroused by the sudden discovery of the letter from Eva Braun.[10]

Because he was forbidden to enter Austria, Hitler was unable to attend her funeral, which was held in Vienna. However, he did get his chauffeur to drive him there that same night. After a lot of cloak and dagger work he was smuggled into the country and laid a wreath of flowers on Geli's grave. Although he had not killed her, he felt a certain sense of responsibility for her death. Above all, though, he was a man in grief and shock.

Two days later he attended a conference of party leaders. He also took an important decision in his personal life. At an inn where he was offered ham for breakfast he looked at it in sudden revulsion and refused to eat. To the startled Goering he announced that it was like eating a dead body. From that day forward he never touched meat.[11]

Meanwhile women continued to find Hitler as irresistible as before. Wherever he went he was besieged by crowds of admirers. In one city two enterprising girls even managed to catch him in his own railway carriage. They went into a state of hysterical ecstasy, sobbing, crying and screaming as if he was a pop star or movie idol.[12]

During the first general election of the two that took place in 1933, Hitler asked one of his *Gauleiters* (regional leaders) to find fifteen young women to join him for coffee. Before long the news that Hitler was staying in a hotel brought in a flood of women on their own account. Soon the fifteen women who had been asked to come arrived and spent the time gaping in rapt adoration at the party leader. Before long the embarrassed Hitler suggested that they move to the Artists Cafe. This turned out to be another mistake. Soon every woman in the cafe was abandoning companions and partners and mobbing Hitler in a frenzy of adoration.[13]

Meanwhile Hitler was dogged by more crises in his personal life. On top of the expected problems of having to inject life into what seemed to have become one election campaign after another, his relationship with Eva Braun, who had been his regular mistress for the last two years, was to receive an unpleasant jolt. In almost a mirror image of the disaster he had suffered with Geli's suicide, Eva shot herself. The desperate Hitler, clutching a hastily furnished bunch of flowers, rushed to her sickbed.

After a long talk with the doctor, Hitler came to a reluctant decision. He told Hoffmann sadly: 'The girl did it for love of me. Obviously I must now look after the girl.'[14]

From that time on Eva was to become a full part of Hitler's life. He moved her into quarters with himself and henceforth devoted as much time to her as he could spare from his increasingly hectic political schedule. The last thing he wanted was another Geli on his conscience.

Once Hitler finally became Chancellor later that year, his new duties took up even more of his time. Though Eva remained his mistress, her status was carefully concealed even from some of his closest friends. Hitler's purge of the SA and other political opponents during the 'Night of the Long Knives' so alarmed Hanfstaengl that he decided to try and stabilise him by finding a potential marriage partner. The woman he chose for this role was the daughter of the American ambassador, Martha Dodd. He rang Martha and pressed on her the importance of using her influence to try and charm Hitler into a pro-Western and pro-peace policy. She was at first intrigued and flattered by the strange suggestion from Hanfstaengl that she should try to persuade Hitler to propose marriage to her. When she met Hitler, his shyness and the odd charm that so many women remarked upon captivated Martha. However, her father, the ambassador, was strongly opposed to Hitler, regarding him as a dangerous madman. We do not know what Hitler thought of Martha, but the whole affair got no further than the initial stages.

Leni Riefenstahl was one of many women who were linked romantically with Hitler during this period. Most of them, like Riefenstahl herself, were actresses. However, he did like being seen in the company of glamorous women, even though he had no desire for the relationship to go any further than company. Meanwhile he had a new admirer, one of the eccentric English aristocratic family, the Mitfords. Unity Mitford became totally infatuated with Hitler on her first meeting with him. Hitler enjoyed her company enormously, but she never became his mistress. This was not because of any unwillingness on Unity's part, but the result of Hitler's obsessive secrecy concerning his romantic entanglements and the unfortunate Unity's inability to be discreet.[15]

After her attempted suicide, Hitler took good care to watch Eva Braun closely. Unfortunately for her, now that he was Chancellor, he had even less time to spare for her than had been the case earlier. What was worse, she had finally realised that he had no intention of ever marrying her. In spite of this knowledge, which devastated her so completely that she became sunk into a more or less permanent state of depression, she still continued to cling to the man she loved. She became even more obsessed with him, and his absences made her even more melancholic, while his rare visits lit up her whole life. After one of them she wrote in her diary: 'I am so endlessly happy that he loves me so much, and pray that it will always be so.'[16]

After six months, during which she swung between ecstasy and despair, Eva had had enough. For the second time in her relationship with Hitler, she felt completely forsaken by the man she loved. In the dark well of sorrow that filled her now, she attempted suicide for the second time. This time, instead of a revolver she used sleeping pills. Her sister found her and sent for her own employer, a Jewish doctor. She also removed the pages from Eva's diary so as to conceal the evidence of her attempted suicide. The doctor, at the urgent promptings of Eva's sister, obligingly described the event as an accidental overdose brought on by tiredness.

Officially Hitler accepted this explanation. However, he was not stupid enough to believe that it was true. During the summer he saw to it that Eva and her younger sister – not the one who had saved her life – were found a place of their own. In a flat only a short distance from Hitler's own home in Munich, they set up home. Hitler paid the rent through an intermediary and furnished it with goods bought at sales.

Although he still tried to maintain the discretion he had employed up to now, his visits could hardly be kept a complete secret. Plain-clothes police patrolled both the building and the surrounding area. Furthermore, Eva's new semi-official status led to problems with her father. Even though she was the mistress of the most powerful man in Germany, her father still felt a sense of shame and disgrace at his daughter's liaison. Her mother also wanted Hitler to break off the relationship. Both parents tried through separate letters to urge this course upon him. The mother's letter reached Hitler and was ignored; her father's was intercepted by Eva herself and destroyed.

Before long Hitler decided that he needed a place where he could keep an eye on Eva without having to employ such public and elaborate security precautions. Now she lived in Hitler's summer 'palace', a place that he loved dearly and so came to more frequently than he had to the flat in Munich.

In 1939, with the imminent possibility of war over Poland coming nearer, Eva was moved into the Chancellery. This office was to become in time the very heart of the Nazi state. She was never allowed to draw the curtains in her bedroom, and even had to go into Hitler's quarters through the entrance reserved for servants. So tight was the blanket of security around their affair that even the majority of Hitler's inner circle had no idea that Eva was his mistress. Although now she saw him every day, she was never allowed to leave her room when Hitler entertained important guests. She was more or less a prisoner, even if a prisoner of love.

When war came at last over Poland, Unity Mitford, who loved both Britain and Germany passionately, became yet another woman who had loved Hitler to attempt suicide. On hearing the news of war, she walked into the English Gardens and shot herself in the head. Amazingly, she did not succeed in killing herself. In fact, she was able to walk into a hospital where she was treated by a surgeon. The bullet which she had fired into her own temple was too dangerously located for surgery to be possible. After the British had managed to extricate their army from Dunkirk, Hitler decided to return Unity to her own country. She travelled through Switzerland on a train, a hopeless invalid and mentally unstable. Eight years later the bullet she had fired into her own head moved of its own accord, and the unfortunate woman died at last.[17]

Following the fall of France, Eva moved back to Berchtesgaden. Hitler now had more time to spend with her. The security precautions which had been so obsessively maintained until that time were now abandoned. Even the staff at Berchtesgaden were now allowed to see them together openly. Both Eva and Hitler used the familiar *du* form with each other in front of everyone. This new openness about Eva's status, though it delighted her, was not at all welcome to some of the inner circle. Ribbentrop's wife completely ignored her, while the wives of Goering and Goebbels were deliberately rude.

Their husbands shared their views of Eva, although in the presence of Hitler himself they were icily polite. Martin Bormann and Eva detested each other. She was beginning to lose weight now, and Hitler teased her that it was because she refused to join him in a vegetarian diet. He also tried to get her to give up smoking.

By 1945 the war was obviously lost, even to the eternally optimistic Hitler's eyes. The doleful Eva, who had been flitting between Berlin and Munich for the last few years, now took a definite decision. In spite of Hitler's orders to remain in Munich, she came back. She told her friends that she was not afraid of death and that if it came she wanted to die by the side of the man she loved.

On 22 April 1945 Hitler finally admitted to the inmates of the bunker that the end was near. Everything was lost and all the women should be evacuated from the city while there was still time. The other women simply stared at him in a state of shock. Eva was the only one to react. She told him quietly that she would never leave his side. On the evening of 23 April Hitler finally married Eva. In spite of what she knew would happen soon, she was full of joy. At least she would die with the man she loved, and at last he had agreed to her dearest wish, to make her his wife.

The staff held a party in the bunker, with drinking and as much gaiety as they could find in the circumstances. Next day Eva got up and gave what few possessions she had with her to her friends. She spent the day talking with them and more or less chain smoking. Even Hitler no longer bothered to tell her to stop. That night there was some dancing in the bunker. The end was very near now.

After lunch on 30 April Hitler, Bormann, Goebbels and his wife, the two secretaries, the cook and Eva all had one last meeting. Hitler, who was crying, shook hands with everyone and mumbled incoherent goodbyes.

It was Eva who reassured the other women and told them to get out while they still could. For herself, she was going to die with the man she loved.

After the farewells, Hitler and Eva retired to their room. After her two previous attempts to kill herself, this time she really meant it. Now that she was married to the man she loved, she was willing to die. She took up the phial of poison that Hitler had obtained for her. Hitler shot himself soon after. That evening both bodies were burned.

It is a striking fact that no fewer than four of the women with whom Hitler had been involved in some way attempted suicide. Geli and Eva were successful, although Eva's suicide in the bunker was a special case. Hitler had the unfortunate tendency of making women become obsessed with him and then not giving them the attention which they felt he owed them. Unity's obsession with Hitler was of course an unrequited love, but all three of the other women who committed or attempted suicide had been involved with him. It was as if Hitler became a drug inside their system which they simply had to possess or they could no longer bear to be alive.

Even though when he was with them, Hitler treated his women quite well, the way in which he picked them up and put them down when it suited him was intolerable to them. Caught in the heat of passion, they could not bear his cold detachment. They loved him, and he claimed to love them. How was it then that he could treat them in the way that he did?

The key to this lies partly in his own nature and partly in the rather old fashioned attitude he had towards women. Hitler was very shy and never felt at ease in the company of women. They always made him nervous. On the 'ideological' front, Hitler really believed that a woman's place was in the home and that she found her truest fulfilment as a wife and mother. He could not understand why women could not be content to be simply wives and mothers.

Although, because it was Hitler's attitude, this view of women became official National Socialist policy, it was one which was not widely shared by the top leadership. Goebbels in particular was scornful of the Nazi attitude towards women. As soon as total war became inevitable, he set out to reverse the policy and use women as freely as men in working roles.

As well as the general bias in favour of marriage and the family, the Nazi state also had a specific commitment towards selective breeding. Hitler had proclaimed in *Mein Kampf* that he rejected 'the idea that what he does with his own body is each individual's own business.' [18]

Although for the most part the Nazi attempts at selective breeding went no further than the outlawing of sexual relations between 'Aryans' and Jews, together with the requirement to provide a record of ancestors to weed out those individuals with Jewish blood, Himmler had far more radical plans. He was an outspoken advocate of polygamy, believing that monogamy was 'the satanic work of the Catholic Church.' Himmler also created the *Lebensborn*, which has often been wrongly described as a state-run brothel, but was actually designed as another means of boosting the birth-rate in Germany and of improving the breeding stock.

The *Lebensborn* began in 1936 with a single home, but as time went on more and more homes were added. Himmler's plans grew more ambitious with the early German victories and he intended, had the Germans won the war, to make it compulsory for all unmarried women of childbearing age to 'volunteer' for service in the *Lebensborn*. He told his masseur Felix Kersten excitedly that 'Nietzsche's Superman could be attained by means of breeding.'[19]

In case it may be felt that Himmler's ideas only represented his own notoriously eccentric beliefs, it is worth pointing out not only that Hitler never opposed them, but that he also allowed him to spend large amounts of public money on these repulsive projects. Certainly Bormann, one of the least cranky and ideological of the National Socialist leadership, supported Himmler.[20]

Perhaps in the end the most devastating comment that can be made upon Hitler's relationships with women is that no fewer than four women tried to kill themselves over him. It has been argued that the true figure is six suicide attempts, for which involvement with Hitler is to blame. Certainly three of them were successful. For all the excuses that have been offered on his behalf, it remains a terrible indictment of Hitler's inability to form successful relationships with women.

Notes

1. Kubizek, *The Young Hitler I Knew*. Perhaps the most curious aspect of all with regard to Hitler's infatuation with Stephanie is that she was Jewish. Jansten was her married name, and her maiden name was actually Stephanie Isak.
2. Ibid
3. For the argument, see King, *Satan and Swastika*
4. Hanfstaengl, *Hitler: The Missing Years*
5. Maurice's comments are recorded in: Nerin Gun, *Eva Braun*, Bantam, 1969
6. Hanfstaengl, op. cit
7. Heinrich Hoffmann, *Hitler was my friend*, Burke, 1955
8. Hanfstaengl, op. cit
9. Gun, op. cit
10. For the various accounts of the episode with Geli, the reader should consult a) Hanfstaengl, op. cit.; b) Hoffmann, op. cit.; c) Henriette von Schirach, *The Price of Glory*, Muller, 1960; d) Gun, op. cit.; e) Frank, *Im Angesicht des Galgens*

11. This incident is recorded in: G M Gilbert, *The Psychology of Dictatorship*, Ronald Press, 1950
12. Incident related in: Sefton Delmer, *Trail Sinister*, Secker & Warburg, 1961
13. Account in: Hans Severus Ziegler, *Wer war Hitler?*, Grabert, 1970
14. Hoffmann, op. cit
15. At least three of the five Mitford sisters were unconventional. Jessica was a keen Communist sympathiser; Diana married Sir Oswald Mosley; and Unity's bizarre unrequited love for Hitler led eventually to her death. See: Jessica Mitford, *Hons and Rebels*, Orion, 1999
16. Gun, op. cit
17. Sir Oswald Mosley, *My Life*, Nelson, 1970
18. Hitler, *Mein Kampf*
19. Felix Kersten, *The Kersten Memoirs*, Odhams, 1956
20. Bormann's Memorandum of 29 January 1944

CHAPTER V

Hitler as Conspirator

After his decision to join the German Workers' Party, Hitler began by try-ing to win wider public support. He had no intention of allowing the tiny group to remain an unknown band of agitators. Most of his fellow-leaders were quite happy to be big fish in a tiny pond. Hitler's ambitions were much greater than that.

He still had no clear plan about how he would achieve power, although both the Russian and German Revolutions had led him to the view that a successful change in government could only come about through a popu-lar uprising. Lenin had done so successfully in Russia, and the German Marxists had come within an ace of turning Germany into a Communist state. Hitler knew that he could never support the conservative forces who wanted to bring back the monarchy and keep the running of the country in the hands of the old aristocracy. He despised those people as reactionaries who were worse than anyone. On the other hand he was no longer prepared to see Germany go Communist. His concept of National Socialism, an amalgam of patriotic and left-wing policies, was genuinely held. Although Hitler was primarily an opportunist who never hesitated to drop a policy if it brought him support, he always regarded these U-turns as strategic retreats rather than a genuine abandonment of his beliefs.

Apart from his brief involvement in the Bavarian Soviet, Hitler's first attempt at conspiracy was his visit to Berlin with Dietrich Eckart during the 1920 Kapp *putsch*. This had come about when various *Freikorps* units, refusing a government order to disband, marched on Berlin instead and installed a civil servant named Kapp as Chancellor. Not unnaturally, the government asked the army to put down this revolt. The army leadership simply refused to do so, their excuse being that soldiers should not be asked to fire upon each other. As a result of their actions, the Kapp *putsch* came within a whisker of success. Hitler and Eckart went to Berlin to see if they could become involved with the conspiracy. Understandably, with the army having openly refused to crush Kapp's revolt, the government was wondering how or even if it could be put down. At this point the workers of Berlin took a hand. They called a general strike which brought the whole city to the brink of collapse. Every service from transport, street cleaning, electricity and water was shut down. Even shops and offices closed in protest against the coup. Faced with the impossibility of maintaining himself in power without shooting the strikers, Kapp panicked. He fled ignominiously and left his co-conspirators to face the consequences. Most of them followed his example.

One of the few who did not was Kapp's press representative and unofficial Foreign Secretary, the bizarre Trebitsch-Lincoln. The career of this extraordinary man deserved, and got, a book written about it.[1] He was at different times in his life a Liberal MP in Britain, a German spy in the First World War, and a Buddhist monk, to name just a few of his activities. When Hitler and Eckart finally arrived in Berlin, the Kapp *putsch* had all but collapsed. In the Reich Chancellery they were received by Trebitsch-Lincoln. He told them that Kapp had run away and that they had better look out for themselves now that the coup had failed. Eckart looked at the Hungarian Jew disdainfully and took Hitler by the arm. 'Come on, Adolf, we have no business here,' he said.

In spite of Eckart's words, he and Hitler did stay behind in Berlin. Both men were anxious to make contacts that would allow them to extend the influence of their party beyond Bavaria. They met Ludendorff and also some members of an ex-soldiers' association, together with various *völkisch* organisations. Eckart also introduced Hitler to Hélène Bechstein on this visit, who was to become a generous provider of funds to the party.[2]

Hitler's and Eckart's meeting with Ludendorff turned out to have momentous consequences for the future course of history. Disgusted by the amateurish fiasco that Kapp's *putsch* had turned out to be, Ludendorff decided to take over himself the business of plotting a military coup against the government. Instead of relying on popular uprisings or ill-disciplined freebooters, Ludendorff decided that the army itself would have to become involved in conspiracies against the government. However, the Kapp fiasco had left the senior generals anything but willing to get involved in any more rash adventures of that sort. Though they were prepared to turn a blind eye to unofficial paramilitary organisations if they did not step too far outside the bounds they considered acceptable, they were certainly not willing to go beyond that. Ludendorff had to remain content with training irregulars into efficient fighting forces. As many of them were ex-servicemen anyway, they soon became quite formidable weapons of destruction. Hitler's rough and ready bunch of bouncers found the new semi-military atmosphere exhilarating.

Meanwhile, simply because of the fortunate accident that Hitler had made his political base in Munich, the special peculiarities of Bavarian politics at that time came to his assistance. Von Kahr, the leader of Bavaria, met with Hitler and extended a relatively friendly welcome towards him. Even though he described him as a 'raging Austrian,' von Kahr felt that Hitler could well be a useful ally in his own battle against the central government.

At this moment in time Bavaria, which had come into the new Germany during the previous century most unwillingly, was seriously thinking about declaring its independence from the Reich. Bavarian patriots mourned the departure of their king and hated the Social Democrats who dominated the government in Berlin. If Bavaria was independent, they felt, they would not have to endure the sad spectacle of a saddler of horses sitting in the Kaiser's place and giving them orders. Von Kahr hoped that Hitler and his growing support could be turned to the advantage of the monarchist and separatist cause.

It was not the first time in his political career that others thought they could make use of Hitler for their own purposes. Even Drexler, the founder of the party which Hitler now dominated, had thought that he could keep his excesses in check. It was a mistake that was, astonishingly, to be repeated again and again throughout the rest of his rise to power. Having survived an attempt to exercise some limits on his control of the party, Hitler turned to the process of creating an effective unit of paramilitaries out of the bunch of roughnecks who acted as stewards and bodyguards for him. The first manifestation of this new disciplined force was known as the Gymnastic and Sports Division of the party. Two months later it was given the far more colourful name of *Sturmabteilung* (SA for short). From the beginning there were disputes over the role and power of the SA. Hitler saw it as a means of maintaining order and intimidating the opposition. Its leader, Captain Ernst Roehm, saw it more or less as his own private army. To Ludendorff, it was an auxiliary armed force to be used in the crusade to overthrow the hated Weimar Republic.[3]

Hitler was quite willing for others to entertain any views they liked about the future course of the SA. He knew that he could control them if it ever came to a struggle over the leadership. In the meantime he turned them from a defensive force into an instrument of terror. A series of minor disturbances of the peace and petty assaults at last culminated in a direct assault upon a political meeting held by a rival organisation. This was the Bavarian League, which was a moderate group of Social Democrat sympathisers who nevertheless wanted home rule for Bavaria. Its leader was about to address his audience when Hitler entered the meeting.

He had already infiltrated numerous SA troops in plain clothes into the audience and his entrance was the signal for them to leap to their feet and cheer him. Before long there was pandemonium and open brawling between the SA and their opponents. The unfortunate speaker was beaten up and the meeting prevented from continuing.[4] Hitler was arrested and prosecuted for a breach of the peace. News of his forthcoming trial only led to fresh outbreaks of violence on the streets. A meeting addressed by Hitler was gatecrashed by Social Democrats and Communists. The SA, outnumbered for once, waited until the trouble started and then waded into the opposition. They succeeded in driving them out of the building after doing heavy damage to the furniture and the people who had been inside it. Hitler finished his speech just before the police arrived to break things up.

The same year saw a string of political assassinations in Germany. This trend was not one which Hitler encouraged. He felt that it was pointless to indulge in individual vengeance rather than trying to destroy the whole system. The following year the German Foreign Minister, hated both for his implementation of the Treaty of Versailles, even though reluctantly, and for being a rich Jew, was assassinated. This act provoked a wide-spread reaction against the political right and nationalist movements generally. Even Hitler condemned it. On the same day that the Foreign Minister was murdered, Hitler himself was imprisoned for causing a breach of the peace. By a curious irony, he was put in the same cell that had once been occupied by Kurt Eisner. He spent five weeks there, which characteristically he used to read and develop his ideas.

Hitler's imprisonment had certainly moderated neither his language nor his conduct. His first public address after being released was a violent attack on the Jews, on the Social Democrats, on the Communists and the financial markets. He urged his listeners to react against the attempts to silence them by open physical violence. He did everything but call for the overthrow of the German government by force. His vehemence, the power of his oratory and the sheer excitement of his storm troopers and their martial music made him a rising star in Bavarian politics.

Meanwhile the Bavarian separatists, headed by yet another civil serv-ant, were planning to overthrow the government of Bavaria. In its place they wanted a dictatorship headed by von Kahr. The Nazis were asked to join the scheme and Hitler, believing it to be the forerunner of a blow aimed at the very heart of the German government, agreed to take part. He sent one of his trusted henchmen off to the north to rally nationalist support there. It was only when he grew puzzled at the lack of any news from Bavaria itself that it dawned on him that its leader had lost his nerve at the last moment. Indignantly, the Nazi leader returned to Munich and challenged him. The would-be conspirator ignored Hitler and promptly went off on holiday. Although the Nazis had been ready and willing to march, none of the other nationalist organisations had risked joining the plot. As a result of his involvement, Hitler was forced to go into hiding for fear of arrest.

When Lüdecke, the man whom Hitler had entrusted with the task of rallying support in north Germany, found his leader again he was seeth-ing with anger. 'I was ready! My men were ready! From now on I go my way alone. One party. One single party. These gentlemen, these counts and generals – they won't do anything. I shall.'[5]

Meanwhile the exploits of Mussolini in Italy were attracting the attention of Hitler. He sent Lüdecke to Italy to observe his progress and see if he might be useful as a future ally. Although Mussolini offered no real support at this time, he did at least receive Lüdecke, who quickly became an admirer. His pointers on how Mussolini was gradually building up his power base to the stage where he would soon take power also interested Hitler. His eyes grew thoughtful when he heard how the Blackshirts marched into Bolshevised towns and took possession, while the garrisons kept benevolently neutral or, in some cases, even quartered the Fascists.[6]

Hitler was particularly impressed by the way in which Mussolini had sent his Blackshirts against the Communists and destroyed them. He decided on a trial of strength at Coburg. Accompanied by some 800 SA men, he set out quietly.

On their arrival at Coburg, the sight of Hitler and his storm troopers stepping off the train caused consternation among the ordinary people. However, the Social Democrats and Communists were furious to see the Nazis invading their own stronghold. A skirmish took place and the Nazis were victorious. They marched through the town like conquering heroes. Next day the combined anti-Nazi forces announced a mass protest. By now almost 1,500 SA men had arrived. The Nazis gathered in the main square, but only a few hundred demonstrators turned up to oppose them. What was of more interest to Hitler was that today the townsfolk were welcoming the Nazis with genuine enthusiasm. Imperial flags were hanging from windows everywhere, and large crowds made a welcoming pathway for the marching storm troopers. Hitler remarked contemptuously that it showed just how spineless the middle classes were. He drew from this victory the dangerous conclusion that he could go right to the top of German politics simply by a sufficiently ruthless display of physical force.[7]

Two weeks later Mussolini ordered his Fascists to march on Rome. He followed them by train and arrived in the capital to find that his bluff had been successful. The Italian government had resigned in the face of violence and the king had asked Mussolini to become Prime Minister. He was to become generally nicknamed *Il Duce*, the Leader, exactly the same title that Hitler, surely not accidentally, was to adopt. Until 1943 Hitler continued to be a warm admirer of Mussolini and for a long time put his abilities and achievements on the same scale as his own. Four days after the success of the march on Rome one of Hitler's own close followers was to address a large crowd and claimed explosively: 'Germany's Mussolini is called Hitler!'

The growing militancy of Hitler's movement began to start alarm bells ringing in the minds of a few concerned individuals. For one, the

American consular staff in Bavaria were convinced of his dangerous abilities but they were unable to get their nervous reports taken seriously in an increasingly isolationist America. Preoccupied with their own worries about prohibition, Al Capone and the Ku Klux Klan, the posturings of an obscure Austrian politician in a German provincial state seemed unimportant to them. Even within Hitler's own power-base of Bavaria, where three-quarters of the police force were open or secret supporters of his, a member of the Ministry of the Interior voiced his fears in a report to the State government. He claimed that the Nazi Party represented a very real danger, 'not only to the present form of government, but for any political system at all, because if they really achieve their dark ideas in regard to the Jews, Social Democrats and bank-capitalists, then there will be much blood and disorder.'

Even the new German Chancellor was warned about Hitler's ambitions by the Bulgarian consul. He had recently had conversations with the Nazi leader which had disturbed him so much that he felt compelled to pass on his fears to the highest authority in the land. Hitler had boasted that Parliamentary government in Germany was about to collapse and that only a dictatorship could save the country. He expected the Communists to take over in the north of Germany and his own party to control the south. Then the rival movements would fight for power and he was not afraid of the conflict.

Meanwhile Hitler was beginning to be taken seriously by some unlikely allies. The French and Belgian invasion of the Ruhr in 1923 inflamed all shades of political opinion in Germany. Many new members flocked to Hitler's party and even the Social Democrats invited him to join a national protest against the occupation. He was determined to stand alone, however, and turned down every proposal for joint action. Instead he announced that his own party would hold twelve public rallies to campaign against the invasion.

Terrified of the consequences of unilateral action by a man who had been hailed openly as 'Germany's Mussolini,' the chief of police in Bavaria told Hitler that his demonstrations could not be allowed to go ahead. Hitler shouted defiantly that he did not care if the police opened fire on his followers. For himself, he would be standing at the front of the crowd.

Hitler kept his word and tore frantically around the city addressing a string of illegal rallies. The audiences who heard him were electrified. Next day 6,000 storm troopers displayed their colours in another action of defiance against the police ban. Although in fact no serious trouble took place, his open rebellion had won him greater support than ever before. It had also made the government of Bavaria look weak and indecisive. The whole affair greatly encouraged Hitler in his belief that the time for a successful grab for power along Mussolini's lines was very near.

Hitler continued his extremely popular campaign against the French troops as well as continuing to try the patience of the Bavarian govern-

1. A sketch of the church and village of Ardoye in Flanders drawn by Hitler during the summer of 1917. (HU63413, IWM, A P Price Collection)

2. Hitler (back row, second from right) convalescing at the Beelitz Hospital, Berlin, recovering from a leg wound received on 7 October 1916 during the Battle of the Somme. (HU63453, IWM, A P Price Collection)

3. Hitler addressing an early meeting of the National Socialist German Workers' Party in Munich, 1922. (NYP68037, IWM)

4. Hitler, Hess and friends during his imprisonment at Landsberg. (NYP68040, IWM)

5. Hitler reviews members of the SA from his car at Nuremberg in 1930. (NYP68041, IWM)

6. Hitler, dishevelled and exhausted, emerges after making a speech to a Nazi Party meeting. (NYP68042, IWM)

7. Hitler sits with followers in a Munich beer garden. (NYP68038, IWM)

8. Geli Raubal, Hitler's niece, sitting on a roof. (00040978 — AKG Images Agency, Ulstein Collection)

9. *Right:* President Hindenburg appointing Hitler as Chancellor of Germany in January 1933. (NYP22518, IWM)

10. *Below:* Members of the German Labour Service, carrying shovels in a military fashion, are reviewed by Hitler. (NYP68056, IWM)

11. The 'Leader' visits his people. 'Jugend um Hitler'. (HU6293, IWM)

12. Eva Braun arm-in-arm with Hitler at Berchtesgaden in the 1930s. (HU63208, IWM, C Perera Collection)

13. Eva Braun in formal pose. (00531698 — AKG Images, Ullstein Collection)

14. Interior view of Hitler's residence, the Berghof, at Berchtesgaden, in the Obersalzburg, after its reconstruction during 1935–1936, showing the Great Study accommodation. (HU63542, IWM, K Butler Collection)

15. Hitler awarding the Iron Cross, Second class, to Alfred Czech, a twelve-year-old Hitler Youth soldier who fought in Pomerania and Silesia in 1945. One of the last known photographs of Hitler. (NYP62569, IWM)

16. The Liberation of Belsen Concentration Camp, April 1945. (BU3810, IWM)

ment. He turned up to meet the Bavarian Prime Minister with the leader of another paramilitary organisation. The two demanded that Bavaria defy the new law that had been passed by the Weimar government following the assassination of Rathenau. If they did not agree to the Bavarian demand to repeal the law, Bavaria should stand alone and declare that it did not recognise it. Three days later the Prime Minister gave his answer. He declared his own opposition to the Weimar law, but stated that he could not defy a legal requirement. Indeed, he would have to enforce it in spite of his own view that it was a mistake.

Hitler immediately called for a mass demonstration. Around 1,300 SA troops turned out to support him. However, this time the government decided to take action. Army and police units converged on the crowd and ordered them to hand over their weapons. In spite of his strong desire to defy the instructions, he backed down. The frustrated storm troopers took out their anger and disappointment on a band of Communists that they met on their way back from the demonstration.

Although he did all he could to try and turn the fiasco into some sort of triumph, even his own supporters knew that it had been a disastrous defeat for them. People who had been following his astonishing rise to fame began to predict that it was the beginning of the end for Hitler and the Nazis. It was not only the revolutionary wing of the party that began to lose faith in Hitler. Drexler, the founder of the party which Hitler now led, had always resented his loss of power and status. He was convinced that the confrontational tactics which Hitler was determined on adopting were doomed to failure. He was also worried by Hitler's new attempts to broaden the base of his support by courting wealthy nationalists. Drexler had always seen the working classes as the backbone of the party and he was convinced that any attempt to forge links with the 'reactionaries' would only lead to the final eclipse of the party.

Realising that his public support was slipping rapidly, Hitler did what he always did when problems started to mount. He held a massive rally in Nuremberg to celebrate the defeat of the French by the Germans in 1870. Although this was a general nationalist festivity rather than simply a Nazi rally, Hitler used it as an occasion to revive his flagging supporters. Swastika flags and marching storm troopers thronged the streets of the city and Hitler's movement provided the largest contingent of the marchers. During this celebration a loose nationalist paramilitary organisation called the German Battle League was formed. It was almost entirely dominated by the Nazis and it called openly for the overthrow of the Bavarian regime and its replacement by one dominated by the Nazis. Hitler was the political leader of the organisation and his new prestige led to a rapid revival in his confidence. He was always a creature of moods and could swing almost instantaneously from depression to total confidence and self-belief. Now he openly announced his intentions, and it is quite incredible that the Bavarian authorities continued to take no serious action against him on the basis of his track record.

This latest piece of arrogance by Hitler infuriated the Bavarian Prime Minister beyond endurance. He declared a state of emergency and appointed former Premier von Kahr as commissar general. Von Kahr immediately banned fourteen meetings by the Nazis which were due to take place the following day. Hitler had to decide how to respond to this sudden display of power by the state. Last time it had happened he had backed down and lost support as a result of his prudence. This time he was determined to resist. To a group of officers in the army he revealed that he planned to march upon Berlin and overthrow the Weimar Republic once and for all. He started to draw parallels between himself and Napoleon. Defying von Kahr to arrest him, he made one inflammatory speech after another.

The unfortunate commissar's problems were made worse by a combination of Nazi sympathisers within his own government, especially among the police and military, and a sudden determination by the authorities in Berlin to break the power of the Nazis before they became too strong to be stopped. When the head of the Bavarian army refused a direct order by the government in Berlin to ban Hitler's newspaper and take action against the Nazis, the Chancellor ordered his dismissal. This perfectly constitutional act plunged the Bavarian authorities into a frenzy which had disastrous consequences. They announced that all military units in Bavaria had to swear allegiance to the state government instead of the government in Berlin. Next day, the whole of the military forces in Bavaria swore the oath of loyalty to the state and renounced their obedience to Weimar. As if this act of open mutiny was not enough, von Kahr demanded that the new government in Berlin, headed by the great German politician Stresemann, should resign. Stresemann, although a nationalist, was a very liberal one. Even so, he was at this time still inclined to see 'reds under the beds' and made some unfortunate comments about Marxist subversives who were trying to destroy Germany.

As for the dismissed head of the army, von Lossow, he declared openly that the only choices were to give in to the government, to declare Bavaria's independence, or to march on Berlin and set up a nationalist dictatorship. Von Kahr and many of his colleagues were seriously thinking about going all out for independence. Hitler, of course, was committed to marching on Berlin. His difficulty was in persuading the Bavarian authorities to go down that road rather than the less dangerous one of open confrontation with Berlin. For a moment he considered a crazy plan to kidnap the pretender to the Bavarian throne and force him to give his support to Hitler's plans. Hanfstaengl talked Hitler out of it but he still had hopes of persuading them to abandon Bavarian separatism for an outright march on Berlin.

His first move in this direction was to try and get the chief of police and head of the army to join with him. He called publicly for troops from Bavaria to march on Berlin and the already nervous Bavarian authorities were increasingly concerned about the unpredictable Austrian. Hitler's request to meet von Seisser, the police chief, probably came as a welcome relief to them.

If they thought that Hitler was now swinging over to a more cautious policy, though, they were sadly mistaken. Von Seisser heard Hitler's plan to drop von Kahr from the government and to join up with his own movement in their campaign against Berlin. He told Hitler that he could not be in any way associated with a movement that aspired to overthrow the government. They were terrified that Hitler's headstrong behaviour would stampede them into another half-baked *putsch* like the Kapp fiasco three years before. After their discussions, Hitler and his allies were formally warned not to take action on their own. The Bavarian government, he was informed, was making plans of its own, which in a very short time would be revealed.

Typically, Hitler took no notice. He met with Ludendorff, Goering and other top-level conspirators to discuss the situation. The decision was taken at that meeting to stage a *putsch* on Sunday 11 November. Not only was this the fifth anniversary of Germany's surrender, but it would also be a day when most government forces would be on reserve strength. Next day the plans were dramatically revised as a result of the sudden and unexpected announcement by von Kahr that he intended to hold a meeting at the beerhall the following night. Although Hitler had received an official invitation that day, he saw the whole thing as a trap.

To this day no one is really sure what the intentions of the Bavarian government were. However, given their reluctance to either challenge the Berlin authorities directly or to accept their instructions, the most probable explanation is that they meant to declare Bavarian independence and the restoration of the monarchy. Such a course of action would undoubtedly have finished any chance of Hitler's political career moving on to the national stage. Filled with a sense of destiny, he persuaded his reluctant co-conspirators to act the very next night. All the top ministers of the government would be sitting on the same platform. Perhaps a show of force could bring them to heel.

The following day all units were gradually moved into position. By the evening the plans were in place. Hitler stood in the beerhall as he waited for his SA bodyguards to arrive. At 8.30 they finally arrived. Quickly the building was surrounded and the police totally surprised. Inside the beerhall the SA units shouted 'Heil Hitler.' Pulling out his gun, Hitler and his co-conspirators moved towards the platform. The exits had been blocked by storm troopers and a machine gun placed in a position where it commanded the entire hall. People began to scramble for cover as they feared a blood bath was about to take place.

Hitler jumped on to a chair and fired a shot into the ceiling. As the crowd fell silent he announced that the national revolution had broken out. Brandishing his gun, he took von Kahr and his two colleagues into a side room and apologised for his unorthodox way of proceeding. He promised all three of them top jobs in the new Germany. None of them seemed worried by the situation.

Hitler for once was unsure what to do. In a moment of inspired lunacy he rushed out into the hall and delivered the speech of his life. The crowd, which had been almost completely hostile towards him at the beginning, found itself being won over by the brilliance of his oratory. They cheered him wildly and when Ludendorff finally arrived he was greeted with even greater applause. Ludendorff was in fact anything but pleased with the situation that he found on his arrival. It should have been him, not the upstart Austrian corporal, who was the leader of the new Germany. Scowling in a not too well disguised fury, he went into the side room to talk with von Kahr and his fellow-ministers. Reasoning as he walked towards the room that he could always use Hitler and then ditch him when he had served his purpose, the Prussian warlord decided to use his influence to persuade the Bavarian ministers to agree to the *putsch* and authorise the march on Berlin by the army.

Ludendorff did have a certain amount of success in his persuasions. The army leader agreed to go along with the plan, and then, more reluctantly, the police chief. It was the civilian von Kahr who proved the most stubborn. All the same, when they did return to the beerhall he spoke first, announcing that he would serve Bavaria as regent for the king. This produced an outburst of wild cheering from the crowd.

Meanwhile the storm trooper units were busy taking over some of the key positions within the city. However, as might be expected, there were a few problems in the seizure of power. The engineers' barracks were having a violent confrontation with the SA units. Hitler, in a display of quite incredibly bad judgement, not only decided to go there himself to calm things down but also left Ludendorff in charge. As soon as Hitler had gone, the army chief told Ludendorff that the three of them had to go and issue some orders on behalf of the new regime. Since he had given Ludendorff his word as an officer and a gentleman that he would return and do nothing against the *putsch* while he was away, Ludendorff let them go. When he returned Hitler was appalled to find his hostages gone. He gave Ludendorff a severe reprimand which the haughty general dismissed with a contemptuous wave of his hand. No German officer would break his sworn word, he informed the former corporal arrogantly.

Hitler, of course, knew better than that. Even so, the storm troopers were having some success in gaining control of key positions. What was even more encouraging was the wholesale defection to the Nazis of 1,000 military cadets. They went to the beerhall to salute Hitler and Ludendorff and then marched off to occupy von Kahr's offices. Before long the army chief gave orders to smash the *putsch* by force if necessary. Incredibly, it had not occurred to the plotters to control the telephone lines so that von Kahr and his allies could not issue such orders to troops from just outside Munich. Von Kahr had just received a message from the pretender to the Bavarian throne ordering him to put down the *putsch* and destroy the Nazi party for good. He promptly went ahead with these instructions, which were very much in line with his own thinking.

After it began to dawn on Hitler and Ludendorff that the *putsch* had failed, the general began to fall apart. He announced in shocked surprise that he would never trust a German officer's word again. Then he more or less retreated into his shell. Both Ludendorff and Hitler claimed credit for the idea to march through the heart of the city and stake everything on one victory or death stroke. Although it is impossible to prove at this late stage, the odds are that it was Hitler's idea. Certainly it was carried out in true Hitler fashion.

The specific details of the failed *putsch* have been covered again and again by numerous historians and it is not really necessary to repeat them here.[8] What mattered was what happened in the main square of the city soon after the march had begun. Police troopers under orders from von Kahr were suddenly facing Hitler and Ludendorff and the SA units behind them.

Essentially, one side or the other – the truth about this has never been established – fired first. The police then opened fire with a volley that killed some of the marchers. Hitler was dragged down to the ground by his bodyguard and a fellow-conspirator who lost his own life at the time. Although Ludendorff later claimed that he stayed on his feet, all eyewitness accounts agree that he hit the ground at the first volley. It was after the momentary silence that the general rose to his feet and marched alone towards the waiting police. He walked into the column and was promptly put under arrest by a lieutenant. Once he had been arrested, the general announced that from now on he would be known as plain *Herr* Ludendorff, since the events of that night had shown him that uniforms had been dishonoured. Before long he was to deny any involvement with the *putsch* at all, claiming with characteristic dishonesty that he had been an innocent bystander.

Hitler's companions helped him to safety. He took refuge in the home of his friends the Hanfstaengls. For a moment he took up his revolver and thought of suicide but Helene Hanfstaengl managed to talk him out of it. He then wrote a series of letters to party comrades, the most important of them being the one which handed over the Nazi leadership to Rosenberg. Eventually the police arrived and took Hitler off to the prison at Landsberg. With another curious piece of symmetry, he was placed in the cell that Arco-Valley, the man who killed Eisner, had been occupying. He had already been briefly imprisoned in Eisner's own cell.

The failed *putsch* was already leading most people to the view that Hitler had overreached himself once too often and that he was now finished as a serious political force. In normal circumstances that should and would have been the case. But Hitler's genius was to reassert itself with a vengeance when the time came. The times themselves, of course, were anything but normal, and the circumstances in which he was to find himself led to a quite unexpected revival in his fortunes. These extraordinary developments will be dealt with in the following chapter.

Notes

1. Bernard Wasserstein, *The Secret Lives of Trebitsch-Lincoln*, Penguin, 1983
2. Otto Dietrich, *The Hitler I Knew*, gives the best account of Hitler's and Eckart's 'involvement' – it hardly amounted to more than a brief visit to an already collapsing regime – in the Kapp Putsch fiasco.
3. For the early years of the SA, the best source is still: Konrad Heiden, *A History of National Socialism*, Octagon, 1971
4. For this first instance of the SA's use as an instrument of political intimidation see: Ernst Deurlein, *Der Aufsteig der NSDAP, 1919 to 1933 in Augenseugen Berichtet*, Rauch, 1968
5. Ibid
6. Ibid
7. Ibid
8. The best works on the Munich *putsch* are: a) Richard Hanser, *Putsch!*, Peter H Wiyden, 1970: b) Harold J Gordon, *Hitler and the Beer-Hall Putsch*, Princeton University, 1972; c) Ernst Deurlein, *Der Hitler Putsch*, Deutsches Verlags-Anstalt, 1962

CHAPTER VI

Hitler the Prisoner

If Hitler's desperate gamble in the beerhall had almost finished his political career, it was his imprisonment and trial that revived his spirits and revitalised the party's fortunes. Partly that was down to luck, partly to the desire of the Bavarian authorities to cover up their own murky past, but mostly it was the result of a brilliant performance by Hitler at his trial. Unlike Ludendorff, who pretended that he had taken no part in the *putsch*, Hitler claimed full credit for his actions and announced that he, and only he, was the true saviour of the German people.

All this, however, lay in the future. At first Hitler simply sat in his cell at Landsberg, brooding darkly over his prospects. The prison doctor had treated his left arm, but his dislocated shoulder and broken upper arm were very painful. In addition he was full of anger and contempt for the people that he had expected would support him. Once again the army, the police, and the upper classes that led Bavaria had betrayed him. Instead of placing themselves at the head of a national revolution, they had turned upon him and crushed his bid for national regeneration.

Drexler found that Hitler, sunk in apathy, had refused to eat for two weeks. He was determined to talk him out of his fast and spent an hour and three quarters urging him to eat something. Hitler had already been urged by Helene Hanfstaengl and Hélène Bechstein to give up his hunger strike, and a party member from the Sudetenland in Czechoslovakia had also demanded that Hitler should give up. Drexler's words finally convinced Hitler that he should save his strength and make one further effort to lead the nation.[1]

Even after he had finally given up his fast, he still refused to say anything to the authorities that might incriminate him. It was only when the assistant prosecutor, who came himself to interview the prisoner, sent away the note-taker and asked Hitler to speak to him off the record, that he finally got him to break his silence. Once he began speaking, it was more like a public oration than a confession, but the prosecutor listened patiently and put in a full report to his office when he returned to Munich.

Meanwhile Hitler's spirits had revived dramatically. He was looking forward to the trial with considerable excitement. His storm troopers, who had gone underground at first, were now being reassembled under other names. Constant streams of visitors were also busy lifting his spirits and promising to continue to work for the national cause within the nation. Lüdecke even went to America to try and raise money for the Nazis. However, he found that the mere mention of Hitler's name led to hoots of laughter. Even the Ku Klux Klan, which was at the height of its popularity and influence at that time, regarded him as a joke. His mission was a complete failure.[2]

Things were not going so well with the Nazi party at home either. Officially it had been declared illegal and Rosenberg had to operate more or less undercover. He was not helped in his efforts to hold the party together by the fact that, with the commanding presence of Hitler removed, factions were beginning to appear within Nazi ranks. Both on personal and political grounds, serious splits began to develop. In Austria, Hanfstaengl, Goering and three other Nazis regarded themselves, even though they were exiled and in hiding, as the real leaders of the party. Drexler also hoped that Hitler's imprisonment could lead to the party returning to the direction in which he wished it to go. Meanwhile the left wing of the party, headed by Gregor Strasser, was anxious to head the party even further in a socialist direction than they had already gone in the early years of the movement. Rosenberg, always the intellectual with no charisma and very little support within the party, did his best to keep things going. Although he was by no means the ideal choice, he was one of the few candidates available for the job of party leader and he was completely loyal to Hitler. This was not something that could be said of some of the other candidates.[3]

Meanwhile Hitler was taking advantage of his imprisonment to brush up on his reading. Always a prolific reader, with plenty of time on his hands he now read voraciously. Scornfully he was to refer to Landsberg prison in a conversation with Frank as 'my education at state expense.'[4] He read Nietzsche, Marx, Treitschke, Houston Stewart Chamberlain, Bismarck and various other political and racist works. He also continued his occult studies.

The newly acquired time that he found in prison led him to reflect on the *putsch* itself. Reluctantly he came to the conclusion that it had been a mistake. It would not have been possible for him to have seized power in Germany in the same way that Mussolini had managed in Italy. The *putsch* had been an improvised, spur of the moment affair, and the machinery for turning it into a genuine bid for power had not been put in place. In addition, he was now as contemptuous of Ludendorff as he had already become of other army officers, and felt that it would have been impossible to work with him. Although that might well have been true, Hitler was hardly the easiest of men to work with himself.[5]

Having regained his old confidence, Hitler was looking forward in a strange sort of way to his trial. It turned out to be one of the worst conducted in legal history. To begin with, Hitler was only the second named defendant in the case, the first name and the supposed ringleader being that of Ludendorff. In spite of this it was on Hitler that all the attention of Germany became focused. He denounced the rulers of his country, admitted his part as the prime mover in the conspiracy and declared, in a ringing phrase that became famous, that he was innocent of treason because it was impossible to commit treason against the 'November criminals'.

The judges in the court were all keen nationalists themselves. The effect of Hitler's words on them was electrifying. Instead of the ragged and inadequate conspirator, motivated by envy, that they had expected to find, they came upon a man whose words and manner spoke of patriotism and the loftiest ideals, and in a way that moved these seasoned servants of law. Before long Hitler had taken over the proceedings completely and turned the trial into a vehicle for National Socialist propaganda. On only one single occasion was any attempt made to halt his flow of words, and then for a brief moment only, by which time the damage had already been done. Not only had Hitler completely taken over the courtroom, but the way in which he had upstaged Ludendorff led to the general becoming even more petulant and sulky than he had been before. Whereas Hitler gave a bravura performance in the courtroom, Ludendorff contented himself with bullying the already intimidated judges. He treated them as if they were on parade and he was the officer reviewing them.[6]

During the trial Rosenberg and Hanfstaengl, who hated each other, visited Hitler. Hanfstaengl came as a friend, and he also took his son along to meet Hitler. Rosenberg's visit was political, concerned with the present direction of the party. He explained to Hitler that he had decided to go along with an idea of Gregor Strasser's and enter candidates as part of a *völkisch* bloc. Hitler was not keen, but Rosenberg, who was full of enthusiasm for the idea, went ahead anyway.

Meanwhile the highlight of the trial was Hitler's interrogation in the witness box of the Bavarian leadership. This deteriorated at one stage into an exchange of insults between Hitler and the army chief, but in fact Hitler made some shrewd points about the intentions of the leadership, which were not lost on the judges. His final summing up was a masterpiece of oratory, which had as devastating an effect on the court as his opening speech. So effectively had he conducted his defence, and so inept had the prosecution been, that people outside the courtroom were actually taking bets that Hitler would be acquitted. It was in fact a very close run thing.

Ludendorff, in spite of the overwhelming evidence against him, was completely cleared of all charges. He greeted the not guilty verdict with yet more sarcasm, describing it as a 'disgrace'. Considering that he had been busy throughout the trial lying about his role and claiming that he was in no way responsible for the *putsch*, his remarks were even more extraordinary.

Hitler was found guilty largely because the conduct of the trial had become such a national scandal that an acquittal would certainly have led to the referral of the case to a higher court outside Bavaria. Hitler would certainly not have been allowed to behave elsewhere as he had been in Munich. Indeed, he would certainly have been given a far stiffer sentence than he could expect to receive from the Bavarian court authorities.

There was too the quite justified suspicion that the activities of von Kahr and his associates had also been at least bordering on treason. For this reason they decided that the safest course of action was to find Hitler guilty but give him a derisorily short sentence, considering the gravity of his crime. He was therefore sentenced to five years in prison, six months being taken off his sentence because of his pre-trial imprisonment. The court also refused to avail itself of its power to deport Hitler to his native Austria as an undesirable alien. His war record weighed heavily in his favour with regard to this decision. He returned to prison, uncertain of how long he might have to spend there.[7]

In his section of the prison, Hitler was top dog. The other prisoners all deferred to him and even mealtimes could not begin until he had seated himself at the table. He continued to read, and now at last he had time to put down his thoughts on paper. The result was, of course, *Mein Kampf*.

Meanwhile Rosenberg's decision to put up candidates for the Bavarian elections turned out to be a triumph. The hastily assembled slate won just under 200,000 votes and became the second largest party in Parliament. A month later the elections to the national Reichstag took place. Gregor Strasser, Ludendorff, Roehm and twenty-nine other candidates were elected. All but two of the *völkisch* slate became deputies to the Reichstag. In normal circumstances, Hitler would have been delighted by such good results. However, although his newly acquired national celebrity was to a considerable extent responsible for the high vote, he could not claim personal credit for this victory. Not only had Rosenberg and Strasser turned out to be right in ignoring his advice, but Ludendorff was now going around Germany claiming all the credit for the result and trying to assert himself as the bloc's leader. The various other nationalist parties that had joined with the Nazis were also trying to submerge Hitler's movement in a wider *völkisch* association.

As if all this was not enough trouble, Drexler was spearheading his own campaign against the imprisoned leader. Convinced, with a certain amount of justification, that Hitler had never treated him with the respect due to the founder and former leader of the party, he began to mastermind a movement for greater democracy within the Nazis. He was in any case very unhappy with the direction in which he felt that Hitler had been taking things. The fiasco of the *putsch* was the last straw for Drexler. The bitter former leader became determined to break Hitler's iron grip on the party and to bring about what he saw as a return to sanity.[8]

It was not only Hitler who was being challenged. Rosenberg's unlikely alliance with Strasser was also provoking considerable dissension within the party. Strasser himself, who represented the party's left, was highly popular with its members. The remote conservative intellectual was probably being used by Strasser to further his own political ambitions. Hitler, appealed to for his support by all the factions within the party, refused to become involved. He had now become converted to the policy of winning power through the ballot box. With regard to the internal running of the party or any policy disagreements between its members, he refused to make any attempt to intervene. During the time that he was in prison, he declared, he would devote himself to writing and would take no active part in politics.

Although this remained true with regard to the world outside, it was anything but true within the prison. Hitler and his fellow-Nazis spent their time inside propagandising to such good effect that the governor and a majority of his staff became converted to National Socialism.

His main activities in prison were spreading the word among prisoners and staff developing new angles on his philosophy of life, and writing *Mein Kampf*. He was greatly assisted in the composition of this book by a close friend of Hess, Karl Haushofer.

Because his son Albrecht was strongly anti-Nazi, even being involved in the German resistance, Karl Haushofer's denials of any real influence upon Hitler have often been believed. Nevertheless, his protestations of innocence were certainly false. He quite rightly claimed that Hitler misunderstood and oversimplified the new ideas to which Haushofer introduced him during the Nazi leader's imprisonment. All the same, his influence over Hitler was profound. It took two main forms, occult training and directly political ideas. The most important contribution that Haushofer made to Nazi political thought was his concept of *lebensraum*, which means 'living space'. This was an idea that he derived from the British imperialist Sir Halford Mackinder, the inventor of the pseudo-science known as geopolitics. Mackinder's work, which first became known in the 1890s, had enormous influence in Germany. Haushofer was also partly responsible for directing Hitler's attention towards Russia, since he had adopted another of Mackinder's ideas, the notion of the 'heartland', which was supposed to be a territory stretching from the Caucasus Mountains to Tibet. Whoever controlled the heartland, so both Mackinder and Haushofer claimed, controlled the world.

Haushofer, along with Eckart, was the man most responsible for the occult training that Hitler followed from before the First World War. He was in terms of his abilities at the very top of the tree. He had tremendous knowledge of magic, which he passed on to his pupil Hitler. Far from being an unwilling and minor player on the sidelines, Haushofer was one of the decisive influences on the formation of Hitler's development into the messianic figure he was to become for millions of Germans.[9]

The main 'constructive' achievement of Hitler's time in prison was the writing of *Mein Kampf*. Originally called *Four and a Half Years of Struggle Against Lies, Stupidity and Cowardice,* Hitler allowed himself to be talked into changing it to the far shorter *Mein Kampf,* or *My Struggle.* He was not too concerned about the attempts by Rosenberg, Strasser, Ludendorff and Drexler to battle for control of the party, as he was confident that he would soon be free and that on his release all sections would fall back into line under his leadership.

Hitler's fairly confident expectations of an early parole, boosted by a very favourable report from the prison governor, were to be surprisingly dashed. The Bavarian authorities remained frightened of Hitler's talent for rousing the people and preferred to let him stay in prison a little longer. They were also still considering deporting him back to Austria as an undesirable alien. The result was that, although Hitler was declared eligible for parole, the early release for which he had hoped was refused. A few of the minor players in the *putsch* were released quietly but Hitler himself remained in prison. It was not until 19 December 1924 that the Bavarian Supreme Court ordered his release. Hitler said goodbye to his fellow-conspirators, gave them what money he had, and left the prison for good. He ordered Hoffmann to take a picture of him outside to commemorate his experience.

He came home to gifts from friends and neighbours, gifts of food and flowers, and a warm welcome from his dog. Hitler was convinced that his time in prison had been an essential step in his development. Not only had it led him to formulate new ideas and put more flesh on some old policies, but also hardened his character. From now on he meant to dominate the party in a way he had never done before. It was from this time on that what was to become known as the *Fuehrer-prinzip,* the leadership principle, came to be an unchallenged and unchallengeable article of faith in the party. This next stage in his career will be considered in the following chapter.

Notes

1. Drexler's account is given in the Bayerisches Hauptstaatsarchiv, MA 104221, Drexler Bericht.
2. Lüdecke, *I Knew Hitler.* It is only fair to point out, however, that Henry Ford, a notorious anti-Semite and a man who had contributed to the Nazi Party from as early as 1920, continued to give them his financial support, even if he did reduce his contributions for the next two or three years.
3. Alfred Rosenberg, *Memoirs,* Ziff-Davis, 1949
4. Frank, *Im Angesicht des Galgens*

5. Harold J Gordon, *Hitler and the Beer-Hall Putsch*
6. One has only to examine even briefly the way in which the trial was conducted to see at once that it was a travesty of justice. The curious may wish to consult the full details in *Protokol der Hitler-Prozess*, Deutscher Volksverlag, 1924
7. Adolf Hitler, *Hitler's Secret Conversations*
8. Frank, op cit
9. For more on Haushofer, see: a) FitzGerald, *Storm Troopers of Satan;* b) King, *Satan and Swastika;* c) James Webb, *The Occult Establishment,* Richard Drew, 1981; d) J H Brennan, *Occult Reich,* Futura, 1974; e) Louis Pauwels and Jacques Bergier, *The Morning of the Magicians,* Mayflower, 1973; f) Ravenscroft, *The Spear of Destiny;* g) Dusty Sklar, *The Nazis and the Occult,* Dorset Press, 1989

CHAPTER VII

Hitler the Politician

It is obvious from the accounts of Hitler's youth by Kubizek that politics became a passion for him during his teenage years. However, it was not until Germany had lost the First World War that he became actively involved in any meaningful way. We have already dealt with Hitler's brief flirtation with Communism, his employment as an undercover agent to German intelligence charged with the job of restoring national pride to the German soldiers, and, of course, the way in which he had taken a party of some fifty members and turned it into a powerful political force within Germany. Now, on his release from prison, his first task was to regain control of the party, which had been in serious danger of splitting into at least three separate groups.

Perhaps it would be more accurate to speak of two main sections within the broad Nazi base, as Rosenberg commanded little support within the party and Strasser was the dominant figure in their alliance. As for Ludendorff, he had lost all credibility as a national leader thanks to his spineless behaviour at his own trial for treason. The moderate faction, headed by Hanfstaengl and Goering, was certainly far from hostile to Hitler, and would probably come to heel without any serious trouble. Their dislike of his anti-Semitism was the main area of disagreement between themselves and Hitler. He was confident that this obstacle could be overcome.

All the same, fresh elections held during the very December of his release showed that there was a real problem to be overcome. The Nazi bloc had lost almost a million votes and the Nazi Party itself was still outlawed. Any political organisation would have to be undertaken very carefully indeed. On the other hand, in spite of the attempts which had been made by the Bavarian Minister of Justice to have Hitler expelled from the country, the Austrian refusal to have him back had put the Bavarian government in a most difficult position. Reluctantly, the deportation proceedings against Hitler were dropped.[1]

Meanwhile Hitler was finding it difficult to adjust to freedom after a year in prison. He kept expecting to find a hand on his shoulder any minute telling him that he needed permission to do anything. Realising that he was not yet in a fit state to begin his political comeback, he spent his time with friends. The Hanfstaengls were a household he always enjoyed visiting and it was there that he spent Christmas Eve. They welcomed him as an old friend and listened to his new thoughts on politics. Unfortunately this soon degenerated into another assault on the Jews and the embarrassed Hanfstaengl felt that his guest had become even more paranoid in his anti-Semitism since his time in prison. In particular he was obsessed with the idea that America was controlled by an international conspiracy of Jewish capitalists – an idea, to be fair, that he probably got from Henry Ford. It was on this particular Christmas Eve visit that he made his unfortunate attempt to seduce Helene Hanfstaengl, after which his relationship with the family was never to be the same.[2]

Meanwhile the political situation did not look good for Hitler. Not only had the elections shown a drop in support for the *völkisch* bloc, but a new government in France was finally prepared to be more reasonable in its demands upon Germany. The economy, which had almost collapsed after the French occupation of the Ruhr, was beginning to recover. Germany was about to enter the brief period of prosperity which was to become known as the 'golden twenties.' In this changed situation Hitler looked like a rabble-rouser who was constantly harping on about the past. People were beginning to forget about the war and the Treaty of Versailles as the Weimar Republic at last began to produce some solid achievements of its own to make its citizens proud once more. The cunning Stresemann, first as Chancellor and then Foreign Minister, led the new Germany into a higher place than she had occupied at any time since 1914. In this climate the Nazis found making converts very heavy going.

On the other hand, the effects of the inflation of 1923 had been quite devastating on certain sections of the German population. Until the Munich *putsch* the bulk of the party's support had come from the working class. With the revival in prosperity, their support began to return to its more traditional home, the Social Democrats. However, the middle classes, who had tended to support the German equivalent of the British Liberal Party before 1923, now began to find the Nazi message attractive. Big business had managed to survive the great disaster of 1923, but the small shopkeepers, the farmers and the small businessmen had been almost ruined by inflation. When Hitler told them that their miseries were due to Jewish capitalists and department stores, many were willing to listen and some were even convinced by his message. There was, then, a potential source of new support for the party. None of this mattered, of course, unless he could get the ban on the Nazis lifted. After a meeting with the new Bavarian Prime Minister, Hitler pledged himself to work through strictly legal means for the goal of the defeat of Communism.[3] Although no decision was taken at the time, he made such a favourable impression that it was only a month later that the ban on the party, its newspaper and its public meetings was lifted.

The day after the announcement, Hitler went to a party convention in the very beerhall where he had launched his abortive *putsch*. All the important Nazi leaders came to greet him, except for Roehm, Strasser and Rosenberg. The first two represented the left-wing of the party and knew that they would stand no chance in the emotional atmosphere to be expected that evening. Rosenberg quite simply felt that Hitler had betrayed him. He had no desire to prostrate himself before the returning hero when he had not even been allowed to meet Hitler following his release. Those who came to hail Hitler were already in a highly charged state of emotion before he spoke. After his speech the whole meeting was solidly behind him. Cunningly, instead of siding with one or other of the factions within the party, Hitler called instead for reconciliation. He would be not only the leader of the party but he himself would in a sense be the programme. He offered a year of crusading politics, promising that if he had not managed to turn things around by then he would resign and let someone else try their luck. 'Everyone for Hitler!' came the carefully planned cry. Naturally, at the meeting that night, everybody was indeed for Hitler.[4]

The day after Hitler's first public meeting since his release, a new German President was elected. This was the aged Field Marshal von Hindenburg, a reactionary monarchist whose very candidacy would have been totally unacceptable to the Western Allies two years earlier.

Hindenburg was a most curious character. A mediocre man, who tried his best to work within the Weimar constitution which he personally detested, his interventions on the political scene tended to be in the conservative interest. He had only won narrowly, but his presence as the new figurehead of Germany made the emergency powers which the President enjoyed under the constitution a source of danger if Parliamentary government broke down.

However, Hitler's own powers of oratory had alarmed the Bavarian government. Only recently out of prison, he was already busily inciting his followers to struggle by all means possible for the regeneration of the German nation. Since Hitler went out of his way to add that, if necessary, this included the use of violence, the result was inevitable. The nervous Bavarian government immediately cancelled some meetings which he had been scheduled to address. Before long they were to ban him completely from any public speaking in Bavaria. Other German states were quick to follow the Bavarian example and the result was that any National Socialist meeting could be held anywhere in Germany as long as Hitler did not address it.

Deprived of his strongest weapon, Hitler was forced to confine himself to the grass roots of the party. He began the work of organising it within

Bavaria and actually managed to meet every single member of the Munich party. His aides, the dubious Esser and the even less appealing Streicher, went out into the countryside, building up a strong base among the discontented peasants and farmers in Bavaria. Outside his Bavarian powerbase he had to rely upon Gregor Strasser and his brother Otto, both brilliant speakers and in Gregor's case a brilliant organiser as well. The only problem was that, in spite of Gregor's public announcement of loyalty to Hitler, he was an extremely ambitious and able politician. Both brothers were also fiercely committed to the left-wing of the party and Otto Strasser was himself a notoriously indiscreet and inflammatory speaker, who had not been above disagreeing violently with Hitler on more than one occasion.

Nevertheless, Hitler had no option but to trust the Strassers. Gregor was not only one of the leading delegates to the German Parliament but was also the only major Nazi who had close and strong support in northern Germany. Many people within the party saw him as a possible alternative leader should Hitler fail. Although both Hitler and Strasser despised the conservative forces within Germany, Hitler's opportunism led him to believe that he might be able to make use of them for his own purposes. Strasser believed that the Nazis were a working class party or they were nothing. He bitterly opposed the German aristocracy and capitalists. Strasser's direction of the party in northern Germany was bringing in disillusioned Communists and Social Democrats, in certain areas with quite spectacular success. Party membership soared as the charismatic Strasser appealed with remarkable persistence to the German workers. The results were undeniable. Even Hitler, who was worried about Strasser as a possible rival, was impressed by his work.

Perhaps Strasser's success had been too sudden and too spectacular. Whether his new importance to the cause went to his head or not, Strasser decided to hold a party conference to push the party in the direction which he felt was the only logical one for it to take. It was certainly not intended as any sort of challenge to his leadership, but the delegates under Strasser's control felt that Hitler was being manipulated by his reactionary advisers from Bavaria and that a special party conference could lead him back on to the right revolutionary socialist road.

At this conference, held in Hagen, his policies were endorsed quite overwhelmingly. These called in essence for what became known at the time as 'national Bolshevism'. Strasser's closest allies at this time were his brother Otto, Heinrich Himmler and Josef Goebbels. Himmler had been acting as Strasser's secretary and was then replaced by Goebbels. Goebbels was fiercely committed to Strasser and his vision of 'national Bolshevism.' Like many Nazis during the 'era of struggle,' he had formerly been a Communist. In essence, Goebbels remained a Marxist throughout his life. It was the internationalism of Marxism which repelled him, however.

When he discovered the Nazis he felt that he could truly embrace a purely German, nationalist brand of socialism. Like the Strassers, Goebbels aimed his oratory and writing at the working classes, particularly Communists and trade unionists.

That November he met Hitler for the first time. Goebbels was bowled over by the Austrian's charisma and wrote in his diaries of how much he idolised him. With another man one might have suspected latent homosexuality, but not with Goebbels. The brilliant but immature 29 year old was only caught up in a typical adolescent bout of hero-worship.[5] Nevertheless, for all his personal adoration of Hitler, this did not stop Goebbels from participating soon after in an open revolt against the party leadership. Strasser had organised a meeting of northern *Gauleiters* – regional party bosses – to draft a new party programme which would have moved the Nazis decisively to the left. This conference was held at Hanover in January 1926.

Hitler himself did not attend, but he sent Gottfried Feder, the man who had drafted the original party programme with Hitler and Drexler, to speak on his behalf. A whole series of radical resolutions were proposed and passed, only one *Gauleiter* voting against them. Feder simply announced that neither Hitler nor he would accept the new programme. The resolutions had called for the confiscation of former royal property, nationalisation of land, breaking up large private estates into tenant farms and wholesale nationalisation of businesses.[6]

Feder's intervention infuriated most of the delegates. None went as far as Goebbels did, however. He sprang up angrily and called for the expulsion of 'the petty bourgeois Hitler' from the party. This open challenge to the leader himself could hardly be ignored, especially when it came from a man with the organisational and propagandist skills of Goebbels. Alarmed by a no doubt highly coloured report from Feder, Hitler decided to act. With the speed and energy that he always displayed when a threat arose, he summoned all party leaders to attend a secret congress at Bamberg in three weeks' time. The Bavarian loyalists vastly outnumbered the nervous north Germans, many of whom felt in any case that Goebbels had gone too far and that a Nazi party without Hitler at its head was inconceivable.

Meanwhile Hitler himself had no intention of turning upon either Goebbels or Strasser. He knew that he needed both men and also realised that they were not fundamentally disloyal to him, simply that they wanted him to take a more leftist approach to politics. Aware of the difficult path that he had to tread, Hitler handled the rebels masterfully. He began by declaring that he was the leader of the party and that he alone could determine the course of its destiny. Policies were to be shaped by him, not by party members. The Nazis were not a democratic party and he expected absolute and unconditional loyalty and obedience from his members. Having set the stage by insisting on the primacy of the leadership principle, he gave a speech which was full of radical and left-wing slogans and rhetoric. He then offered a vision of himself as the man who stood above all political differences as the saviour of Germany, the man who was both revolutionary and yet preserver of all that was good about the nation's past. He reassured those members of the middle classes who were beginning to find the Nazi message attractive while renouncing none of his revolutionary and socialist rhetoric. As for the idea that new policies could be added to the existing party platform, he firmly declared that the twenty-five points of the original party programme were 'the foundation of our religion, our ideology'. In no way could it be abandoned or altered. The movement had its manifesto that stood written as firmly in stone as the tablets of the Mosaic Law. But Hitler could and would lead the movement to triumph, and when he had done so a truly national socialism would be created in Germany.[7]

Strasser knew when he was beaten. Faced with the choice of abandoning his fight for greater socialism within the party or of founding a new party himself, he capitulated. It was not the first time that Strasser was found wanting in resolution when his continued opposition might have made a difference. Nor was it to be the last. In the end this fatal indecisiveness in his character was to lead to his own death on the orders of Hitler and his henchmen. Goebbels showed rather more courage, chanting a number of slogans from time to time. He wrote in his diary of his intense disappointment at the result.[8] Goebbels was made of far tougher material than his boss Strasser.

Though he had won the contest, Hitler was in the mood for neither vengeance nor complacency. He respected the abilities of both men and knew that they had already proved their worth by bringing thousands of working class members in to the party. With this in mind, he set out to woo both men over to his side. Strasser was the first to yield, issuing a letter to his supporters in March in which he announced the abandonment of his own programme.

Goebbels proved a rather more difficult man to convert. It took two days of a personal visit by Hitler to bring him round to his point of view. Gradually, under the spell of Hitler's relentless barrage of charm, Goebbels began, not only to give way, but even to see his own beliefs as being compatible with Hitler's own. The brief but dangerous flickering of revolt within the party had been snuffed out by the neutralisation of its leaders.

Now secure in the leadership, Hitler discovered a new occult adviser, Erik Jan Hanussen. Like so many people who were to become involved with the Nazi party in its early years, Hanussen was Jewish, his real name being Herschel Steinschneider. Haushofer, who was Hitler's main occult adviser between 1924 and 1942, had a Jewish wife. Hanussen was noted for his clairvoyant gifts and his extraordinary predictive abilities.

Unlike many occult practitioners, Hanussen's gifts were more genuine than faked. However, he was undoubtedly a showman, and did not lack confidence. When he first met Hitler at a society hostess's reception in Berlin, he actually suggested to the Nazi leader that he ought to learn how to speak properly. Considering that even at this stage of his career Hitler was noted as one of the most powerful orators in Germany, this was a remarkable statement to have made to him. What was even more remarkable, though, was Hitler's reaction. Instead of denouncing the clairvoyant indignantly for his presumption, he asked him how he could improve his presentation as a public speaker.

Hanussen told him that, although his delivery and timing were impressive, he needed to learn to use gesture and body language to emphasise his message and have a greater impact upon his audience. Over the next few years Hanussen and Hitler met regularly, and the Jewish clairvoyant taught Hitler how to make the most of his talent for public speaking. So trusted a confidant did he become that he was even allowed to advise Hitler on his choice of colleagues, based on his clairvoyant and astrological gifts.[9]

Meanwhile Hitler once again needed to consolidate his position in the party. The threat of open revolt had been laid to rest, but he needed to find some way of using Strasser and Goebbels without allowing them to become serious rivals to himself. With this aim in mind, he decided to adopt a twin-track approach. At a party meeting in the Munich beerhall, Hitler alone was given formal power to choose all his subordinates, that no checks upon his power could be placed in any way by the party, and that the original twenty-five point manifesto was the unalterable ideology of the party. On the personal front, he had already decided that it was in his own interests to divide his two dangerous rivals from one another. Strasser and Goebbels together were a formidable team, but perhaps if they could be broken up the old political trick of dividing and ruling might prove successful.

Of the two men, it was now Goebbels, whose own opposition to Hitler had been both more open and more consistent, who had become convinced that Hitler was the new German Messiah. As such, he was more amenable to persuasion than Strasser, who still held considerable reservations about Hitler. Hitler dealt with the problem by bringing Strasser into the inner circle of the party leadership. As for Goebbels, he appointed him the *Gauleiter* of Berlin. This was a task which the young intellectual was more than happy to take on. Berlin was the 'Red city' *par excellence*, dominated by the Social Democrats and the Communists. The Nazi party in Berlin was derisorily small, saddled with large debts and having made no impact whatever on the citizens. From Hitler's point of view he had not only removed a dangerous rival but also sent him to a place where he would have his hands full keeping the party going. If he could make any headway as well, that would be a bonus. There was just one small problem which needed to be ironed out. Before he left for Berlin, Goebbels broke off his engagement to a young girl who was half-Jewish.

Even though this was the height of the Weimar Republic's 'golden twenties' Nazi membership had increased by 10,000 during the year. This does not sound much, and the party remained one of the smallest in Germany, but it was superbly organised and men such as Goebbels and Strasser were giving it slightly more cutting edge than the crude thugs like Esser and Streicher who had been dominating it for some years.

The end of 1926 also saw the second volume of *Mein Kampf* published. It was less autobiographical than the first volume, more a political history of the party – in a highly selective version, naturally – and containing more questionable political diatribes. Curiously, it demonstrated a new shift in Hitler's thinking on foreign policy. At the end of the First World War he had been convinced that France was the natural enemy of Germany and that even Bolshevist Russia was worth consideration as an ally against the French. Now he had elevated the Soviet Union to first place on the list of Germany's enemies. He spoke of the need for *lebensraum* and claimed that only in the wide lands belonging to the Soviet Union could Germany find this necessity. Once this had been achieved, the headquarters of world 'Jewry' would have been destroyed and the 'Jewish menace' eliminated for good. According to Haushofer, Hess asked him to review the second volume of *Mein Kampf*. To Hess's surprise the professor refused. He claimed that his own ideas on *lebensraum* were nothing like the crude imperialism that Hitler was advocating. He also claimed that he was repelled by Hitler's obsessive anti-Semitism and that he was also personally offended by it as his own wife was Jewish.[10]

In March 1927 the ban on Hitler's public speaking was finally lifted. Four nights later he made an impassioned speech, this time in a more measured, deliberate fashion, using all the new tricks he had learned from Hanussen. As the Jewish clairvoyant had predicted, it increased Hitler's effectiveness as a speaker. For two and a half hours he spoke to an audience which was wildly enthusiastic at the beginning and by the end had worked itself up into a state of frenzy.

During this particular speech, and indeed many subsequent ones, Hitler continued to push the socialist aspects of National Socialism. All the same, it was to Strasser and especially Goebbels that he now looked to win over the working classes to Nazi ideas. Goebbels had left for his new job as *Gauleiter* of Berlin, where he found the party in total disarray. To turn things round in a city where the Social Democrats and Communists dominated politics, he began by rigorously reorganising the party, insisting on strict discipline and also shaking up its finances, turning it from a debt-ridden and shambolic organisation into a financially sound and highly effective movement. The Nazi party in Berlin had been a joke before the arrival of Goebbels. Before long, it was to become both respected and feared.

Unfortunately for Goebbels, his newly disciplined storm troopers were rather too prone to indulge in pitched battles in the streets. Before long this was to lead to the banning of the Berlin party by the police. Forced to find other avenues to get his message across, he published a weekly paper, *Der Angriff*, 'the attack'. Although at first the standard was low, even Goebbels being disappointed with it, before long he had turned it into a medium which enjoyed real success in promoting Nazi ideas. Goebbels was now finding himself the most respected and popular man in the Berlin party. This led to the beginnings of a feud with Strasser, his former friend and boss. Although Goebbels was increasing support for the Nazis in Berlin, it was obvious that the party could not really afford such a public dispute between two of its most prominent members.

Hitler decided to intervene personally in the matter. He went to Berlin and met with both Goebbels and the Strasser brothers. Although Otto was bitterly hostile to Goebbels, Gregor was much more willing to compromise. Hitler had not only brought him into the inner circles of the party, but was planning even greater advancement for him. Unlike his brother, Gregor Strasser believed that he could handle Hitler and that the Fuehrer valued his advice and had even changed his mind after listening to his own arguments.[11]

It was particularly important for Hitler that inter-party squabbling should stop as 1928 was to see a new general election. It would be hard enough for the party to contend with the climate of economic prosperity in Germany at that time without its own members being more interested in pursuing mutual jealousies rather than the common cause of winning seats. As it happened, it made less difference than Hitler imagined. Goebbels was elected to the Reichstag, on a very left-wing platform largely directed at the working classes and very strong on socialist rhetoric. The party as a whole lost 100,000 votes and two seats. This was not really a disaster; the vote had held up surprisingly well in the unfavourable conditions of the time. To some extent the fact that it had held so relatively steady is largely to the credit of the better regional organisers, men such as Goebbels and Strasser. All the same, the mood in the party as a whole was sombre.

To the surprise of his followers, Hitler was not only not disappointed but even seemed quite upbeat about the result. He stressed the big increase in support for the Social Democrats and the Communists, contrasting it with the poor performances by the liberal and conservative forces. Hitler seemed to feel that the election results pointed to a future in which the 'old' parties would be swept away and the radical, left-wing parties would be the leading forces in Germany's future.

Meanwhile he had been working on another book. For reasons which can only be guessed at, it was not to be published in his lifetime. In it he linked the concepts of *lebensraum* with racism and especially anti-Semitism. The law of life, he claimed, was that of a struggle to survive. This was as true of races and nations as it was of individuals. Racial purity was an essential ingredient of a nation's strength. When 'inferior' races were allowed to intermingle with 'master' races, the only result could be the decline and eventual disappearance of the superior stock. He also claimed that the Jews were different from all other peoples on the earth since they had no nation state to call their own, nor were they simply a religious group of many differing racial origins. In fact, their goal was not just the conquest of the world, but also to destroy all superior racial stock.

The reason why this book was never published in his lifetime will never be known. It has been suggested cynically that it was not published because it was not worth publishing, but that never stopped him from inflicting the vast tome of Mein Kampf on the world. It has also been suggested that the logic of his comments pointed so inevitably to the Final Solution that he might have thought it unwise to be so clear about his long-term intentions. Most likely of all, though, is that the work was felt to be too heavy in comparison with Mein Kampf, likely to appeal only to the 'intellectuals' within the party.[12]

Meanwhile the year 1928, which had begun with a relatively disappointing performance at the general election, saw the new policy of giving Goebbels and Strasser their heads bear quite remarkable fruit. From a membership of just 40,000, the two populists turned things round so spectacularly that the end of the year saw the party membership stand at 100,000. With all the unfavourable conditions they faced, this was a remarkable tribute to the ability of Goebbels and Strasser to attract working-class support.

Hitler was still trying to appeal to other new sources of membership besides the working class ones that Goebbels and Strasser were delivering so conclusively. He had made a small impression on the impoverished middle classes whose savings had been wiped out by inflation and was also having some success in gathering support from among pensioners and others on fixed incomes. There remained two principal groups upon which his message had not yet made much impact.

The first of these was what might loosely be called the intelligentsia. Although the Nazis had a surprisingly strong following among young university students, it was rather more high-powered intellectual support that they wanted. In December 1928 Hitler gave a talk to the students of Berlin University. An eyewitness described how the students were spellbound when they heard him speaking. He wrote: 'My first impression of him was that of a consummate showman. I came away from that meeting wondering how a man whose diction was by no means faultless, who ranted and fumed and stamped, could so impress young intellectuals.'[13]

It was at this particular meeting that Hitler was to make one of his most important converts. A young man from a middle-class family, Albert

Speer, listened to Hitler speak and came away entranced. As Lochner, the eyewitness just quoted, suggested, many of the students who had heard his speech seemed to be hypnotised. It was no accident that Hitler had always been a keen student of hypnosis himself and was also gifted in what used to be known as mesmerism.[14]

The second group on which Hitler had only been able to exercise marginal influence were the upper-class nationalists and German businessmen. He had been trying in vain for the last few years to break into those circles of power within Germany.

It was the Young Plan, a new formula for the payment of German reparations left over since the First World War, which presented Hitler with his opportunity at last. Essentially, it reduced the level of payments that had to be made by the German government, and gave them longer to pay off the remaining debt. The German Nationalists, a small and ineffective party of extreme reactionaries, which stood for upper-class privileges and a restored monarchy, under their new leader, the wealthy businessman Alfred Hugenberg, wanted to campaign for a popular referendum on the Young Plan. He hoped that he would be able to persuade the German people to reject it, but even the arrogant and out-of-touch Hugenberg knew that neither he nor the Nationalists could possibly reach out to enough supporters on their own. What he needed was a man with the common touch, and who enjoyed strong support among the working classes. The only man who fitted that bill and was also impeccably nationalist in his opinions was Hitler. With the staggeringly naive judgement so often shown by Hitler's opponents, Hugenberg believed that he could make an alliance of convenience with him and use the Nazi leader for his own purposes. Hitler, of course, had no intention of being used by anyone.

Thanks to Hugenberg's bad judgement, Hitler suddenly found that doors which had been closed to him for years suddenly swung open. Money for which he had pleaded in vain suddenly began to pour into his coffers. From a relatively poor party, the financial position of the Nazis began to improve dramatically.

Hitler was not slow to take advantage of the new opportunities which had opened up for him so suddenly and so surprisingly. The Hugenberg press and media empire, which had either ignored him completely or else treated him as a mad socialist revolutionary, suddenly praised him as a patriot and a man of vision. All for the sake of a referendum on a reparations plan which even Hitler knew had no chance of succeeding, Hugenberg threw away the one advantage which his party had hitherto held over the Nazis, that of their monopoly on money from big business and support from the aristocracy, the upper middle classes, and the media circles which represented them. Hitler was now able to tap into a completely new source of support, the most powerful organisations in Germany. He had no real interest in the Young Plan and he certainly had no interest in being seen as a junior partner to Hugenberg in nationalist politics.

The only possible problem might be to hold the party's left-wing in line when he was engaged in this alliance with the most reactionary elements in German politics. Hitler was confident that he could keep them loyal, however, and certainly the inner circle of socialists, like Goebbels and Strasser, were well aware that the alliance was seen by Hitler as nothing more than a marriage of convenience. They knew that Hitler was not in the least a reactionary and had nothing but contempt for people like Hugenberg and the sort of attitudes that his party embodied. His whole aim was to take advantage of this unexpected opportunity and to use Hugenberg as ruthlessly as the media magnate so naively thought that he could use Hitler.

When the referendum on the Young Plan was finally held, the allies were only able to secure six million votes. Without the powerful advocacy of Hitler and especially Goebbels, it would not have won even that amount of support. Stresemann, in one of his last political triumphs, had seen off the unlikely combination of the Nazis and the Nationalists. Hugenberg was devastated by the defeat, but Hitler, having got all that he wanted from the magnate, rubbed salt in the wound by immediately breaking off their alliance. Now that he was able to reach people whom he had tried in vain before to approach, he no longer needed the Nationalist leader. Henceforth he was to bid strongly and confidently for supreme power in Germany. General elections were not due for a while but the peculiar circumstances of 1929 suddenly came to his assistance yet again.

That year, the Wall Street crash led to a general depression all round the world. Germany was hit as hard as any country. The Social Democrats had been in a stable coalition for a relatively long time but the recession led to the break up of the alliance. The coalition partners could not reach agreement on whether or not to cut unemployment benefit as a way of reducing government spending. The Social Democrats opposed this measure, but the more conservative and liberal parties within the coalition felt that it was essential. Since no agreement could be reached on this matter, the result was an unwise and ultimately disastrous decision to call fresh elections.

Almost all political commentators at the time dismissed the Nazis out of hand. They were felt to be a party that could never be more than a minor eccentricity, and the idea that they might actually win power would have been universally laughed at. Such views ignored the new confidence which Hitler had developed over the last two years, his new access to money and contacts in the upper echelons of German society, and above all the extent to which Goebbels and Strasser had already mobilised a strong and solid base among the working-classes.

At the time of the 1930 elections in Germany, the Nazis had only twelve seats in the Reichstag. However, by that time there were already three million unemployed people in Germany and the new Chancellor's policy of economic austerity and reducing public spending was not only losing him support but was also making the economic crisis even worse. Throughout the Western world the recession was leading governments to persevere with old-fashioned economic remedies which were totally unsuitable. Two years later the Americans were to reject Hoover's failed policies decisively and elect Franklin Roosevelt on the most radical programme ever to be put before an American electorate and succeed in winning their support.

Hitler, like Roosevelt, had his own unorthodox solutions to the problems of the economic depression. Unlike the conventional parties, who argued about where cuts in public spending should be made, Hitler spoke instead of the regeneration of German industry and agriculture, the restoration of dignity to those who had been robbed of it by inflation and unemployment, the end of the outdated class structure which still dominated Germany at that time – these themes were uppermost in his campaigning. Many observers noted how little difference there was in his speeches to the workers of Germany from those made by the Communists.

It was also remarkable how little anti-Semitism was mentioned during the campaign, presumably because Hitler did not want to lose votes through pressing the issue too hard. There were, of course, occasional references to Jewish capitalism and Jewish Marxists, but such utterances played almost no part in the main thrust of his campaign. Hitler wanted to be seen as the man who stood above all the sectional interests with which the other parties were identified, the man who simply wanted to unite Germany and bring about a new golden age of prosperity and glory.

The very fact that the Nazis genuinely were a party which included, and in a sense represented, almost every class within the country made them quite unique in Germany at that time. The Democrats represented the middle-class 'liberal intellectuals', the Nationalists the upper and upper-middle classes, the Centre Party the Catholics, the Social Democrats and Communists the working classes, and the National Democrats the enlightened middle-class conservatives. Only the Nazis had no specific interest group with which they could be in any meaningful way identified. As such, Hitler's claim that he was the saviour of the whole nation, not simply a section of it, was both new and extremely appealing to the electorate.

Another difference between the Nazis and all their political rivals except the Communists was the extent to which they went out and campaigned actively, tirelessly, until the last polling station had shut and the last vote had been counted. Most of the parties in the Reichstag, even the Social Democrats, would have found such tactics a little beneath them. This policy of aggressive and persistent canvassing, mass meetings on an enormous scale, even the most effective use ever made of aircraft for political effect, all these combined with the years of organisation which the party had built up to make the Nazis an altogether more formidable challenge than the established parties realised.

Even within the Nazi party there soon developed two schools of thought with regard to the question of entering a possible coalition government. Hitler himself, supremely confident that it was only a matter of time before he was appointed Chancellor, held out doggedly against any kind of deal. Others within the party ranks were not so sure. With the Weimar electoral system of proportional representation, it seemed inconceivable that the Nazis could ever win enough votes to form a government on their own.

Among those who did advocate coalition, again there were divisions. Men such as Gregor Strasser dreamed of a united socialist front of Communists, Social Democrats and Nazis. This would undoubtedly have produced a working majority within the Reichstag but it was never really practical politics. Nevertheless, to the reactionary elements in Germany it was a very real and frightening possibility. Hitler skilfully played upon their fears with the intention of enticing them towards an accommodation with the Nazis. He let men like Goering and Hanfstaengl put the moderate, conservative side of the party forward to the nationalist groups who still distrusted the Nazis as a bunch of wild radicals.

Meanwhile Captain Ernst Roehm was recalled by Hitler to head up the SA once more. The Berlin branch in particular, infuriated partly by Goebbels' deliberately provocative behaviour towards the organisation, was in a state of virtual revolt. Hitler needed the threat generated by the SA but could not spare the time to keep them under control. Reluctantly, he turned to the one man he knew could enforce discipline within the SA. In return, he was forced to give Roehm carte blanche to run the organisation as he saw fit. However, as with so many of Hitler's decisions, this was only a temporary tactical manoeuvre.

In late February 1931 Hitler, obeying a decree from the central government, ordered both the SA and SS to stop fighting with Communists and Jews, at least in the streets. At the end of March the frustrated SA in Berlin decided that there should be no capitulation to the authorities.

Faced with an open challenge to his authority, Hitler turned to the SS. For the first time Himmler and his forces were asked to discipline members of the rival Nazi organisation. It was not to be the last time. Himmler's troops smashed all opposition inside twenty-four hours. Goebbels, who had been largely responsible for the trouble in the first place, was given a private reprimand by Hitler against becoming involved in any kind of unilateral action but was not otherwise disciplined. A few SA men were thrown out of the organisation and more reliable ones brought in by Roehm. With the danger from the always rowdy SA over for the time being, he felt free to concentrate his attention on the next election.[15]

Along with the tightening of control on the SA, Hitler had also made sure that his already watertight position within the party itself was made even more secure. It was at this time that the continuing crisis in German politics came to his assistance. For just over a year the German Chancellor had been forced to rely on emergency decrees signed by the President to get his legislation adopted. The deliberately obstructive tactics of the Nazis within Parliament had made his task almost impossible. Now he was approached by General von Schleicher, one of Hindenburg's closest advisers, with a view to arranging a meeting between Hitler and the President. Schleicher had reluctantly come round to the view that the best chance of ending the chaos in German politics was by bringing the Nazis into government. As well as trying to win over Hitler, Schleicher had also begun cultivating Strasser, largely for his strong support among the left-wing of the party. Perhaps it might be possible to split the Nazis into factions and persuade some of them to join the government and end the turbulence of Brüning's Chancellorship.

The meeting between Hitler and Hindenburg turned out disastrously. The aged President with his loud voice and intimidating manner completely unnerved Hitler. Hindenburg in his turn was both bored and irritated by Hitler's continual tendency to address him as if he was making a speech. The first meeting between the two had failed dismally.

Meanwhile 1932 was to become a double election year. The first was the scheduled Presidential elections. Largely out of fear of splitting the anti-Nazi vote, the Social Democrats, Catholics, liberals and moderate conservatives decided to back Hindenburg for re-election. The Nazis, of course, fielded Hitler. Both the Nationalists and Communists also put up candidates, neither of them being even remotely credible challengers. In essence, then, Germany had to choose between Hindenburg and Hitler. The race turned out to be very close indeed, and went to a second ballot. The results of that second ballot were a personal triumph for Hitler and a deep humiliation for Hindenburg. A quarter of the Communists switched their votes on the second ballot to Hitler. Most of the Nationalist votes also went to the Nazis rather than to Hindenburg. Although he was narrowly re-elected, it had been a chastening experience for Hindenburg. For the first time he began to take Hitler altogether more seriously. The same could not be said of his Chancellor, who proceeded to commit political suicide by – presumably thinking that Hitler had shot his bolt – banning the SA and SS. Not only the Nazis opposed this move; Schleicher did so as well. Brüning, with no majority in the Reichstag and now having lost the confidence of Hindenburg, was forced to resign.

What followed then was an interlude which turned out to be half way between farce and tragedy. An obscure aristocratic nonentity called Franz von Papen was persuaded by Schleicher to take over as Chancellor and rule by emergency decree. At least Brüning had been a member of the

Catholic Centre party in the Reichstag. He was to be the last democratically elected Chancellor until after the war.

Schleicher had intended that Papen should simply be a front for his own behind-the-scenes rule. Unfortunately the inept Papen, once installed as Chancellor, developed delusions of grandeur. However, this was not entirely his own fault. The feckless Hindenburg was completely captivated by the shallow charm of Papen. Suddenly the nonentity was wielding more power than both Schleicher and even Hindenburg himself.

Meanwhile Hitler's demands were arousing opposition even within his own party. Both Goering and Strasser protested that what was needed now was to get into some sort of coalition, not to make unrealistic demands. Goebbels, on the other hand, was urging Hitler to use the SA and SS to take over power by force if Hindenburg refused to give in to the Nazi demands.

With the SA – the largest paramilitary force under Hitler's command – put on emergency alert, Hindenburg and his advisers discussed the increasingly tense situation. Papen offered to resign, but Hindenburg absolutely refused to replace him with Hitler. The compromise proposal was agreed upon to offer Hitler the position of Vice-Chancellor, Papen remaining as Chancellor.

Although he refused the offer out of hand, after a further meeting with Hindenburg he began to weaken in his determination. No doubt he was beginning to listen to the advice of Strasser and Goering to take something rather than nothing. However, just when it looked as if he was ready to agree to the proposal, a newspaper story about the meeting appeared, so soon after it had taken place that it had obviously been written before the event. It was in fact a typically brash and ill-advised piece of insolence by Papen. Even Schleicher had known nothing about it. Frantically he tried to revive his own contacts with Hitler, but the infuriated Nazi leader would have nothing at all to do with him. Goebbels was busily urging him to use the SA to rise up in revolution and sweep the insecure government away once and for all. Hanfstaengl, Goering and Strasser were trying to urge more cautious counsels.

In the end, Hitler, perhaps remembering the fiasco of Munich, decided against a *putsch*. He sent all paramilitary units on two weeks' leave. This open display to Papen that he had decided to persist with purely legal means of winning power brought a fairly swift response. Papen sent one of his closest aides, Ribbentrop, to see Hitler. Unfortunately he was so overwhelmed by the Nazi leader's personality that Ribbentrop became a fervent disciple and promptly joined the Nazi party.

Meanwhile Hitler had decided that the rowdy behaviour in Parliament by the Nazis should be ended. Instead he made a secret arrangement with the Catholic Centre party by which they supported Goering's candidacy as Reichstag President, a post equivalent to the Speaker of the House of

Commons. The new modus vivendi between the Nazis and the Centre Party offered a possible source of political stability. However, this was soon to change when Hitler decided to support a motion of no confidence in the government. Papen's administration was defeated by the biggest margin in German history. The result was yet another general election. This time the Nazis lost two million votes and thirty-four seats.

Even though the Nazis were in decline, Papen's government was doomed. Hindenburg reluctantly accepted his resignation and for the first time began to consider appointing Hitler as Chancellor. Hugenberg argued him out of this but Papen – still caretaker Chancellor – began to talk openly about resolving the situation by establishing a military dictatorship. It was Schleicher who pointed out the difficulties of this risky proposal, which could involve civil war against both the Nazis and the Communists, each with their own well-equipped and trained private armies. Instead, he suggested, he should play on his own contacts with Strasser and try to form a coalition with his supporters, together with the Social Democrats and what moderate parties remained in the Reichstag. The result was Papen's forced resignation as Chancellor and Schleicher's appointment as his replacement.

Strasser was promptly offered the Vice-Chancellorship by Schleicher. He went to discuss the matter with Hitler, who, encouraged to believe the worst as a result of Goebbels' insinuations, flew into a rage and accused Strasser of betraying him. Strasser protested hotly that he was only a messenger, not a traitor. By now Goering had changed his mind about settling for anything less than a Hitler Chancellorship. After a furious discussion Strasser stormed out and resigned all his party offices. Hitler, stunned, alternately raved about betrayal and wondered if he should make it up with Strasser. In the end he decided to try and end the feud, but the dispirited Strasser had already left for Italy, having told a friend darkly that he was doomed to death now.[16] Stunned that he had come so close to losing his iron grip over the party, Hitler appointed the pliable and totally dependent Hess to most of Strasser's former posts.

Even though the threat of a party split seemed to have been avoided, it was still hard to see how Hitler, whose party was now practically out of funds and was at last losing significant support from the general public, could ever hope to win power. Roosevelt received an intelligence report, which stated firmly: 'Hitler's influence is waning so fast that the Government is no longer fearful of the growth of the Nazi movement.'[17]

On any rational assessment, Hitler's party was finished as a serious political force. He had probably peaked too soon and the recent murders by a group of SA men of a Communist in front of his family, and Hitler's strong defence of them, had outraged moderate opinion. On the very brink of the abyss, the German electorate had started to turn away from the Nazis.

However, what few people knew was that Schleicher's intrigues to remove Papen from power had incensed the former Chancellor's vanity. Papen therefore approached Hitler secretly with a view to forming a joint administration. Hitler would be Chancellor but both men would exercise equal power.

Meanwhile Schleicher had been guilty of the same blind arrogance and poor judgement that had ruined Papen's government. He had been skilfully manoeuvring up to then with an unlikely alliance between the Social Democrats and the Nationalists, together with a lukewarm show of tolerance from the Catholic Centre party. Now, at a stroke, all his good work was undone by one rash act. He had, at the prompting of the Social Democrats, supported the confiscation of bankrupt noble estates in East Prussia. When Hindenburg refused to agree to the measure, Schleicher broke with the Nationalists. The Social Democrats were also furious at the way in which he had raised their hopes, and it was now inevitable that Schleicher would have to go.

Taking advantage of Schleicher's almost impossible position, Papen went to Hindenburg and urged upon him the idea that he should make Hitler his Chancellor but surround him with a majority of non-Nazis, including himself as Vice-Chancellor. Schleicher, who of course had his own spies, now went to Hindenburg and urged upon him the necessity of a military dictatorship. Not only did the President refuse, but he also saw to it that the plans were leaked. This finally finished the uneasy accommodation that the Centre and Social Democratic parties had made with Schleicher's regime. Having already upset the Nationalists as well, he was finished for good. His last hope was to persuade Hindenburg to dissolve the Reichstag. When even this request was turned down, Schleicher had no choice but to resign.

Hitler was now called upon by Hindenburg to form a coalition that included Papen and various non-Nazis. His price was new elections, which, as Chancellor, he was now confident of winning. What had seemed an impossible dream not so long ago had finally come true. Hitler had been appointed Chancellor, and even though there were only three Nazis in the Cabinet, effectively the party was at last in power. Opponents trembled and waited to see what would happen; supporters were jubilant. Among the great mass of German people, the general reaction was one of relief. Perhaps now that Hitler was in power he would at least put a stop to the endless elections and parliamentary crises of the past three years. They were to be proved right in that assumption, of course, though in anything but the manner in which they had expected. Once he had achieved power, Hitler never let go of it until the day he died.

Notes

1. For the period immediately following Hitler's release, the best sources are: a) Hoffmann, *Hitler Was My Friend*; b) Hanfstaengl, *Hitler: The Missing Years*.
2. Hanfstaengl, op. cit
3. Otto Strasser, *Hitler and I*, Jonathan Cape, 1940
4. Lüdecke, *I Knew Hitler*
5. Josef Goebbels, *The Early Goebbels Diaries*, Weidenfeld & Nicolson, 1962
6. Ibid
7. Dietrich Orlow, *The History of the Nazi Party 1919–1933*, David & Charles, 1971
8. Goebbels, op. cit
9. For more information on Hitler and Hanussen, see: a) FitzGerald, *Storm Troopers of Satan*; b) Sklar, *The Nazis and the Occult*; c) Sheila Ostrander and Lynn Schroeder, *Psychic Discoveries behind the Iron Curtain*, Bantam, 1971
10. This incident may well be yet another example of Haushofer's later attempts to distance himself from his once close relationship with Hitler and Hess. There is no evidence that Haushofer was in fact asked to review this book, and even if he had been, it might have been Hess, not Hitler, who thought of him as a suitable reviewer. In any event, it is doubtful that Hitler would have been concerned about Haushofer's refusal to review his book. Haushofer's own version is given in: H A Walsh, *Total Power*, Garden City, 1943
11. The fullest account of this dispute is given in: Otto Strasser, *Mein Kampf*, Heinrich Heine, 1969
12. The book in question was Adolf Hitler, *Hitler's Secret Book*, Grove Press, 1961. For the various theories about why it was never published, see: a) A J P Taylor, *The Origins of the Second World War*, Penguin, 1965; b) Eberhard Jäckel, *Hitler's Weltanschauung: A Blueprint for Power*, Wesleyan University Press, 1972. There has been comparatively little more recent speculation about the reasons for the book's non-publication.
13. Louis Lochner, *What About Germany?*, Dodd Mead, 1942
14. For Speer's account, see Albert Speer, *Inside the Third Reich*. On the question of Hitler's hypnotic powers, see a) FitzGerald, op. cit.; b) Greiner, *Das Ende des Hitler-Mythos*
15. For an account of the so-called 'Stennes *putsch*' see Hanfstaengl, op. cit
16. For Strasser's last days in the party, see Hanfstaengl, op. cit
17. Orville Bullitt (ed.), *For the President, Personal and Secret*, Houghton-Mifflin, 1972

CHAPTER VIII

Hitler the Messiah

The vain and shallow Papen had been the prime mover in the squalid intrigue which had brought Hitler to power. He had done this largely out of his jealousy and resentment at Schleicher's own intrigues. Even though he was not the new Chancellor, Papen was quite convinced that Hitler was his catspaw. The Nazi leader, of course, had entirely different ideas on the subject. It did not matter to him that Papen boasted openly to his right-wing friends about 'hiring' Hitler. Hitler knew that he would be the master of Germany until he died.

What was even more striking was the way in which his followers reacted to the news of his appointment. In spite of all the reams of paper which have been wasted by conspiracy theorists in a vain attempt to 'prove' that the Nazis were a party of the upper and middle classes, the facts simply do not bear this out. Most party members were very ordinary people, from working-class or lower middle-class backgrounds. Also contrary to the myths, the amount of money which the Nazis received from business sources has been grossly exaggerated. The bulk of the party's income up to 1934 came from membership subscriptions and donations by party members, by no means always the better off ones either. To these ordinary Germans, bewildered and angry at a country that seemed to have no use for them, Hitler's sudden appointment as Chancellor, which had been totally unexpected, came as if a miracle had delivered them from their sufferings. They went wild with joy.

That same evening of 30 January 1933, with his usual audacity and flair for catching the headlines, Goebbels organised a torchlight parade in the capital. Thousands of SA and SS men were hastily called upon to wear their uniforms and march to the Chancellery to pay their homage to Hitler. Massed bands playing martial music in accompaniment to the torchlight procession of paramilitary Nazis made a stunning spectacle. Even Hitler was astonished, commenting, 'How on earth did he conjure up all these thousands of torches in the space of a few hours?' Goebbels had also managed to get a running commentary on the scene broadcast on national radio.[1]

To the SA and SS men in particular that night seemed like the coming true of an impossible dream. These men had endured hunger, poverty and constant violence and imprisonment, many of them for years. Now, at last, the party in which they believed was in charge of the country. It was their turn to rule; the old order of aristocrats and the wealthy would see its power broken for ever with the coming of the new German revolution. They were to receive their reward for this loyalty very soon.

Hitler had become Chancellor on 30 January. By the middle of February he was confident enough to authorise Goering to instruct the police 'to avoid at all costs anything suggestive of hostility to the SA, SS and *Stalhelm*.' This licensed the Nazi paramilitaries to wreak vengeance upon their opponents, and countless scores of Communists, Social Democrats and Jews were beaten up on the streets or even arrested. Not surprisingly, the SA in particular also abused their new semi-legal powers to settle personal grudges. The newly legitimised 'Storm Troopers' swaggered around the country like a band of robbers and thugs. Not even the mildest of protests at their outrageous behaviour came from Hindenburg, Papen or any other non-Nazi in government. All the same, effective instrument of intimidation that it was, Hitler knew that he could not rely simply on the SA or even the SS to enforce his rule. He needed above all to control the armed forces and the police. The reorganisation of the police force he left to Himmler and Goering, with results that have become notorious. As for the army, he resolved to deal with that himself.

Four days after becoming Chancellor, Hitler met with key leaders in the armed forces. He spoke of the economic crisis which the country faced, and told them that he believed that rearmament and wars of conquest in the East were the only long-term solution. Three of the generals present were hostile to this surprisingly candid foreign policy, and two of them were very nervous indeed at the talk of foreign wars of conquest. Most of the generals and admirals were impressed by Hitler's talk, however.[2]

His next step was to use the emergency powers under the constitution to bring in a law that restricted press freedom and also laid down controls on political meetings. Once again no protest came from Papen or the other non-Nazis within the cabinet, although this time Hindenburg did at least question the law. Faced with unanimous cabinet support, however, he had little choice but to sign the decree. Soon after that he was presented with Hitler's second move towards dictatorship, the appointment of a new government in Prussia. Since Papen had already taken over the running of the province during his own chancellorship, and as Hitler had shrewdly proposed Papen as the figurehead of the new Prussian government, Hindenburg could hardly refuse to sanction that law.

The Nazi Party was busy trying to consolidate power lower down the chain of command. For the first time in German history, men from lower-middle and working-class backgrounds found themselves wielding immense power over the lives of their local communities. Their loyalty to the party was now rewarded with jobs and positions of authority. At village and town level, they encountered almost no resistance. The provincial governments were a different matter. Profoundly jealous of their local rights, they formed the next barrier that Hitler had to cross in his march towards assuming full power in Germany.

Meanwhile the Communists were mounting the only effective opposition to the Nazis. The liberals and moderate conservatives had all fallen silent or even begun to wonder if there might not be some things to be admired in the Nazis. The Social Democrats appeared to be in a state of shock, and were too paralysed to do or even say anything. Hitler was cleverly wooing the Catholics, and the Nationalists were in government with him. There is no doubt that the relationship between the Nazis and the Communists had always been a curious one. Although they fought each other constantly, each secretly admired the other. Both were violent and ruthless, both despised the ruling classes of their country, and both were committed to a radical socialist ideology. Throughout the 'period of struggle' it was very common for supporters to switch from Nazi to Communist or vice versa, often several times.

Many Communists had already joined the Nazis after Hitler's triumph. The fact that so many members were turning to Hitler alarmed the Communist leadership enormously. There is no doubt that it played a significant part in their decision to raise the political stakes suddenly. Instead of running a purely political campaign, with the usual accompaniments of street violence and industrial unrest, they began to call openly for revolution. The official party newspaper, in language that would have frightened a less paranoid person than Hitler, violently incited their followers to rise up in the following terms: 'Workers, to the barricades! Forward to victory; Fresh bullets in your guns. Draw the pins of your hand grenades.'[3] The Nazi response to this call was swift and forceful. Communist party headquarters in Berlin were raided on 24 February, following which Goering authorised the release of a statement that plans for a Communist uprising had been discovered.

Three days later an extraordinary event occurred, over which historians still disagree. Even some of the facts of the matter are still in dispute. It is certain that Hanussen, giving a séance in Berlin to a number of important people, announced that a large Berlin building would be engulfed in flames. Next day, three days after the raid on Communist headquarters, the Reichstag – the German Parliament building – was set on fire.

There have always been three theories concerning the conflagration: one that the Nazis organised the fire themselves, the second that it was the work of a lone psychopath, and the third that it was organised by the Communists. The strongest argument in favour of the Nazi hypothesis is that there was a tunnel to the Reichstag that led directly from Goering's palace. The mass arrests which followed the blaze led to a general feeling among both opponents and foreign governments that the fire had been started to provide an excuse for rounding up enemies of the regime. Finally, there was Hanussen's curious prediction that a large building in Berlin would catch fire.

The most compelling argument for the Communist hypothesis is that the incendiary, van der Lubbe, was himself a Communist, or rather a member of a splinter group known as International Communists. There is also no doubt that the Communists had been calling violently for revolution and armed struggle.

The strong probability, though, is that the fire was the unaided work of van der Lubbe. He was already a serial arsonist, and on the day before Hanussen's prediction had tried to burn down no fewer than three government buildings. There is no doubt that he bought fire lighters on the day of the fire from a shop and that a neutral observer saw him breaking the glass of the building and carrying some sort of burning material in his hand. Fire engines were summoned and tried to put out the blaze.

The reaction of the Nazi leaders was anything but in tune with the idea that they had organised the fire themselves. Hanfstaengl was the first to inform them, ringing Goebbels to give him the news. Goebbels was furious at what he thought was a joke in poor taste. He spoke to Hitler, who also refused to believe it. Hanfstaengl grew angry, and insisted that the fire engines were already trying to put out the flames which he could see leaping from the Reichstag building. Even this did not convince the Nazis. It was only when Hitler saw the flames himself that he set off with Goebbels to find out what was happening. By now the news had reached Goering, who was busy trying to direct the rescue operation.

Hitler immediately leapt to the conclusion, understandable in the circumstances, that the Communists were behind the fire. Before long most of the important local and national officials were present, as well as journalists. Then Diels, the head of the Prussian political police, arrived. He informed the assembled notables that the arsonist had been arrested and identified. By now Hitler had become extremely excitable. He made wild threats to execute all Communists and Social Democrats. Diels could not even attract his attention to give him the details the police had uncovered. At last he told him that the fire was almost certainly the work of a single lunatic. Hitler stared at him coldly and ignored his comments. He kept on attacking the Communists, who had obviously been planning to use the fire as the first step in a national uprising. Diels tried to repeat his view that the fire was not the work of the Communists, but his claims were brushed aside contemptuously. Hitler and the Nazis genuinely believed that they were threatened by a Communist uprising, and firmly ignored all evidence to the contrary.[4]

Next morning Hitler moved quickly to take advantage of the unexpected turn of events. At a cabinet meeting he called for a new emergency decree, which announced stringent controls on the press, freedom of assembly and freedom to organise, as well as mail censorship and telephone tapping. The Minister of the Interior was authorised to take control of any state government which could not maintain law and order satisfactorily. Nobody opposed this drastic violation of civil liberties, and only Papen made any protest about the suspension of states' rights. Even then he backed down quickly and Hindenburg signed this suspension of the Weimar constitution without even making any comment on the matter.

Meanwhile thousands of Communists were being arrested. Some Social Democrats were also taken into custody. However, Hitler, even in the height of his fury, was still a cunning politician. He did not make the mistake of banning any political party, not even the Communists. It was his intention to avoid the risk of Communist voters switching to the Social Democrats if their own party had been banned. Now, in the hysterical atmosphere engendered by the fire, he called fresh elections. The Nazis won just under forty-four per cent of the votes, and the eight per cent of their Nationalist allies was enough to give them a majority in Parliament.

Immediately he sent the SA to those states which were still not controlled by the Nazis. They were instructed to hand over to Nazi-approved leaders. In spite of some protests, they gave way. There was now no effective democratic machinery available to check Hitler's drive towards dictatorship. His next move was to put before the Reichstag the so-called Enabling Law. This removed whatever limited legal checks remained on his authority. It gave him, even though in theory only temporarily, the legal right to absolute power over the nation.

Such a radical change to the constitution needed the support of two thirds of the parliamentary deputies. There was no way on paper that such a figure could be achieved. Even though the Communist deputies had been excluded from the Reichstag by force and were languishing in prison, the Social Democrats, the Catholic Centre Party, and some smaller groups had the numbers to block the measure. The only groups that mattered were the Social Democrats and the Centre. The Social Democrats could never be brought to vote for the measure, so Hitler set out determinedly to woo the Centre vote. To their eternal discredit, they fell for his promises and supported the Enabling Law. Only the Social Democrats had the courage to vote against the measure. Democracy within Germany had now been voted out of existence by the members of its own Reichstag. The curious fact was that the majority of German people seemed quite happy to see the destruction of their civil liberties. Democracy was, after all, a relatively recent development, and one which had become associated with the Treaty of Versailles, inflation, unemployment and crisis. Perhaps a more authoritarian government would restore order and prosperity to Germany. They were certainly willing to let the Nazis try.

Hitler had been consciously setting out to present himself as the German Messiah, the strong man who could and would save the country. Goebbels and his powerful propaganda machine did all they could to see to it that this message was so emphasised that in time it became a part of the ordinary consciousness of the German people.

Hitler, who had taken a keen interest in Roosevelt's New Deal policies in America, began to put in place a raft of measures designed to bring down unemployment. In direct contrast to what every other regime in Europe was doing, which was cutting government spending and reducing borrowing, as well as creating tariff barriers against imports, he increased government spending, borrowed extensively, and tried to set up trade deals with other countries.

Hjalmar Schacht was the man chosen to be Hitler's instrument for the revival of German business. He was appointed President of the Reichsbank and promptly promised to give as much money as was needed 'to take the last unemployed off the streets.' He was as good as his word, creating an ingenious system under which unlimited credit was made available to the regime without any actual cash changing hands. Before long Schacht was to become nicknamed 'the old wizard' because of his success at bringing about a revival of the German economy, almost entirely through the mechanism of actually releasing funds – or at least credit on a vast scale. This enabled the oil necessary to lubricate the economy to be productively employed.

It was to a considerable extent the regime's success in dealing with the unemployment problem that led to the growing support for Hitler among the vast majority of Germans. However, it was not only on the material level that Hitler won their confidence. He gave the nation back its pride, its self-confidence, its self-respect. Under Hitler people began to feel positive and optimistic again. Nor must the extent to which the Nazi government brought about a social revolution be underestimated. Hitler did more to smash the antiquated feudal and class system than all the democratic governments of Weimar put together. Under the Nazis, ordinary people were for the first time able to enjoy opportunities which they had only been able to dream of before. For all these reasons, they began to treat Hitler as more than simply a successful politician, but as a truly messianic figure.

In addition to all the material and social benefits which the Nazi takeover brought to the majority of the German people, the part played by what might be called the spiritual dimension of Nazism must not be overlooked. The Third Reich was led by a whole cluster of men who were deeply steeped in occult and magical practices, even very murky religious views. Hitler, Goering and Himmler were the most prominent party members subscribing to various kinds of unorthodox and semi-occult beliefs. Hess's own eccentricities are well known, and other senior leaders with at least a sprinkling of occultism were Bormann and Goebbels, as well as the party's official ideologist, Rosenberg.

We have seen already the extent to which Nazi rallies were staged in a consciously and deliberately invoked religious atmosphere. Hitler was presented quite openly as the saviour of Germany, the man chosen by God himself to lead his country back to greatness. This religious dimension was played on for all it was worth, with hardly a breath of criticism from the Christian churches. The mayor of Hamburg, for instance, made the quite extraordinary statement that 'we can communicate directly to God through Adolf Hitler.'[5] An even more astonishing statement was issued by a group of German Christians in 1937, which claimed that 'Hitler's word is God's Law.'[6]

If those who were *not* involved in the inner circle of the party said this, it is hardly surprising that even more extreme claims were made by those who were. Himmler, Hess and Rosenberg were particularly prone to these excesses, but even such an enlightened figure as Baldur von Schirach, head of the Hitler Youth, and one of the most liberal members of the party, could say honestly that: 'The service of Germany appears to us to be genuine and sincere service of God; the banner of the Third Reich appears to us to be his banner; and the Fuehrer of the people is the saviour whom he sent to rescue us.'[7]

However much Hitler was able to project his chosen image of himself as the Messiah upon the German people, he still had to deal with real problems and real political enemies. The Reichstag fire, for which he was not responsible and of which he knew nothing until it had already taken place, made him widely distrusted abroad. In the same way it was not Hitler, nor even Himmler, but an obscure SA officer named Edmund Heines who first introduced the idea of the concentration camp to Germany. There is a certain ironic justice in the fact that he was one of those murdered by the SS during the notorious 'Night of the Long Knives.'

Once again, this ruthless slaughter of the leadership of the SA and various opposition leaders has been blamed on Hitler's lust for power. A careful study of the evidence, however, shows that in fact Hitler was almost alone in *not* wanting to massacre Roehm and his SA comrades. Only Goebbels also opposed the slaughter, since he shared Roehm's left-wing views. It was Himmler and Goering who joined forces to destroy the power of the SA. For all their persuasiveness, it still took three unexpected events to bring Hitler reluctantly round to the view that the SA and other potential rival power groups should be violently eliminated.

The first of these was a plan by Roehm to abolish the old armed forces and merge them into a new citizen's militia dominated by the SA. Not only did this stand no chance of being adopted; it also brought from the army leadership a thinly veiled threat to carry out a coup d'état if the SA's power was not reduced immediately. Although Hitler managed to pacify them, the implied threat remained. The second unexpected development was that Roehm started holding secret meetings with Schleicher.

It is impossible to know what his reasons for these meetings were, but Schleicher had certainly contemplated a coup to prevent Hitler from achieving power. Even if they were wholly innocent – which seems unlikely – they must have looked sinister to Himmler and Goering.

The final unexpected development was a speech at Marburg University by the vain and shallow Papen. Foolishly hoping that the Nazis had shot their bolt, he called upon the German people to resist the calls from the party's left wing for a 'second revolution.' The speech infuriated both Hitler and Goebbels, but won widespread praise and support in the country. When Goebbels denounced it indignantly as reactionary and treasonable, Papen and some of his close colleagues in the still largely non-Nazi Cabinet offered their resignations. Without their support, Hitler's fragile coalition was doomed. Hindenburg would never support Hitler against Papen. The only choices open to him were to risk civil war by backing Roehm and the SA or to follow the advice of Himmler and Goering, and crush the brown-shirted storm troopers by force.

The most prominent people to be murdered during the 'Night of the Long Knives' were Roehm, Gregor Strasser and Schleicher. Papen was placed under arrest and only escaped with his life because Hindenburg asked for it to be spared. Goering was furious when told that he could not shoot him. The 'Night of the Long Knives' marked the end of the power of the SA and the triumph of the conservative forces among the Nazis over the socialist wing of the party. It also led to the institutionalisation of the SS and the Gestapo, and their methods of brutal violence, as part of the everyday life of Germany. Finally, it intimidated some of the few officers in the army who had been thinking about getting rid of Hitler. From now on, even the army was afraid of the Nazis.[8]

Even this wholesale slaughter, which for a moment ripped away the mask of legality from the Nazis, did not shake Hitler's popularity. Most people seemed willing to accept that the unruly SA had been getting out of hand and needed to be brought to heel. Even if the means employed were drastic, perhaps only violence could have broken such a powerful paramilitary organisation. Or so at least they tried to rationalise the appalling events to themselves. Hindenburg, in spite of stories to the contrary by his apologists, was not at all disturbed by the massacres. His only complaint was that if Hitler had acted against Roehm sooner, less blood would have been shed.

There was to be no further public violence in Germany until 1938. Instead the secret brutality of concentration camps and the Gestapo replaced such massive and open displays of the dark side of the party. Throughout this period Hitler's popularity continued to grow. In spite of the fact that the Nazis did employ an extensive machinery of terror, which undoubtedly intimidated many potential opponents of the regime, his appeal could not have endured for so long had it been based on fear alone.

The plain and unpalatable fact is that the majority of the German people believed in Hitler and continued to support him even during the dark days when Germany was obviously losing the war. It was very common for people to say that, although things were bad, Hitler would manage to find a way out. It was even common for people to say, if only the Fuehrer knew what was going on in his name! Others might be blamed, but rarely Hitler himself.

Only Goering and Goebbels, who were the only Nazis apart from Hitler to enjoy any popularity between 1933 and 1945, ever held any even remotely comparable influence over the German people. Neither of them, however, was ever elevated to such semi-divine status as Hitler in the eyes of the ordinary person. Nor is it possible to imagine them having had even the remotest chance of success if they had made any such attempt. Only Hitler could have pulled off such a conjuring trick so successfully. No other Nazi leader could have done it. Only Hitler ever succeeded in getting himself regarded, not just as a successful and popular politician, but as the saviour of his country.

Notes

1. Hoffmann, *Hitler was my Friend*
2. Robert O'Neill, *The German Army and the Nazi Party*, Heinemann, 1966
3. This quotation from *Red Sailor*, the official organ of the KPD, is given in:
      Charles Bewley, *Hermann Goering and the Third Reich*, Devin-Adair, 1962
4. The definitive work on the subject remains: Fritz Tobias, *The Reichstag Fire*,
      Secker, 1963
5. Cited in: Walter Langer, *The Mind of Adolf Hitler*, Basic Books, 1972. Langer
      needs to be treated with some caution as a source. He is prone to embroider
      a little too much. Even his psychological profiling is questionable when set
      against contradictory and more reliable evidence.
6. Ibid
7. Von Schirach, giving evidence at the Nuremberg Trials. See *Trials of the Major
      War Criminals*, vol. xiv, May 1946, p. 481
8. Most of the above from a) Rudolf Diels, *Lucifer ante Portas*, Deutsche Verlags
      Anstalt, 1950; b) Hans-Bernd Gisevius, *To the Bitter End*, Jonathan Cape,
      1948; c) John Wheeler-Bennett, *The Nemesis of Power*, Viking, 1967. Both
      Diels and Gisevius also need to be treated with some caution as sources.
      Diels's accounts are fairly accurate but tend to paint his own actions in the
      best possible light. Gisevius's book is a far more colourful mixture of fact
      and fiction. However, where, as with the massacre of the SA leadership and
      others, it is supported by other witnesses, I have made use of his account.

CHAPTER IX
Hitler the 'Green' Leader

Neither Hitler himself nor his Nazi Party are generally thought of as pioneers of environmental concerns, yet in fact between 1933 and 1942 there was a sustained attempt at the highest levels of government in Germany to introduce and encourage a whole range of what would nowadays be considered 'green' policies.

Much of the credit for the surprisingly modern measures taken under the Nazis must go to the Agriculture Minister, Richard Walther Darré. He owed his astonishing success in forcing through ecological concerns upon German industry and agriculture to the combination of his own exceptional personal abilities and Hitler's romantic notions about agriculture. In particular, Darré was able to harmonise his own 'green' vision of Germany's future with the Nazi fantasy of a Nordic super-race and a new, Aryan, Garden of Eden.[1]

Hitler was captivated by Darré's portrayal of a Germany that resembled a glorified rural idyll with flaxen-haired maidens and strong Teutonic swains toiling on the land. Less creditably, Darré cynically appealed to Nazi anti-Semitism by blaming the Jews for the pollution of Germany. He was not the first Nazi to suggest this line of criticism to Hitler; the unstable Dietrich Eckart had done so many years before. Curiously, Eckart, one of the more intelligent (if less rational) of the early Nazi inner circle, was both fascinated and repelled by the ideas on organic farming of Rudolf Steiner. What Steiner called 'biodynamics' appealed greatly to both Eckart and other Nazi leaders. However, since Eckart was also convinced that Steiner was one of the leading members of the 'Jewish conspiracy', he approved of his ideas while detesting the man himself. Until his death in 1923, Eckart was probably Hitler's closest friend and adviser. Hitler imbibed the ideas of Steiner through his friend and was quite prepared to be sympathetic to Darré's even more radical plans when he became Chancellor in 1933.[2]

Hitler defended Darré's schemes against fierce howls of protest from industrialists, farmers and capitalists. He ignored their objections completely. In Landsberg prison, Hitler had also read Count Herman Keyserling, the most famous German philosopher of his time. Keyserling not only approved of Steiner's theories of 'biodynamics' but allowed Steiner to use them to rid his estate of rabbits, apparently successfully. With the approval of the thoroughly 'Aryan' Keyserling for the methods, Darré was pouring out his ideas into the ears of a Hitler already predisposed to agree with him.[3]

What perhaps even Hitler did not realise was quite how radical Darré's views really were. It is not too much to claim for him the title of the father of the modern environmental movement. It is also quite certain that Nazi Germany, at least until 1942, was the 'greenest' country in the world.

Darré was fortunate to be able to put nearly all his proposals into effect when the Nazis came to power, including many that were so unorthodox that they raised howls of protest, all of which Hitler completely ignored. One of the earliest measures to become law when Hitler was appointed Chancellor was a proposal of Darré's aimed at preventing the confiscation of smallholdings from their owners as a result of bank foreclosures. During the last four years of the Weimar Republic, this had been a major issue of concern. Farms were being seized all over Germany by the banks as the unfortunate farmers, crushed by the world recession, were unable to meet their interest payments.

Hitler, at Darré's prompting, introduced a law forbidding all speculation in land. It also gave generous State-funded debt relief to peasants, coupled with low interest rates if they needed to borrow further, and, crucially, to the fury of the bankers, made it unlawful for banks or indeed any other creditors to foreclose on a farmer for any debts he or she owed. Such debts could now only be paid for out of current receipts, and Hitler's government agreed to write off all existing borrowings in exchange for 1% of the annual farm value and 2% interest on the loan issued. This astonishing, even revolutionary measure, more or less saved the German farmer from extinction. Almost everyone welcomed it except the bankers and the aristocracy.[4]

A more controversial proposal by Darré was also enshrined in law. It became known as the Law of Hereditary Entailment, and declared the widespread practice of dividing up smallholdings among the various members of a family to be illegal. Only one person could become the 'designated heir', though the other family members would be compensated for their loss of inheritance rights. This aspect of Darré's legislation drew a very mixed response from German farmers. Some were enthusiastic about it, while others fiercely opposed it. It certainly meant that smallholdings remained viable, and the combination of land security, debt relief and readily available low interest loans transformed the future of the German farmer overnight.[5]

One aspect of Darré's plans that was opposed by almost all farmers, however, was his insistence that each farm had to be run for the benefit of the German people as a whole, not simply for the purpose of private profit. Smallholdings were actively encouraged and both collective farms and large private estates were discouraged and frowned upon. Once again, the extent to which both Darré and Hitler genuinely believed in the 'socialist' side of National Socialism shines through.

On the food front, all food producers were brought under State control and forced to conform to the most rigorous regulation that they had ever known. Higher prices were also placed on meat and particularly fat, with the result that the German diet, to the astonishment of other countries, became one of the healthiest in the world. As part of the drive for self-sufficiency in food, imports were actively discouraged and even the domestic production of certain items was severely restricted. Instead of the massive overproduction that Darré found when Hitler came to power, he introduced measures to conserve livestock and dairy produce. By 1936 Germany had become 81% self-sufficient in food.[6]

Soil improvement was encouraged, and in particular the reclaiming of land for agricultural use. Vegetable production was also encouraged, rather than the traditional dependence upon pigs and cattle. Better drainage of land led to a more fertile arable soil, and the feeding of grain to farm animals was strictly forbidden. Flood protection measures were also undertaken.

There was also very little mechanisation of agriculture in Germany compared with other countries. Darré actively encouraged this non-mechanised approach to farming rather than the quick 'techno-fix' so fatal to American agriculture at the same period of time, which had turned much of the US farmlands into 'dust bowls' through intensive cultivation of the soil to the point of exhausting its capacity to regenerate itself.

Another great contribution of Darré's was his crack-down on the prevalent practice of adulterating food. A nationwide organisation was set up with the responsibility for regulating the production, marketing and pricing of all farm produce. It had the power to fine or even close down businesses found guilty of adulteration. In another clear demonstration of the 'socialist' side of National Socialism, it even had the power to fine or close businesses for profiteering. It was not for nothing that Herbert Backe, the man who eventually succeeded Darré as Agriculture Minister in 1942, remarked to an agrarian assembly in Germany as early as 1934 that 'German agricultural policy was now based on organic concepts'.[7]

Darré even seems to have invented the term 'organic farming'. Certainly the earliest use of the phrase appears to have occurred in a speech he gave to the National Peasant Council on 20 June 1940. Darré may have chosen to coin the expression because the existing German name for the practice, 'biodynamic farming', had been invented by Rudolf Steiner. Hitler, of course, largely under Eckart's influence, was deeply suspicious of Steiner or anything that appeared to derive from him in any way. Darré, though he actively propagandised on behalf of Steiner's idea, adopted the new term 'organic farming' in an attempt to make Steiner's views more acceptable to the regime. It is questionable how many contemporary environmentalists and advocates of organic farming realise that both the term and the practice were invented and actively pursued by a Nazi Minister.[8]

Darré's ideas aroused bitter hostility among industrialists, large farmers, owners of the big estates and the German aristocracy. They also, curiously, infuriated the 'modernising' wing of the Nazi Party, whose visions of a future reminiscent of *Brave New World* were completely at variance with Darré's concept of Germany. The modernisers saw him as a hopeless romantic.

Darré, in fact, seems to have been alone in the Nazi Party in terms of being both a moderniser in general and a conservationist when it came to the land. His ideas were founded upon a deep conviction that the very soul of a nation resided in its soil. It was his policies that became known as *Blut und Boden*, 'blood and soil', often known disrespectfully as *Blubo*.[9]

Though Darré unquestionably was something of a romantic in his attitude towards the land, he was anything but a naïve dreamer. Before being appointed Agriculture Minister, he had been a wealthy and successful businessman. Hitler had a far more romantic vision of agriculture than the practical Darré. Unlike his Chancellor, Darré was simply a man ahead of his time when it came to the state of the environment.

Hitler, like Darré, was profoundly influenced by one of the oddest books ever to have had a major impact upon important thinking. The book in question was *Civilisation: Its Cause and Cure*, which was written by the eccentric Edward Carpenter and first published as long ago as 1889, the year of the future German Chancellor's birth. Carpenter envisioned a Utopia based upon strict vegetarian principles and a return to a rural life. His book was enormously popular and sold widely all over the world. It was particularly influential on thinkers in Britain, America and Germany.

Carpenter, like other influences on Hitler's thought, was part of the sidestream of the Social Darwinist movement that inclined towards the return to a simple life rather than the grasping way in which capitalists of the time tended to interpret it and use it as a justification for greed and inhumanity. [10] Other important thinkers of this 'naturalistic' wing of Social Darwinism included Ernest Thompson Seton, G Stanley Hall and the German writer Ernst Häckel. Hitler was familiar with all three writers and admired their work enormously. He was particularly impressed by the emphasis they laid upon children developing in a steady evolutionary spiral, and how much this process could be actively assisted by having the child growing in harmony with Nature. He was particularly keen on their association of this evolutionary process as being connected with the 'perfected state of race-maturity'.[11]

Häckel claimed to have invented a new principle of biology, which he named the 'Biogenetic Law'. According to Häckel, children should be encouraged to mirror in their lives each stage of the human evolution towards greater achievement. This would lead them to progress from one stage in the evolutionary tree to a successive and higher one.[12]

The founders of the 'Order of Woodcraft Chivalry', Ernest Westlake and his son Aubrey, were both regularly in touch with German contacts and exchanged views about evolution, organic farming and, regrettably, at times their shared Nordic fantasies. It is only fair to add that the Westlakes did not succumb to the anti-Semitism that was increasingly becoming attached in Germany to 'back to the land' movements. In their introduction to *Woodcraft Way*, the Westlakes wrote:

A complete education means the living over again by the individual of the experiences passed through by his ancestors. As man's progenitors inhabited fruit-producing regions along with other animals, so his children should begin life in an orchard-garden along with pet animals, whether wild or domesticated.

When the time comes for them to break out of this garden, they will proceed to lay a solid foundation of Palaeolithic culture by betaking themselves under adult guidance to some suitable cave or rock-shelter.[13]

This reads like pure fantasy today, but it was profoundly influential in its time. Hitler was aware of the Westlakes and indeed most of the important contributors to the organic farming movement. Far from being uninterested in agriculture, Hitler felt passionate about the issue. He did not simply let Darré get on with imposing his ideas on Germany out of boredom with the whole subject. On the contrary, Hitler shared Darré's views on the subject and enthusiastically supported his Agriculture Minister against the opposition of the bankers, the industrialists, the aristocracy, and the majority of his own Cabinet. Hitler really *did* believe in 'green' environmental policies.

Hitler was particularly fond of the ideas of the naturalist Seton, who appealed to him not only because of the American's emphasis on harmony with Nature and his commitment to a Social Darwinist ideology, but above all Seton's attempt to paint the Native Americans as environmentalists living a pure and natural life. Some examples of Seton's romantic notions about the Indians include his portrayal of them as 'the great prophet of the outdoor life' who 'taught the sacred duty of reverencing, beautifying and perfecting the body' and 'sought for the beautiful in everything'.[13] Seton also claimed, quite falsely, that the Native Americans held all natural resources in common and that there was neither poverty nor greed among them. [14] His books were profoundly influential. Not only Hitler but most Germans in the 'youth movements' and environmentalist sympathisers read them. Several ecologically-minded German movements were founded in direct response to the influence of Seton's books.[15]

Seton had been inspired to found his movement after the writer Rudyard Kipling laid upon him the solemn charge of the 'regeneration of the Anglo–Saxon race'.[16] This aspect of his thought also made his philosophy popular with Hitler and the Nazis. Seton wrote, admittedly referring to the USA: 'I should like to lead this whole nation into the way of living outdoors for at least a month each year, reviving and expanding a custom that as far back as Moses was deemed essential to the national well-being'.[17]

The Westlakes were also influenced by ideas of 'racial improvement', but the general thrust of their thinking was directed towards the betterment of humanity through the natural development of the individual child. Others in their circle thought differently. The neglected but in his time profoundly influential English thinker and politician John Hargrave wrote, as early as 1919, 'The time has now come when we can control and use that process of natural selection known as Evolution'.[18] This saying, like many aspects of Hargrave's thought, was to be enthusiastically adopted by the Nazi Party. Again, Hitler was familiar with Hargrave and broadly approved of most of his ideas, though the approval was certainly not mutual.

Eugenics, as genetic engineering proposals were referred to in those days, became one of the most astonishingly influential bad ideas of all time. It was particularly popular in America and Britain. As early as 1915, a dozen states in the USA had introduced laws to compulsorily sterilise 'eugenically unfit' people. In 1910, the Eugenics Record Office advised the British government 'concerning the eugenic fitness of proposed marriages'. The Eugenics Society, in a grim and thoroughly distasteful but by no means accidental anticipation of Nazi policy, proposed that there should be compulsory sterilisation for 'stock' with 'bad heredity and inferior capacity'. Even the distinguished scientist and politically liberal Julian Huxley argued fiercely in favour of 'racial improvement', and continued to do so long after the Nazi excesses had made this view anything but politically correct.[19]

Hitler had been exposed to Social Darwinist and eugenics enthusiasts during his time in Vienna. He felt profoundly in sympathy with them, particularly in the light of their close connection with what are now recognised as racist attitudes. For a man who read constantly that leading scientists believed 'racial hygiene', 'improving the stock' and 'eliminating lesser breeds' could bring about a radical leap forward in human evolution, how could he not feel that his own ideas on the superiority of the Germans and the innate inferiority of Jews and Slavs were supported by the finest scientific minds of his day?

In the same way, the people he had read or otherwise been influenced by during his early years in Austria and Germany associated racial improvement with a rural lifestyle. The concepts of 'blood and soil' became inextricably bound up in Hitler's thinking. The phrase may have come from Darré, but the philosophy was entirely in tune with Hitler's own ideas. It may seem strange today that environmental ideas were so closely intertwined with racist views, but at the time they all seemed part of a general philosophy of living in harmony with Nature, Social Darwinism, eugenics and racial betterment. In Hitler's time, the association of what now seem to us to be ideas at the opposite ends of the political spectrum seemed perfectly reasonable.

A German academic, Heinz Reichling, author of a paper on the influence of Seton on European thought, attended a conference of the Woodcraft Folk in 1933 at the Wye Family. He came away deeply impressed and passed on his impressions to his German colleagues.[20]

The German *Bünde* and *Wandervögel*, together with the *Musikheim*, were at the forefront of both the youth movements in the country and the growing emphasis on environmental concerns. They liaised regularly with Hargrave, Rolf Gardiner, Leslie Paul and other leading English exponents of what (minus the racist elements) was almost indistinguishable from views put forward by *völkisch* spokespeople in Germany. Hitler was familiar with the work of most of the British environmentalists, and he had a high regard for both Gardiner (who spoke fluent German) and Hargrave, as did Darré. Throughout the 1920s and 1930s, the principal influence on the *Bünde* was Hargrave. His works were translated into German and had a profound effect on the thinking of his European contemporaries, particularly Darré and Hitler.[21]

'Blood and Soil' was paralleled in Britain by a very similar though less effective movement which became known, at least by its opponents, as 'Muck and Mysticism'. The continual and deep links between the German and British campaigns had a profound effect on the future direction of post-war environmentalists. Almost all the early leaders of the European 'Green' movement first learned their principles either directly from the Nazi example or else from others who had enjoyed strong links of friendship with them. In 1934, for instance, Gardiner had a personal interview with Rudolf Hess to exchange ideas on how Britain and Germany could pool their resources and jointly work towards an 'organic society' based on 'biodynamic' principles.[22]

Hitler was a passionate advocate of 'blood and soil' policies. He genuinely believed in the deep spiritual value of a nation's land. Hitler felt that the soil and landscape of a country also encapsulated the cultural heritage of its people. It is hardly surprising that he devoted considerable time and attention to 'the revitalising of peasant culture', a phrase first used by Darré but adopted enthusiastically by Hitler. Hitler frequently spoke of Darré's ideas as being the basis of German life, and that the German race could only truly be regenerated through a renewed contact with the soil on which they lived.[23]

Hitler set up a National Peasants' Assembly, decreed that a Harvest Festival should be held each year on the first Sunday after Michaelmas, encouraged the promotion of local and peasant art, and ordered the design of and wearing by local peasants of regional costumes. He also favoured an activity known as 'Germanic dances', rather similar to the Morris Dancing of British folklorists. Hitler also authorised the setting up of a government agency known as the *Kreisbauernschaft* to collect rural folklore, songs and dances. This soon expanded its role by inventing new 'customs' and rituals for peasant life. Some peasants were offended by the often implicitly pagan nature of the ceremonials, though most considered them a piece of harmless 'townie' eccentricity. Besides, in the Third Reich, neo-paganism was everywhere, especially in any activity where Himmler or Darré took a hand.[24]

One of the most important aspects of Hitler's concern with agriculture and the environment was the establishment of Goslar as the 'National Peasant Town'. The example of this place, and the general realisation that Nazi Germany, whatever else might be objectionable about it, was beyond any doubt leading the world in ecological concerns, led to Goslar becoming a place of pilgrimage for other environmentally-oriented thinkers, especially from Britain. Under Hitler, for the first time since Germany had become a unified country less than a hundred years earlier, the needs of rural Germany and the issues of conservation and protection of the environment were firmly placed at the very centre of national politics. A campaign to turn the often sadly neglected rural areas into flourishing and living communities was spearheaded by the 'model village' project. Any rural area which created a swimming-pool, a sports ground, a Hitler Youth hostel, a village hall and a first-aid station was awarded the title of a 'model village'.[25]

Before 1933 German unemployment had been frighteningly high. Now, under Hitler, there was no longer a shortage of jobs. As well as the sudden security of tenure enjoyed by smallholders and tenant farmers, a national campaign began, aimed at persuading young people to move to the countryside and to ensure that those who lived there already remained.

All members of the Hitler Youth and the League of German Girls had to work on the land as part of what was known as 'Land Help' for the boys and 'Duty Year' for the girls. Even though they offered only unskilled labour, and very few went on to develop a desire to follow a career in agriculture, it still enabled German farmers to rely on extra hands to help with the farm chores and ensure that the harvests were brought in successfully and on time.[26]

In addition to this temporary assistance, crèches and kindergartens were set up in villages to look after the children, so that the farmers' wives could work on the land themselves. A three-year vocational course in agriculture was also set up, leading to the award of a 'Landworker Diploma'.

This in itself gave farmers and even farm workers enhanced status. Similar training courses were also provided for shepherds and herders.[27]

Not only had Hitler introduced a law forbidding the banks to repossess a farm that fell into debt; he also enacted a law, in the teeth of furious opposition from capitalists and big business, which forbade the dismissal of farm labourers without the consent of the Labour Exchange, which was very rarely given. Farm workers enjoyed greater rights against unfair dismissal than any other group of employees under the Nazis.[28]

Another way in which Hitler planned to regenerate the land was through the campaign to encourage settlers to move to the relatively empty and inhospitable eastern part of Germany. The proposed settlers had to fulfil some pretty tough criteria, not only in terms of racial origins but also their health, financial soundness, and being either married or engaged. Those who satisfied the requirements were given free land and offered every assistance by the State. There was even a special department of the Labour Corps devoted to helping the wives of settlers in the east. [29]

In 1935 Germany experienced an exceptionally bad harvest. Before Hitler's appointment as Chancellor, the result would certainly have been the total ruin of most German farmers. There would also have been widespread famine throughout the country, and the volume of debt would have risen to a crushing level. Because of Hitler's policies, none of these things happened.

Hitler's policies for agriculture were, of course, part of his general economic policy, given the overall name of *Wehrwirtschaft*. This involved fixing prices to prevent either inflation or depression, and this protected farmers and businesses. They also introduced legislation against profiteering, involving the compulsory investment in government loans of all profits above 6 to 8 per cent. Food rationing was introduced to ensure that all Germans were able to enjoy a healthy and sufficient diet for the first time in four years. Consumption was also controlled by central allocation of necessities and government campaigns to promote healthy food.[30]

Under the influence of these measures, agricultural production rose from 10 billion marks in 1932 to 14 billion in 1939. National income rose from 45 billion in 1932 to 100 billion. The figure of 6,000,000 unemployed in 1933 not only disappeared completely but gave way to a shortage of labour. Workers' earnings increased by 15% in 1933 alone. Guaranteed paid holidays for everyone were introduced and labour courts provided for appeals against unfair dismissal. When economic problems led to slowdown or closure, workers received guaranteed unemployment support. Farmers were able to pay greatly reduced interest rates on their borrowing. The price of fertiliser was reduced, and they were guaranteed higher retail prices than they could have received on the world market, where unregulated 'competition' still prevailed. A campaign to avoid waste also led to a vast expansion of domestic raw materials in the country.

By 1938 Germany had the highest national income in its history, some 88 billion marks. The rationing system, contrary to myth, applied with equal rigour to rich and poor alike. An otherwise hostile observer of Hitler's regime was forced to admit that:

The labourers doing manual work were better off in respect to food than the rich. The well-to-do still had their fine houses, apartments and estates, but they lived in them far removed from the style to which they were accustomed. Like everybody else they could obtain only the same rations of all the necessities of life, including food and clothing, as the mass of the population... the drift was unmistakable. [Referring to the growing socialisation of the German economy under Hitler.[31]]

The weekly ration allowance for all Germans, rich or poor, is given in the following table:

	Grams
Meat	300
Meat products (e.g., sausages)	200
Butter	125
Lard	62.5
Margarine	80
Marmalade	100
Sugar	250
Cheese	62.5
Coffee (generally *Ersatz*)	150
Eggs	1

Bread and grain were also rationed, but Germany had plenty of bread of its own. So plentiful was bread grain that the practice of mixing bread with potato flour was abandoned. Milk was given to children up to the age of 10 and also to pregnant women. Only vegetables and fruit remained unrationed. A 'Christmas' bonus was also introduced, comprising 125 grams of butter, 125 grams of *ersatz* honey, one egg, some chocolate cake and sweets. Spices and food flavouring for Christmas baking were also allowed to be obtained free of rationing. In addition, manual workers, in which category farm labourers were included, received extra food rations.[32]

Another hostile critic, this time from the Communist rather than liberal side of politics, in spite of desperate attempts to twist the facts when the statistics contradicted his belief that workers in Germany were worse off than those in Britain and the Soviet Union, was forced to admit that they *seemed* to be better off in Germany than Britain but they were really worse off. In terms of political freedom and the absence of the Gestapo, British workers were undoubtedly better off than their German counterparts. In terms of pure economic status and wages, however, they were certainly worse off. As for his figures for the Soviet Union, they were based on Stalin's wholly fictitious statistics.[33]

The same critic also gives an interesting table, reproduced here:

(Prices in Pfennigs)		
Commodities	January 1933	January 1938
Rye bread	56.1	56.1
Wheat flour	6.7	6.4
Rice	9.0	10.4
Split peas	8.6	13.4
Potatoes	15.0	20.5
Carrots	3.5	5.8
Sauerkraut	5.0	6.5
Fat home-produced bacon	9.1	10.6
Margarine	10.0	15.0
Imported lard	7.7	No figures
Sugar	8.9	9.3
Milk	6.0	6.0
Salt	2.1	2.1

As can be seen from the above table, the cost to an ordinary German of feeding himself or herself was in most cases virtually the same as it had been in 1932. Some items had come down in price; others (mainly imported foods or items that the government wished to discourage for health reasons) went up. None, however, had gone up sufficiently to make the prospect of either hunger or malnutrition realistic. Britain certainly had a malnutrition crisis throughout the 1930s, and in the Soviet Union, literal starvation was common. In spite of all the attempts that have been made to present the Nazis as a party that stood for the interests of capitalism, the facts simply do not bear them out.[34]

Hitler's Agriculture Minister Darré faced, from the very moment of his appointment in 1933, the almost united opposition of the industrialists, the banks, the financial capitalists, the aristocracy, the large farmers who wanted to mechanise and run their farms as 'agribusinesses', and most of the senior leadership of the Nazi Party. In spite of this, his success in maintaining his own unorthodox agenda and getting most of it adopted in the teeth of such fierce and powerful opposition is astonishing. Darré even became one of the few men in Nazi Germany to take on Martin Bormann and win. Only three members of the government even supported his proposals, yet he won the battle of wills and saw his ideas adopted as official policy. The reason for this is that he was able to persuade Hitler of the need for his measures, and once Hitler approved a project, other Ministers simply had to fall in with his wishes. Darré's influence on Hitler remained a dominant one until the invasion of Russia, when the needs of a war economy overrode all other considerations. Hitler's passionate commitment to an admittedly romantic environmental vision is one of the many curious facts about his leadership which appears to have disappeared completely from the history books.

Even in terms of art, Hitler elevated 'folk art' to a high position. At the House of German Art, built in Munich in 1937, much of the exhibits dealt with 'blood and soil'. Peasant life was also extensively represented, often in a highly idealised version, but it was still accorded status and value.[35]

The example of Goslar inspired ecological pioneers throughout the West, particularly in Britain. On his own return from the 'National Peasant Village', Gardiner was so inspired by it that he launched the first popular movement for organic farming.[36]

Under Hitler, organic farming methods became the dominant tendency within German agriculture, in spite of fierce opposition from the larger farmers. Attempts were made to prevent soil erosion, and some measures to protect the water table were also taken. The active hostility shown under Hitler's government to factory farming methods was years ahead of its time, and the discouragement of artificial fertilisers and chemical treatment of pests and soil was also strikingly forward-thinking. Vast areas of German farmland that would otherwise have been lost were saved for farming, and much land was actually reclaimed for agricultural use, even against the fierce opposition of firms as powerful as Krupp. Hitler's support of these radical and deeply unpopular policies undoubtedly saved German agriculture.

In the same way, Hitler's awareness that 'intermediate' technology was preferable to the large-scale model advocated by almost everyone else in Germany went right against the orthodox wisdom of his time. Even more remarkable was his willingness to avoid the use of unnecessary technology. His belief that small-scale undertakings were in principle to be promoted rather than the huge models supported by big business was also remarkably perceptive. It took real vision to see beyond the obvious *fact* of rapid technological progress and to recognise that it might pose serious difficulties for later generations. Under the influence of Darré, Hitler pursued policies that the majority of his own supporters disagreed with. The very term 'organic farming' was invented by the Nazis.

Had it not been for the war, Germany might have blazed a trail for the world in its pursuit of 'green' policies. It is no accident that the post-war environmentalist movements drew most of their inspiration from the Nazi example, however understandably reluctant they were to admit this unless pressed. It also seems quite logical that the German Green Party was founded in 1974 by ex-Nazi August Haussleiter, a man who had joined the 1923 Munich *Putsch* in support of Hitler. It is also not surprising that one of the first Green Party members elected to the West German Bundestag was the ex-Nazi General Gerd Bastian. Indeed, Rudolf Bahro, the East German dissident, went further in 1980, calling openly for what he called 'eco-fascism'. His example has also been followed by two Finns, one an 'eco-feminist' who calls for an unlikely combination of feminism, ecology and an otherwise essentially Nazi political programme. An even more bizarre spin on the 'eco-fascist' model also comes from Finland, where the Finnish 'green' Pentii Linkola claims that the main challenge facing the modern environmental movement is to save the white race!

However repellent it may be to contemporary Greens, however much they may have moved their agenda on from its early beginnings, and however much they may seek to deny their ancestry, Nazi Germany between 1933 and 1942 was the 'greenest' country in the world. Hitler consistently supported 'green' policies in the face of sustained opposition from the most powerful sections of German society. He refused to allow the bankers, the aristocrats, the industrialists or even the modernising wing of his own party to turn him away from the course he believed to be the right one for Germany. Hitler was the first 'green' leader to come to power in any major country. His example was widely influential, in spite of the tainted nature of the source.

Notes

1. See, for example, Walther Darré, *Das Bauerntum als Urquell der nordischen Rasse*, Eher, 1929
2. For more on Eckart's and Steiner's relationship with Hitler, see: Michael FitzGerald, *Storm Troopers of Satan*
3. For more on Keyserling, Steiner and Hitler, see: a) Fitzgerald, op. cit.; b) Count Herman Keyserling, *Travel Diary of a Philosopher*, London, 1925; c) Keyserling, *The World in the Making*, London, 1927
4. Stephen H Roberts, *The House that Hitler Built*, Methuen, 1937, is one of the few writers to have dealt with the importance of environmental and agricultural issues under the Nazis, even though he is violently critical of the policies they adopted and gives a highly selective reading of the facts, often amounting to serious distortion of them, to support his position. The fact that the aristocracy, industrialists and bankers were all vehemently opposed to Hitler's agricultural policies is one of the clearest proofs that Roberts is not simply biased, but wilfully mistaken. A comment from Graf von Arnim, for example, being informed of Hitler's views on agriculture, was to say carefully that although of course the Führer's own views were beyond criticism, his Agriculture Minister Darré had wildly radical ideas which amounted to 'a slap in the face of the nobility'.

5. *Reichserbhofgesetz*, 29 September 1933. It was primarily aimed at farms between 12 and 125 hectares, but applied to all farms in Germany. It also prevented the proprietor from selling or mortgaging his smallholding. About a million farms were immediately affected by the new law, and many more chose to adopt its proposals voluntarily. See: a) Roberts, op. cit.; b) Frieda Wunderlich, *Farm Labour in Germany*, Princeton University, 1961; c) Gustavo Corni, *Hitler and the Peasants*, Berg, 1990

6. This achievement is once again criticised in Roberts, op. cit., on the grounds that it only made sense as a prelude to war and that it was bad for the German economy. In 1937 neither statement was true, and once more Roberts resorts to selective reading of the figures to support his claims.

7. Anna Bramwell, *Blood and Soil*, Kensal Press, 1985. The definitive account of Darré's life and work.

8. Richard Walther Darré, *80 Merksätze und Leitsprüche über Zucht und Sitte aus Schriften und Reden von R Walther Darré*, Goslar, 1940

9. The best expression of this viewpoint is once again given in: R Walther Darré, *Um Blut und Boden*, Eher, 1940. Darré did not invent the expression 'blood and soil', which was first used in the early 1920s by a Social Democrat politician, August Winnig. In 1927 Georg Kenstler, an exile from Transylvania, launched a magazine entitled '*Blood and Soil*'. Darré may not have invented the term, but he did more to popularise it than either of his predecessors.

10. Edward Carpenter, *Civilisation: Its Cause and Cure*, London, 1889

11. The most influential books by these three writers and thinkers were:
Ernest Thompson Seton, *Trail of an Artist-Naturalist*, Hodder, 1951
The Book of Woodcraft and Indian Lore, Stevens, 1997
Woodcraft, International Law and Taxation, 2001
G Stanley Hall, *Adolescence*, Ayer, 1970
Ernst Häckel, *The Riddle of the Universe*, Prometheus, 1992
Häckel, incidentally, invented the term 'ecology' in the late 19th century.

12. Introduction to *Woodcraft Way*, Series no. 1, Ernest and Aubrey Westlake

13. Seton, *Trail of an Artist-Naturalist*

14. Seton, *The Book of Woodcraft and Indian Lore*

15. The definitive account of Seton's enormous influence on German *völkisch* thinking remains: Heinz Reichling, *Ernest Thompson Seton und die Woodcraft Bewegung in England*, Bonner Studien zu Englische Philologies, Volume XXX, Bonn, 1937

16. John Hargrave, interview with the historian James Webb

17. Seton, *The Book of Woodcraft and Indian Lore*

18. John Hargrave, *The Great War Brings It Home*, London, 1919

19. Julian Huxley, *Evolution, the Modern Synthesis*, Allen & Unwin, 1963

20. Reichling, op. cit

21. One of the key channels of transmission of these shared environmentalist ideas was Rolf Gardiner's liaison and close friendship with the German

thinker Georg Goetsch, founder of the *Musikheim* at Frankfort-an-der-Oder. The close relationship was strengthened still further when Goetsch married one of Gardiner's 'disciples', Katherine Trevelyan. A good account of this (and many other neglected aspects of the British 'underground' culture before the hippies) is given in: Katherine Trevelyan, *Fool in Love*, London, 1962.

22. *North Sea and Baltic,* Spring 1935
23. Ibid
23. Even the tendentious Roberts, op. cit., admits the genuineness of Hitler's belief in *Blubo* and his deep personal commitment to Darré's ecological vision.
24. Bramwell, op. cit
25. Ibid
26. A vivid description of young boys and girls preparing for their stint on the land is given in: William Teeling, *Why Britain Prospers,* Right Book Club, 1938. Teeling gives an account of a procession of youngsters at Nuremberg in September 1937, being reviewed by Hitler, and proclaiming their eagerness to help the peasants cultivate the land. According to Teeling: 'They spent a good deal of time in moving their spades from the shoulder to the ground'. Teeling also describes some of the work they carried out, including building dykes, reclaiming land for agricultural production, draining marshes and even constructing canals. The young girls were as eager as the boys to work on the land, though many ran a crèche or kindergarten instead to free the farmer's wife for labour in the field.
27. Otto D Tolischus, *They Wanted War,* Hamish Hamilton, 1940
28. Ibid.
29. Ibid.
30. Ibid
31. Ibid
32. Ibid
33. Jürgen Kuszynski, *The Condition of the Workers in Gt. Britain, Germany & the Soviet Union 1932-1938,* Left Book Club, 1939
34. Ibid
35. Roberts, op. cit
36. *North Sea and Baltic,* Spring 1935

CHAPTER X

Hitler and 'Strength through Joy'

Physical strength and sporting achievement were always very important to Hitler. One obvious reason for this is the advantages it brings in terms of soldiering, but there were far deeper reasons for his interest in the subject. It was partly because of the reflected glory that he felt it would bring his nation, but even that was only a small part of it. Perhaps it may not be entirely coincidental that Hitler's best subject at school was gymnastics.

The principal driving force behind his obsession with physical strength and sport, however, sprang, like so many of his plans, from the Social Darwinist ideas he had picked up during his years in Vienna. It would be unfair not to mention that such attitudes were enormously popular throughout the world at that time, particularly in the United States. In Germany, the philosopher Nietzsche, who spent most of his life as an invalid and ended up in a mental hospital, praised strength and denounced weakness in vicious if powerful prose. Hitler, as we know, was a great admirer of Nietzsche, even if he only took what he wanted from the philosopher's thought.[1]

From the 1880s onwards, millions of Germans began to engage in some form of physical education. The *Arbeiterturnerbund* (Workers' Gymnastic Association) set out to extend to the ordinary German disciplines and facilities that had previously only been available to the wealthy. By 1914 their membership had reached 1.25 million. There were also another 1.25 million from the middle and upper classes who belonged to the *Deutsche Turnerschaft*.[2]

The *Arbeiterturnerbund* was formed in 1896 as a breakaway from the *Deutsche Turnerschaft*. This working-class group attracted 50,000 members within the first four years of its existence. Another split came with the formation of the anti-Semitic *Deutscher Turnerbund* in 1889.

Sports and games were also introduced into Germany, almost exclusively from Britain. Football, boxing, tennis, wrestling, swimming, water-polo, even mountaineering, rowing and athletics, were taken up enthusiastically by Germans but were all borrowed from British sources. Generally the source of their adoption was British students living in Germany who introduced the games they loved to the local people. British membership of the gymnastic clubs was also high and resulted in a split between the British emphasis on athleticism and grace in contrast to the previously dominant German tradition of rigid movements. The result was that the working-classes followed the British example and the middle and upper-classes did not. The traditionalists made extreme nationalist and even racist posturings on the subject.

In addition to the gymnastic organisations, there were literally millions of Germans who simply swam, rowed and skated or skied for pleasure, without belonging to any club. Hiking, of course, and even mountain climbing to an extent, also became tremendously popular outdoor activities.

With the formation of the International Olympic Committee in 1894, the issue of the Olympic Games divided German athletes and gymnasts. The traditionalist *Deutscher Turnerschaft* flatly refused to become involved, denouncing 'sport' and 'the spirit of competition' in terms that sound strikingly similar to so-called progressives today. In spite of not having been involved in the organisation of the Games, Germany was still invited to participate in the inaugural Olympics of the modern era at Athens in 1896. The *Deutscher Turnerschaft* flatly refused to send a team. This raised such an outcry in Germany that a 'Committee for Participation in the Olympic Games' was formed in defiance of them, and from 1900 onwards, teams of gymnasts did take part in the Olympics in spite of the wholesale and continuing condemnation of the event by the *Turnerschaft*.[3]

The man who harnessed the vast amount of sporting talent in Germany was Carl Diem. He became General Secretary of the German Olympic Committee in 1906, and launched a crusade for the provision of adequate sporting facilities for German youth. He hired an American trainer for the 1912 Olympic Games, with the aim of improving the poor showing of German athletes in previous Olympics. The results were not immediately impressive, German athletes making no real impression in that year. However, Diem was not in the least deterred. Observing for himself the dominance of Americans in track and field events, he went over to the United States to study the conditions there at first hand. On his return, he published a book, *Sport and Physical Education in America*, which painted a grim picture of the inadequate state of affairs in Germany compared with the American set-up. Considering that Berlin was due to host the 1916 Olympic Games, Diem felt that urgent action was required.

1913 did see the building of the Berlin Stadium. However, the outbreak of the First World War put an end to further developments in this field. After the war, Diem returned to the task of improving German facilities, this time with great success. In 1921 he created the Gymnastic-and-Sports Badge, awarded on the basis of five tests. Three were flexible, but running and swimming were compulsory. Badges were also awarded to women and children, with slightly easier tests. Over a quarter of a million badges were awarded between 1921 and 1933. The German people took up sport and outdoor pursuits with real enthusiasm. By the 1920s Germany was becoming nicknamed by many observers as the 'Land of Sport'.[4]

Nor was it only men who pursued these activities. German women found that doors which had been closed to them previously suddenly opened under the Weimar Republic. They pursued running, swimming, skiing, skating, walking and jumping activities with particular enthusiasm. German women were emerging as a new sporting force.

The Catholic Church in Germany became concerned at this new display of freedom by the country's women. An assembly of German bishops met at Fulda to discuss the issue of women's participation in sport. They ended up by passing a series of futile resolutions, demanding that women should not be allowed to exercise in public, to wear clothes that emphasised their figures, to take part in displays, or to bathe or even walk in the company of men. These absurd ideas had absolutely no impact, even on Catholic women.[5]

Hitler was passionately attached to the idea of sport and physical prowess in general. He believed that it weeded out the weak from the strong and could help in creating a future 'élite'. Though his attitudes towards the place of women in society were in general antiquated, he had no such objection to their taking part in sporting activities. He even approved of women boxing and wrestling.

Hitler was a great admirer of Diem, though the admiration was certainly not mutual. Not only was Diem not a supporter of the Nazis, but his wife, a talented athlete, was Jewish. In spite of these serious defects from his own distorted point of view, Hitler recognised the immense ability Diem had displayed over many years in raising the standard of German sport from poor to good and finally, outstanding.

Even before Hitler became Chancellor, he placed great emphasis on the development of physical prowess. The SA organised its own 'Sports Badge' and 'Reich Sports Contests.' They even invented their own version of football, known as *Kampfball* (Fight Ball). It was a violent and bloody pursuit, often resulting in severe injuries to the participants. [6] They also created mock-battles, known as *Kampfbahnen* (Battle Stations), in which grenade-throwing, pistol shooting, sprinting in gas masks, and attempts to take 'enemy' positions were prominent features.

In the same way, Hitler actively encouraged physical activities in general and sporting ones in particular among the various Nazi youth organisations. Not only the *Jungvolk* and Hitler Youth, but also the *Bund Deutscher Mädel* all regularly took part in physical exercise and competitive sport. This included 'ground agility,' scouting, shooting, boxing and wrestling.[7]

Following his appointment as Chancellor, Hitler set to work energetically to push the physical development of German men and women right to the top of the national agenda. He knew that the Olympic Games were due to come to Berlin in 1936 and was determined to show the world that Germany, even in the brief three years of his Chancellorship, had indeed begun the process of building its new 'Master Race'.

As well as the obvious measures of improving German sporting facilities, training élite athletes and subsidising clubs from State money, Hitler felt that it was essential to create a new climate in the country. He knew that he needed to build from the bottom upwards to achieve the lasting success which he craved. To this end, he appointed SA Group Leader Hans von Tschammer und Osten as the new *Reichssportsführer*. Diem, who would in normal circumstances have been the obvious choice for the job, was debarred from consideration because of his Jewish wife. Tschammer, as he was known, worked closely with the Hitler Youth and the other youth groups under von Schirach's control. Diem's advice was sought on a range of issues, but he was rarely given any credit for the results.[8]

Hitler also appointed Wilhelm Rust as Minister of Education. He had a profound effect on the direction of education in Germany, mainly (and surprisingly) improving it. In this chapter we shall look at how his measures affected sport, and consider the remainder of his educational policies in the following chapter.

Rust attached advisers on physical education to all school departments. He made a daily period of physical education compulsory in all schools. All classes had to be taught separately, rather than en masse. One of the PE periods was to be devoted to team sports such as football. All schools were required to include athletics, boxing, swimming, gymnastics and team games in the curriculum.[9]

As well as the state schools, Hitler also created an entirely new category of school, the 'Napolas'. In *Mein Kampf*, Hitler had shown a surprising admiration for the British public school system. He envisaged his 'Napolas' as German equivalents but minus the class basis. They were designed to train future leaders of the new Germany but entry to them was based strictly on ability, not on social or other considerations, except of course the usual criteria of 'racial purity' and 'National Socialist ideals'. Napolas were usually placed by lakes or the sea, and their facilities were superb. Physical training and politics were the two principal subjects on the curriculum. Girls as well as boys were allowed to join the Napolas, another curious example of how Hitler's attitude to women was more complex than has generally been assumed.[10]

Perhaps the two most famous examples of the development of a culture of physical fitness in Germany are the *Kraft durch Freude* (Strength through Joy) movement and the 1936 Berlin Olympic Games. Myths have grown up about both and *Kraft durch Freude* has been particularly ridiculed by historians, quite unjustly.

It was run by the German Labour Front, the Nazi organisation that replaced the independent trade unions of the Weimar Republic. *Kraft durch Freude* was extremely popular, and undoubtedly one of the most remarkable features of the Nazi regime. Under its auspices, for the first time in their lives, working-class Germans were provided with subsidised holidays, access to sports facilities and all kinds of other benefits. Hitler was determined that ordinary Germans should not be excluded from leisure activities. He expected them to work hard but saw no reason why they should not be rewarded for their efforts with the benefits of leisure and healthy living.

Kraft durch Freude gave the workers subsidised films, dancing, concerts, exhibitions, theatre and adult education. The most striking aspect of the movement was its programme of subsidised holidays. Two cruise ships were built on behalf of the German Labour Front and a further ten chartered by it. They offered cruises at extraordinarily cheap rates. A ten-day cruise to Madeira cost only 25 dollars. Ordinary Germans, for the first time, could travel abroad. One coal miner told Shirer:

> For the first time ever, a labouring man and his family could afford to take an ocean cruise or loll on the beaches for a week or go skiing in the mountains. Maybe in America a worker made enough to afford such vacations, but never in Europe, never in Germany.[11]

By 1937 no fewer than 6,000,000 Germans a year were travelling abroad on subsidised holidays.[12]

Working conditions were also improved, workplaces becoming lighter, less overcrowded, and cleaner. Flowers were placed in all offices and factories to brighten the workers' surroundings and thereby lift their spirits.

Within four years of taking power in Germany, Hitler had raised the health of his people so dramatically that foreign observers were genuinely amazed. Infant mortality dropped, and illness in general showed a decline. The astonished Sir Arnold Wilson, MP, remarked:

> Tuberculosis and other diseases have noticeably diminished. The criminal courts have never had so little to do and the prisons have never had so few occupants. It is a pleasure to observe the physical aptitude of the German youth. Even the poorest persons are better clothed than was formerly the case, and their cheerful faces testify to the psychological improvement that has been wrought within them.[13]

All this was deliberately designed by Hitler to raise the physical fitness of the nation. He knew only too well that it was not enough to get workers back into employment; they also had to be given opportunities for rest and refreshment.

The *Kraft durch Freude* movement, like many other aspects of Nazi rule, was also an expression of Hitler's deeply-felt and quite genuine hatred of the rigid German class structure. He despised the old aristocracy even more than he did the middle classes, seeing himself as a man of the people at the head of a movement that he regarded as the deepest expression of the German working class spirit. On the cruise ships, for example, manual workers mingled on equal terms with 'white-collar' workers and even with employers. This revolutionary change was directly ordered by Hitler.

In a speech to the *Reichstag*, he told the delegates: 'A radical transformation has taken place and has produced results which are democratic in the highest sense of the word, if democracy has any meaning at all'.[14]

In an interview, Hitler also remarked:

> The bourgeois must no longer feel himself a kind of pensioner of either tradition or capital, separated from the worker by the Marxist idea of property, but must aim to accommodate himself as a worker to the welfare of the community'.[15]

In Nazi Germany, the worker was glorified and presented as a hero of the nation every bit as much as he or she was in the Soviet Union. Hitler habitually addressed workers in factories with the familiar plural form *Ihr*, claiming that he, like them, was a simple man of the people.[16]

The most marked aspect of Hitler's drive for social equality was shown in the Youth Labour Service. This compelled young men and women aged between 17 and 25, irrespective of their wealth or social origins, to work as farm hands or common labourers for a year as a sign of their duty to their country. Again, besides the astonishing success of the measure in breaking down class barriers, neutral and even hostile observers remarked how much fitter and better-fed the Germans had become since Hitler took power.

Girls, again irrespective of their family's wealth or social position, had to spend a year working as farm labourers, in what was known as *Land Jahre*. There was also a 'Household Year', during which they had, again regardless of class and of money, to spend a year working as domestic servants.

One of the by-products of these 'work placements' was best expressed by a ribald song among the people:

In the fields and on the heather
I lose Strength through Joy

The number of illegitimate children conceived during these periods of service was quite high. Although marriage increased under Hitler, partly because of his drive for a 'traditional' role for German women, partly to help provide full employment for men more quickly, so too did unmarried births. As in Stalin's Russia, Hitler was anxious that no blame should be attached to women who became pregnant under such circumstances. Once again, Hitler demonstrated his strong and genuine commitment to social equality.[17]

Meanwhile Hitler was determined to make the Berlin Olympics, due in 1936, the most magnificent the world had ever seen. In spite of his enthusiasm, he faced a number of serious problems.

The first obstacle was the open hostility towards his regime shown by calls to boycott the Olympics by anti-Nazis in France, Britain and the United States. In 1933 both the American Athletic Union and the US Olympic Committee voted not to take part in the Games unless Jewish competitors were allowed to represent Germany.

The following year, Avery Brundage, President of the US Olympic Committee, went to Germany to ask the German organisers whether or not Jews would be allowed to compete for their country. Receiving assurances that they would be, on his return to America he gave his recommendation that US athletes should not boycott the Games.

Not everyone was convinced by Brundage's reassuring statement, however. The tide of protest rose so high that a second delegate from the Committee, General Charles E Sherrill, was despatched to Germany in 1935 for a second look. In spite of the fact that, while he was there, the infamous Nuremberg Laws were passed, which effectively robbed all Jews in the country of their civil rights, Sherrill was happy that he had succeeded in his 'mission'.

As he saw it, the demands for boycotting the Games were bringing politics into sport rather than displaying the true Olympic spirit of friendship between nations. This argument was rather flawed by the fact that the Soviet Union was still excluded from membership of the Olympic Committee and therefore unable to take part in the Olympic Games themselves, no doubt to the delight of athletes from other countries. Sherrill's 'mission' did result in an early instance of the policy of 'tokenism', and he was able to claim triumphantly, 'I went to Germany for the purpose of getting at least one Jew on the German Olympic team, and I feel that my job is finished'.[18]

As it happened, Hitler was far too aware of the propaganda value of hosting the Olympics to allow even his anti-Semitism to provide an obstacle. It would have been a major disaster for him if America, Britain and France had boycotted the Games and he decided that, since it was necessary for Jews to be involved, he might as well go the extra mile and make their participation one genuinely based on merit, not simply tokenism. Hitler's attitude was, if he had to have Jews involved, at least let them be the *best* Jews. He could have simply chosen Jews who stood no chance of winning medals and would not therefore have posed a threat to his fantasy of 'Aryan' superiority. Instead, he ordered that Jews should be chosen to compete for Germany who were actually capable of winning medals.

There were already two world-class Jews who had represented Germany in the field of sporting achievement, and both were chosen for the Olympics. One was Rudi Ball, the hockey player; the other was one of the greatest woman fencers of all time, Helene Mayer. Mayer had won the individual international competition for ladies' foil in Britain in 1927 and 1930; Olympic gold in the same event in 1928; and the World Championship for the foil in 1929 and 1931, a title she recaptured in 1937.[19]

Mayer's inclusion made it certain that more than tokenism was involved. In the same spirit, Dr Theodor Lewald, another Jew, was allowed to remain in his post as President of the German Olympic Committee, in a public if perhaps cynical display of 'inclusiveness'. In an even more surprising gesture, another Jew, Captain Wolfgang Fürstner, was put in charge of the development of the Olympic Village itself. [20]

Diem, in spite of his Jewish wife, was the obvious choice to run the organisation of the events, and he remained in his post as Secretary of the German Olympic Committee. It is largely due to the supreme competence of these 'non-Aryans' or, in Diem's case, 'Aryan traitors', that the Berlin Olympics turned out to be such a triumph of organisation.[21]

Since Hitler had done more than simply put one token Jew into the German team, but had also allowed Jews and, in the case of Diem, 'Aryans' married to a Jew, to virtually take over the running of the event, the American Olympic Committee recommended full participation in the 1936 Games in Berlin. However relieved they may have been to escape from a difficult situation, there was no excuse for the disgraceful and untrue statement immediately issued by the Secretary of the US Olympic Committee, Frederick W Rubien, who claimed: 'The Germans are not discriminating against Jews in their Olympic tryouts. The Jews are eliminated because they are not good enough as athletes. Why, there are not a dozen Jews in the world of Olympic calibre'.[22]

Hitler also ordered the removal of anti-Semitic notices from Berlin and all roads leading into the capital. Throughout Germany, in fact, anti-Semitism fell strangely silent. Even Streicher's *Der Stürmer*, a magazine dedicated exclusively to anti-Semitic propaganda of the lowest possible level, suddenly disappeared from newsstands. All foreigners in Germany, even Jews, were greeted with an effusively enthusiastic welcome. Hitler was determined to avoid any possibility of actions or behaviour that would lead to bad publicity for 'his' Games.[23]

The opening ceremony on 1 August 1936 was generally regarded as the finest to date, though some observers regarded it as a typical Nazi piece of 'overkill'. Hitler entered the stadium followed by the two Olympic officials, then the king of Bulgaria, the crown princes of Italy, Sweden and

Greece, and Mussolini's sons. On arrival at the stadium, the orchestra, led by the great composer Richard Strauss, played *Deutschland über Alles*, followed by the 'Horst Wessel Song', and then the 'Olympic Hymn', specially composed by Strauss for the occasion. 110,000 people were present in the stadium to hear Hitler officially declare the Games open.[24]

Those who imagine that political gestures did not enter the Olympics until the 1960s might ponder the fact that the Austrian delegates chose, in spite of their country's independence, to give the Nazi salute. The Bulgarians, again an independent kingdom, not only followed suit but also goose-stepped. The French competitors gave what was described by observers as a 'Roman' salute, and received, surprisingly, a greater cheer from the spectators than the German team. The British team refrained from saluting anyone, which offended many of the Germans in the crowd. The Americans were greeted with cat-calls and stamping of feet when they refused to dip their flag to the Tribune of Honour.[25]

The next day saw the first of many German successes in the Games. Hitler congratulated Hans Wülke on not only winning the shot put but breaking the Olympic record at the same time. He was also able to congratulate Tilly Fleischer, who won the women's javelin, and her fellow-countrywoman who took the silver medal. As well as these German successes, he also congratulated the Finnish runners who had taken gold, silver and bronze in the 10,000 metres. As it fell dark, Hitler, understandably tired, left the stadium. He was not in the Olympic stadium when three Americans won the high jump, two of them being black.[26]

Immediately howls of protest were raised and Hitler, following advice from Diem and Fürstner, met with the President of the International Olympic Committee to discuss the situation. He told him, probably truthfully, that no slight on any athlete had been intended and that it would be very time-consuming for him to have to congratulate every single athlete. The President of the IOC gave him a choice of meeting all the victors or none; Hitler chose to meet none of them. In view of the marked success German athletes enjoyed during the 1936 Games, this deprived him of meeting many impeccably 'Teutonic' victors, but he was certainly not guilty of 'snubbing' any athlete, white, Jewish or otherwise.[27]

One of the abiding myths of the 1936 Games is that Hitler turned his back on the great black American athlete Jesse Owens, the winner of four gold medals in Berlin. Owens himself, who knew all about racism in his home country, publicly denied the story. He stated firmly: 'When I passed the Chancellor he arose, waved his hand at me, and I waved back at him. I think the writers showed bad taste in criticising the man of the hour in Germany'.[28] Far from snubbing Owens, Hitler publicly paid him a tribute for his athletic prowess.

In spite of the outstanding performance by Owens, there was no doubt that the 1936 Olympics were an unqualified triumph for the Germans.

They won thirty-three gold medals, as well as taking most silver and bronzes, and pushed the Americans into second-place in the medal table by a wide gap of fifty-seven points. The only sign of anti-Semitism during the Games was shown by the American team, who chose at the last minute to drop two of their Jewish athletes in the 400 metre relay race. Admittedly, Owens, one of the men chosen to replace them, amply justified his selection, but the other non-Jew had never run as fast as the man whose place he took. Helene Mayer, in almost her last appearance as a representative for her country, took the silver medal in the ladies' foil, the last Jew to appear for Germany in any international competition until after the war.[28]

The Games might have been an unqualified triumph in a sporting sense, but they culminated in deep personal tragedy for some of the individuals who had been involved in them. Having led the German team to its greatest triumph, Diem was summarily dismissed as Secretary of the German Olympic Committee. Lewald was also removed from his post as President. Mayer, in spite of her medal, prudently decided to leave Germany, and when she won her last world championship in 1937, she was already an exile.[29] Most tragic of all was the fate of Captain Fürstner. His organisation of the Olympic Village had been a triumph, and his summary dismissal after the Games led the unfortunate man to commit suicide with his own pistol.[30]

Leni Riefenstahl, already world-famous following her film of the Nuremberg Rally in 1934, was now commissioned to produce a documentary of the Olympic Games. The result, *Olympia*, was a 3½ hour film in two parts. Part 1 was *Fest der Völker* (Festival of the People) and Part 2, *Fest der Schönheit* (Festival of Beauty). It took Riefenstahl eighteen months to edit the film, which had its world premiere on 29 April 1938 in Berlin, to celebrate Hitler's 49th birthday.

The film was recognised as a cinematic masterpiece. Later that year it won the Gold Medal at the Venice Film Festival. Riefenstahl was, of course, neither free of official constraints during the making of her film, nor entirely free of bias in favour of the Nazi regime and especially bias on behalf of her own country. Even so, she made no attempt to remove the footage of Jesse Owens triumphing on the track, nor were attempts made to propagandise Nazi ideas in any overt way. The impression left by her film is of strength, beauty, and the search for a kind of ideal, perfect physical achievement. Riefenstahl herself claimed that in all her films:

I can simply say that I feel spontaneously attracted by everything that is beautiful. Whatever is purely realistic, slice-of-life, which is average, quotidian, doesn't interest me. I am fascinated by what is beautiful, strong, healthy, what is living. I seek harmony. When harmony is produced I am happy.[31]

The cult of physical perfection reached its zenith under the Nazis. Other civilisations, most notably the Greeks and Romans, also worshipped the human body, but none took its adoration to the same absurd lengths as the Germans did between 1933 and 1945.

Perhaps the most remarkable example of the curious attitude the Nazis displayed towards the body is the phenomenon of 'naturism' or 'nudism'. This had been enormously popular under the Weimar Republic, and perhaps one might have expected the often puritanical side of the Nazi regime to outlaw it. Initially, Goering tried to impose a total ban on nudist practices. However, he raised such a storm of protest from people with impeccably *völkisch* credentials, including *Die Deutsche Freikörper*, the magazine of the National Socialist naturists, that the law soon became a dead letter. Hitler himself, asked to give a ruling, surprised the conservatives by suggesting that incorporation, rather than banning, was the answer. [32]

Hitler, yet again, showed himself a more complex individual than some supposed. He could at times be surprisingly modern in his outlook and his attitude to nudism was yet another sign of his 'progressive' side. The result was that, instead of driving 'naturism' underground, the Nazis took it over and ran it in yet another example of the Party's all-pervasive influence on German life. Henceforth all German nudists had to become part of the *NS-Verband für Leibesübung* (National Socialist Union for Physical Exercise).[33] More than that, Hitler authorised the re-issue of a 1924 book by Hans Surén, originally published under the title of *Die Mensch und die Sonne* (*Men and the Sun*), to coincide with the Berlin Olympics of 1936, the title being changed to *Mensch und Sonne: Arisch-olympischer Geist.* (*Men and the Sun, the Aryan Olympic Spirit*). Despite the use of the masculine pronoun, naked females were portrayed as freely as men.[33] In another example of Hitler's tolerant attitude towards nudism, Riefenstahl was allowed to show naked bodies in *Olympia*.[34]

1938 saw the *Bund für Leibeszucht* (Federation for Physical Improvement) allowed to hold an open-air summer camp, which they had been forbidden to do since 1933.[35] A naturist film, *Natürliche Leibeszucht* (Natural Physical Improvement) was even given the official Nazi seal of approval by being recommended as 'educative for the people'.[36] In 1942, admittedly at a time when the German people had more pressing concerns on their mind, naked bathing, which had been officially outlawed for some years, was legalised again.[37]

In the same way, Hitler's normally Victorian attitude towards women was at least partly a pose. He admired Riefenstahl greatly, and for her achievements as an artist, not simply for the effectiveness of her work as propaganda on behalf of the Nazi cause. In the same way he was a great admirer of women who displayed sporting prowess. Gisela Mauermayer, for example, who took the gold medal for the discus at the 1936 Berlin

Olympics, was held up by him as an example of 'true Aryan womanhood' yet his official stance was that of *Küche, Kinder, Kirche*. [38]

Nowhere was this clearer than in the way women and particularly girls were organised in Nazi Germany. Hitler instructed Robert Ley, the leader of the German Labour Front, to create a Women's Labour Service on the same model as the men's. The first women's camp opened at Schurmbach in 1935, soon followed by others. The girls mainly worked on farms, milking cows, making cheese and other agricultural chores. They got up at 5.30 in the morning, after which they were made to do exercises and sing songs until 7 o'clock. Then they had breakfast, and from 7.30 onwards, they worked until 3.00 p.m., having half an hour for lunch. After 3 o'clock, they had an hour's rest, followed by classes until 6.30. The evening then saw them either singing or listening to lectures, and they had to be in bed by 9.30.

A Labour Service Corps official complained that the Chancellor had made his task much more difficult than necessary. He explained that Hitler insisted that the women's leaders must be approximately the same age or only slightly older than the girls in their care, which made it difficult to recruit leaders of the right calibre.[39]

Hitler's concern to raise the population of Germany led to a big drive for motherhood. He outlawed abortion, forbade campaigns in favour of contraception, made it compulsory for husbands to leave their property to their wife and children, and instituted a system of 'marriage-loans'. Under this arrangement, each couple received a loan of a thousand marks, in the form of certificates to buy furniture. They were only allowed to be redeemed at small stores, large chains being specifically forbidden to process the certificates. Each child born released the debtor from a quarter of the loan, so if a family had four children, they paid nothing. Twins counted as two children. By the end of 1936, no fewer than 700,000 people had taken advantage of the scheme, at a total cost of 420,000,000 marks. Each child also brought a 15% reduction in income tax.

Hitler also organised a National Health Service, based on the principle that the State should look after the healthy, not the sick. This radical measure was introduced in July 1934 and occupied itself, as well as the obvious areas, with such less apparent practices as ensuring that farmers kept their herds clean and healthy and that insects did not enter public baths!

Hitler was determined to raise a generation of healthy Aryan men and women. Even by 1937, only four years after he had come to power, neutral and even hostile observers were forced to admit that the health of the nation had dramatically improved. As Roberts put it flippantly, 'The Nazis are raising a generation of blonde physical beauties'.[40]

The initial success of National Socialism led to many examples of absurd behaviour by German conservatives who mistakenly assumed that the Nazis were a party of the right. They seized the opportunity to persecute women who behaved in what they considered 'unfeminine' ways. Police chiefs in many German cities actually put up notices forbidding women to smoke. The police chief in Erfurt, in a display of even greater stupidity, called upon the people of his city to physically stop women who were smoking and 'remind them of their duty as German women and mothers'.[41] Women who wore 'inappropriate clothes', lipstick or make-up were also subjected to harassment by local police. Curt Rosten, one of the Nazi 'ideologists', proudly announced:

> But German men want *German* women again, and quite rightly. Not a frivolous plaything who is superficial and only out for pleasure, who decks herself with tawdry finery and is like a glittering exterior that is hollow and drab within. Our opponents sought to bend women to their dark purposes by painting frivolous life in the most glowing colours and portraying the true profession allotted to woman by nature as slavery.[42]

This sort of nonsense soon attracted protests. Germany, even under Weimar, had very little in the way of a feminist tradition, but Hitler was appalled at the absurdities that were being perpetrated in the name of National Socialism. He soon took a hand in the matter, announcing that, while motherhood was of course the highest calling for German women, they must also be strong like the Valkyries of legend. As Gertrude Scholtz-Klink, who led the largest women's group in Germany, commented rather quaintly, 'Even if our weapon is only the wooden spoon, its striking power shall be no less than that of other weapons'.[43]

Hitler, partly as a general move towards control of every aspect of German life, and partly out of irritation at the way in which conservatives were trying to push their own agenda under the guise of his movement, asked Ley to set up a national umbrella group to Nazify women. Its first leader was the formidable Lydia Gottschewski, who called for a 'fighting front' of women on behalf of the new regime. Gottschewski herself was regarded even by men who knew her as a terrifying figure who utterly intimidated them with her domineering personality. The *Bund Deutscher Mädel*, far from being an organisation devoted to cake-baking and homespun talks, was as physically energetic and even combative as its equivalent in the boys' movements. As well as the physical activities they were made to perform, fights broke out among the girls on a regular basis.[44] When news of them was brought to Hitler's attention, he only laughed and commented that it showed how tough German women were compared with the weak specimens in other countries.

Under Hitler's influence, and with the full approval of such leaders as Gottschewski and Scholtz-Klink, a new ideal of what came to be known as 'Aryan maidenhood' was drawn up. Hitler himself was never consistent in his attitude towards women and the women's groups in part reflected his own confused mixture of traditional and modern thinking.

Ilse Koehn, a former member of the *Bund Deutscher Mädel*, remembers how the leaders of her Labour Camp for girls described the ideal woman as having a body 'tough as leather, hard as Krupp steel, swift as greyhounds'.[45] Hitler liked to emphasise the pursuit of an outdoor, 'natural' life for both sexes, and exalted farming as an ideal occupation for women. He also praised and possibly also found sexually attractive the image of the slim, athletic female body. Girls were positively encouraged to be 'sporty' and strength, speed and physical prowess were not seen as 'unfeminine' in any way by Hitler. In this respect his attitude towards women was far more modern than many of his colleagues.

Under the auspices of Gottschewski and Scholtz-Klink, acting on the principles laid down by Hitler himself, 'physical invigoration' was seen as one of the prime functions of the Labour Camps for girls. Exercise, callisthenics and 'proper harmony of a healthy body' were key skills that were drummed into the girls remorselessly. Diet was also given great attention and fasting was condemned in favour of 'healthy eating'. As Gottschewski herself recognised, women had to play a new role in Nazi Germany that was not simply that of wife and mother. She said the following in her book: 'The German Woman's Front, incorporated into the front of the nation, is not a purpose in itself; it recognises only service to the whole and demands willingness to sacrifice. Our motto is: "Germany must live, even though we die!"'[46]

Germany's army of female labour is one of the most striking examples of how Hitler's thinking combined an astonishing mixture of old-fashioned and modern ideas. He might have spoken publicly of *Kinder, Kirche, Küche,* but he actively encouraged German women to fulfil a much wider and more challenging role.

An enthusiastic Nazi propagandist put it as follows: 'What a present the Führer has given the young by bringing them together so that they can learn to know and love their people through a community of their own!'[47]

Perhaps the most remarkable of all Hitler's ideas concerning German women, and the one that demonstrates strikingly how his real attitude towards females has been caricatured by too many previous writers, was his proposal for 'Women's Universities for Wisdom and Culture'. This was something he discussed in great detail with Himmler, and the list of courses to be pursued, as well as the final goal of the education, is quite at variance with the normal view of Hitler as an antiquated misogynist.

The girls' education was to include, not only the expected skills in cookery and homemaking, but sport, fencing, shooting, and training in foreign diplomacy. On graduation, they would be awarded the title 'High Woman'. Hitler commented acidly to Himmler that they ought to replace 'the wives of most of our National Socialist leaders', who were no more than 'good, trusty housewives, entirely in place during the time of struggle but no longer suit their husbands today'. Hitler envisaged these women as among the future leaders of Germany, not simply at the level of Gottschewski or Scholtz-Klink but perhaps even in his own role at some point.[48]

Hitler presided over an enormous improvement in the health, physical fitness and self-confidence of the German nation. Contrary to myth, he also raised rather than lowered the status of women and young people. None of these gains applied to the Jews, however, and the political repression and brutality that accompanied his regime far outweighs the positive achievements. A National Health Service that excluded Jews could hardly be seen as truly 'national'.

Notes

1. For instance, Nietzsche described the Jews as 'the strongest, toughest, cleverest race in Europe'.
2. J G Dixon, 'Prussia, Politics and Physical Education', from: J G Dixon, P C McIntosh, A D Munrow and R F Willetts, *Landmarks in the History of Physical Education*, Routledge, 1975
3. Ibid
4. Ibid.
5. Ibid
6. Gregor Zeimer, *Education for Death: the Making of a Nazi*, OUP, 1942
7. Dixon, op. cit
8. Ibid.
9. Ibid
10. Eugen Kogon, *Der SS Staat*, Heyne Verlag, 1988
11. William L Shirer, *The Nightmare Years 1930-1940*, Bantam Books, 1985. Shirer, who was certainly anything but sympathetic to Nazism, was forced to admit that the *Kraft durch Freude* movement was a remarkable example of a positive side to the regime. He complained that the holidays were 'over-organised' but admitted that the Germans seemed to prefer their recreation in that fashion.
12. Stephen Roberts, *The House that Hitler Built*
13. The quotation from Wilson is given in: Cesare Santoro, *Hitler Germany*, International Verlag, 1938
14. Speech by Hitler to the *Reichstag*, 30 January 1933
15. Quoted in: David Schoenbaum, *Hitler's Social Revolution*, Doubleday, 1967
16. Ibid
17. Shirer, op. cit
18. Ibid.

19. Milly Mogulof, *Foiled: Hitler's Jewish Olympian – The Helene Mayer Story*, RDR Books, 2002

20. Richard D Mandell, *The Nazi Olympics*, Macmillan, 1971

21. Dixon, op. cit

22. Rubien, quoted in Shirer, op. cit. As Shirer pointed out, the American team alone that took part in the Olympic Games included no fewer than five Jews, and the representatives from other nations brought the total to well above the 'dozen' Rubien mentioned.

23. Mandell, op. cit.

24. Ibid.

25. Ibid.

26. Ibid.

27. Ibid.

28. Ibid.

29. a) Mandell, op. cit.; b) Mogulof, op. cit.

30. Mandell, op. cit.

31. Riefenstahl, interview with *Cahiers du Cinéma*, cited in: Brandon Taylor and Wilfried van der Will, *The Nazification of Art*, Winchester Press, 1990

32. Taylor and van der Will, op. cit.

33. Ibid

34. Ibid

35. Ibid

36. Ibid

37. Ibid

38. Roberts, op. cit., quotes the following piece of doggerel, which he claims was attributed to Hitler by contemporary Germans:
    'Take hold of kettle, broom and pan,
    Then you'll surely get a man!
    Shop and office leave alone,
    Your true lifework lies at home'.
    Since this poem bears no resemblance to any of Hitler's known effusions in verse, and seems also rather superficial compared with the Runic darkness of what survives of his poetry, we can safely concur with Roberts' view that Hitler's authorship is improbable!

39. Roberts, op. cit

40. Ibid

41. Clifford Kirkpatrick, *Nazi Germany: its Women and Family Life*, AMS Press, 1979

42. Curt Rosten, *Das ABC des Nationalsozialismus*, Berlin, 1933

43. Scholtz-Klink, address to German women at the 1937 Reich Party Rally

44. Male Nazis commented patronisingly about the fights among the girls that 'Of course you can't expect a women's camp to have the discipline and seriousness of a men's camp'. Quoted in Roberts, op. cit

45. Ilse Koehn, *Mischling Second Degree: My Childhood in Nazi Germany*, New

York, 1977. It is only fair to add that Koehn found few of her leaders measuring up to the standards they demanded of the girls in their charge!

46. Lydia Gottschewski, *Die Frau im Neuen Staat*, 1934. Equally anxious to promote the 'Valkyrie' image of women was Guida Diehl, *Die Deutsche Frau und der Nationalsozialismus*, 1933. A fine biography of Diehl has been written by Silvia Lange, *Protestantische Frau auf dem Weg in den Nationalsozialismus: Guida Diehls Neulandbewegung 1916-1935*, Verlag J B Metzin, 1998. Both Diehl and especially Gottschewski have recently been 'reinvented', not to say sanitised. Gottschewski in particular is regarded in some quarters as a feminist icon, even a feminist heroine. A website, feminist.com, includes her among its 'Women of Wisdom' and describes her coyly as a 'German political activist' without giving the name of the party on whose behalf she was politically active!

47. Hans Retzlaff, *Arbeitsmaiden am Werk*, Leipzig, 1940

48. Hitler and Himmler's conversations on this project are found in: Felix Kersten, *The Kersten Memoirs*, Odhams, 1956. On the subject of Hitler's attitude to women in general, and in particular the place he saw for them in the Third Reich, an important work has destroyed a number of myths in this respect: Martin Durham, *Women and Fascism*, Routledge, 1998. Durham's book supersedes all previous studies in the field.

CHAPTER XI

Hitler and German Youth

The Nazi Party was in many respects an expression of youthful idealism, however mistaken. Not only the Nazis made this claim about their movement; both neutral and hostile observers also regarded the party as standing for the younger generation. It was not uncommon for those who did not share Nazi views to dismiss many of the 'excesses' of the movement as resulting from the 'wildness' of youth.

Certainly the Nazis attempted to portray themselves as being a 'young' party in contrast with the other political groups in Weimar. There is also no doubt that they appealed disproportionately to the younger generation of Germans, though the same is also true of the Communists. Hitler deliberately directed much of his efforts into the recruitment of young people. Many of the SA were young, often ex-soldiers.

German youth, even before the First World War, had begun to pursue its own agenda, hiking, climbing and generally adopting an outdoor life. The *Wandervögel,* as the loose associations of youngsters were known before the war, also often advocated and practised 'naturism'.[1]

Following the war, which saw the death of so many young men, there was a positive explosion of youth movements. The *Bündische Jugend,* the collective term under which the post-war movements came to be known, was more of a cohesive organisation than the looser *Wandervögel.* It represented a general tendency, with certain vague preconceptions but certainly nothing resembling any kind of coherent programme. In no sense can it be seen as a direct precursor of the Hitler Youth, but it displayed many features which led its members to become sympathetic towards the Nazis or a Nazi-style movement. Its desire to escape from the harsh realities of war, depression and urban life into a rural idyll led it to distrust democratic politics,

This phenomenon was not of course confined to Germany, British youth also adopting a similar attitude. On the whole there was no real political dimension to the movement in Britain, with the exception of Gardiner's Springhead Ring and Hargrave's Kindred of the Kibbo Kift. In Germany, by contrast, such groups were almost entirely dominated by people whose thinking was bitterly hostile to the Weimar Republic and its generally liberal political stance. The Nazi Party quickly grasped the importance of the young. In the short time, they campaigned hard for their votes; in the longer term, they sought to influence their minds in favour of their own agenda.

Gregor Strasser and Goebbels were particularly effective at appealing successfully to German youth. Strasser actually wrote an article with the provocative title, 'Make Way, You Old Ones!'[2] Baldur von Schirach, head of the Hitler Youth, announced triumphantly, 'The NSDAP is the party of youth'.[3] Ludwig Stahl wrote, 'With the exception of the National Socialists all German parliamentary parties have a pre–war programme and so they lose the young'.[4]

Hitler was only 31 when he became leader of the Nazi Party. Even when he became Chancellor in 1933, at the age of 43, he was the youngest leader of any major country in the world. Most of his friends and associates were his own age or younger. Von Schirach was only 23 when Hitler charged him with the mission of inspiring young Germans with the Nazi 'vision'. The *Daily Mail*, partly in surprise but mainly admiration, wrote in a leading article: 'Youth has taken command. A flow of young blood gives new life to the country'.[5]

From the earliest stages of the movement, Hitler directed much of his propaganda efforts towards the young. It was not until 1926 that he decided to create the Greater German Youth Movement. A Nazi called Kurt Grüber had set up a cell of children in Plauen, Saxony, and Hitler, deeply impressed by the results, appointed Grüber the National Leader of what became the 'Hitler Youth'.

The name of the movement was at first a matter of debate. It was Julius Streicher who came up with the name 'Hitler Youth'. Grüber was so successful in promoting the new group throughout Germany that it was banned in Bavaria, Hanover and Hesse. 1928 saw a new venture, the establishment of a similar organisation for girls. Originally the girls' group was called the *Schwesternschaften* (Organisation of Sisters) but it was renamed the *Bund Deutscher Mädel* (League of German Girls) in 1930. A new group for boys aged 10 to 14 was also created, known originally as the *Jungmannschaften,* later renamed the *Jungvolk.*[6]

In 1929 Hitler decided to link the Hitler Youth directly to the 'Storm Troopers'. From that time on, a boy passed from the Hitler Youth at the age of 18 into the Nazi Party and the SA. That year saw Grüber triumphantly lead 2,000 members of the Hitler Youth past the Führer at the party rally. Hitler presented him with banners for each of the provinces in which he had established groups of Hitler Youth and the associated organisations. The sight of children marching with their red flags and hammer and sword insignia stirred the imagination of many youngsters who observed it.

As well as the Hitler Youth, the League of German Girls and the *Jungvolk,* the Nazis also set up a Union of Students and even a Union of

Scholars. Not only the university students but even schoolchildren were directly targeted through these organisations and introduced to Nazi ideas through them. By 1932 the Hitler Youth alone had reached a membership of 35,000, and frightened the German government enough for them to make it illegal that year.

The previous year saw Hitler and Grüber fall out over the aims and organisation of the Hitler Youth. Hitler first ordered that the headquarters of the movement should be moved from Saxony to Bavaria, enabling him to exert much greater control over it. He also divided up the whole of Germany into ten regions each with its own Youth Group.

In late 1931 Hitler appointed von Schirach head of all three Nazi youth organisations. Grüber resigned in protest, and in June 1932 von Schirach was formally appointed National Leader of the Hitler Youth.

Von Schirach was a young man completely under Hitler's spell. He worshipped the Führer and determined to make his youth movement an instrument for achieving political power in Germany. Following one of Hitler's many suggestions, von Schirach planned to run his children's groups almost as an army in waiting, with himself as Field Marshal.

Von Schirach created an organisational structure modelled on the SA, with a group of ten being known as a *Kameradschaft* (loosely, a 'comrade-ship'). Further layers of leadership were installed, up to the *Gau* (province) and even the nation as a whole. Before long, von Schirach had trained and motivated his young charges so well that they became actively involved in the violent street brawls between the SA and rival groups. In a particu-larly tragic case, 15-year-old Herbert Norkus was murdered by a gang of Communists. By 1933 twenty boys from the Hitler Youth had lost their lives in these street battles.[7]

In spite of, or perhaps even because of, the danger to which the young-sters found themselves exposed, membership swelled from its 1932 figure of 35,000 to just over 1,000,000 six months later. Hitler himself publicly commended von Schirach for his success in recruiting youngsters for the Nazi cause.

Once Hitler became Chancellor in 1933, he determined to bring all existing youth movements under the umbrella and overall control of von Schirach's organisation. One by one, the existing groups were forced into the Hitler Youth, or 'integrated', to use the official jargon. Some groups, most notably the Bismarck Youth, resisted this process. Von Schirach, acting on Hitler's orders, dissolved them and made them illegal. By 1934 there were 6,000,000 members of the Hitler Youth, their parade that year displaying 600 banners.

Even outside Germany, the movement attracted widespread support. The Hitler Youth set up camps, to which no fewer than fifty-three coun-tries with German residents sent their children, dressed in the brown shirts and shorts of the movement. It was without doubt a genuinely popular organisation and caught the imagination of young Germans. Von Schirach was a 20-year-old art student when the future Chancellor discovered him. Hitler became a close friend, and before long gave him positions of responsibility within the Nazi Party.

Hitler placed enormous emphasis, not simply on persuading young people to vote Nazi and join the party's various youth groups, but on developing them in the direction he saw as the only possible one for the future of Germany. In essence, he wanted to train boys to become the soldiers of the Reich and women to become the wives and mothers of future troops. He remarked in this context:

> My teaching is hard. Weakness has to be knocked out of them. In my *Ordnunsburgen* a youth will grow up before which the world will shrink back. A violently active, dominating, intrepid, brutal youth — that is what I am after. Youth must be all those things. It must be indifferent to pain. There must be no weakness or tenderness in it. I want to see once more in its eyes the gleam of pride and independence of the beast of prey. In this way I shall eradicate all the thousands of years of human domestication. Then I shall have in front of me the pure and noble natural material. With that I can create the new order.[8]

The importance of the *Wandervögel* and *Bünde* in creating a new atmosphere in which such repulsive views could be seen as acceptable and praiseworthy can hardly be overstated. Most of their members subscribed to the fantasy of the *Volk*, and many were deeply steeped in *völkisch* ideology. Even before the First World War, they had been strongly nationalist, though not in general racist.

Following Germany's defeat in World War One, the appeal of *völkisch* thought grew, particularly when it was combined with bizarre occult theories that offered cloudy 'spiritual' hope to a despairing people. It may even have been through Ludendorff that Hitler got the idea of targeting youth, for the General's wife Mathilde ran a *völkisch* occult society known as the *Tannenberg Bund,* named after her husband's famous victory over the Russians in 1914. Other similar groups were Feder Mühle's *Gottesbund Tanatra,* which among its other claims to 'fame', seems to have invented the slogan of 'a Thousand Year Reich'. Artur Dinter, who wrote a best-selling novel on the 'evils' of intermarriage between Germans and Jews, was also involved in another such group.[9] A member of one of these youth movements explained:

> Mysticism and everything mystical had dominion over us. It was in our ranks that the word Führer originated, with its meaning of blind obedience and devotion. The word *Bund* arose with us, too, with its

mysterious undertone of conspiracy. And I shall never forget how in those early days we pronounced the word *Gemeinschaft* [society] with a trembling throaty note of excitement, as though it hid a deep secret.[10]

The use of the swastika, an ancient symbol of the sun, was also extremely popular among the youth movements. Though Hitler had become familiar with it himself through Guido von List during his years in Vienna, the widespread use of it by the young undoubtedly influenced him in choosing it as the most immediately recognisable Nazi symbol.

World War One, and the German Revolution of 1918 that followed it, radicalised a whole generation of the country's youth. Though they still clung to a vision of a rural Germany, the war and the civil strife that followed turned their attention to politics. In the majority of cases, they were attracted to either the Communists or the Nazis. The Social Democrats had their own youth wing but it never managed to achieve the same popularity with the young.

From 1918 onwards, many disillusioned youngsters joined the *Freikorps*, many of whose members were soon to join the infant Nazi Party. One former member explained:

One often hears the question why it was that youth spontaneously rallied to Hitler. But the experiences of war, revolution, and inflation supply an explanation. We were not spared anything. We knew and felt the worries in the house. The shadow of necessity never left our table and made us silent. We were rudely pushed out of our childhood and not shown the right path. The struggle for life got to us early. Misery, shame, hatred, lies, and civil war imprinted themselves on our souls and made us mature early. So we searched, and found Adolf Hitler. What attracted us like a magnet was precisely the fact that he only made demands of us and promised us nothing. He demanded of every person a total commitment to his movement and therefore to Germany.[11]

It is worth reflecting that 15,000 members of the *Wandervögel* fought for Germany during the First World War. Only 5,000 of them returned. The effect of the war upon these young men was profound. They saw in their deaths a kind of holy offering, a dedication to duty, to country, to self-sacrifice rather than self. When the Nazis, almost certainly with purely cynical motives, appealed to the same idealism that had led so many young men to die, they found many who caught an echo of the comradeship of the trenches and the loyalty even to death which they had practised during the war. They were profoundly affected by Hitler's call to duty in the service of the nation.[12]

One famous remark by one of the 'youth leaders' was quite certainly at least pointing the way in which the movement was heading after the war. It ran as follows: 'Youth knows today where it will not be led: into the dirty, muddy and sluggishly flowing canals of the liberal party system. For this reason youth gravitates to the *Bünde*'.[13]

One marked difference between the *Bünde* and the *Wandervögel* was that the post-war movement had a tightly-knit structure. The pre-war youth had been escapists, dreaming their rural idylls; the *Bünde* were run almost on military lines. They certainly took the soldier as the figure representative of their highest hopes and dreams, and instead of simply walking, the *Bünde* began to march. One of their members proudly declared that the 'German Trinity' was 'God, myself and my weapons'.[14]

One fundamental difference between the *Bünde* and the various Nazi youth organisations was the lack of élitism in the latter. The Hitler Youth in particular was overwhelmingly working-class in its membership, whereas the members of the *Bünde* were almost entirely middle or even upper class in origin.[15]

Thousands of ordinary Germans, normally excluded by snobbery from the *Bünde*, found in the easy camaraderie and genuinely classless atmosphere of the Hitler Youth a new self-confidence and sense of 'belonging' that they had never experienced previously. Hitler might have designed his movement with the deliberate intention of moulding the minds of impressionable youngsters, but there were compensations for those who joined. The members of the Nazi youth movements were healthier, stronger and enjoyed more recreation than the majority of working-class German youngsters.

Hitler, of course, knew only too well the benefit to his party of moulding the minds of future generations. He said of the Hitler Youth, in connection with its intentions and methods:

This youth learns nothing else than to think German, to act German, and if these boys enter our organisation at the age of 10, then four years later they come from the *Jungvolk* into the Hitler Youth, and we keep them there for another four years, and then we certainly don't give them back into the hands of the originators of our old classes and estates, but take them straight into the party, into the Labour Front, the SA or the SS, the NSKK, and so on. And if they are there for another two years or a year and a half and still haven't become complete National Socialists, then they go into the Labour Service and are polished for another six or seven months, all with a symbol, the German spade. And any class consciousness or pride of status that may be left here and there is taken over by the Wehrmacht for further treatment for two years, and when they come back after two, three, or four years, we take them straight into the SA, SS, and so on again, so that they shall in no case suffer a relapse, and they don't feel free again as long as they live. And if anyone says to me, yes, but there will always be a few left over: National Socialism is not at the end of its day, but only at the beginning![16]

The attempt to 'educate' youngsters in the Nazi view of the world began from birth. Hitler was described as 'the man sent from Heaven' who had undone the injustices of the Treaty of Versailles, led Germany to first place among nations, and was crusading against the Bolshevik and Jewish enemies of the people. This fantasy view of the world was deliberately impressed upon children from as young an age as possible. Naturally, teaching in schools throughout Germany also reflected the official Nazi positions. The result, inevitably, was that by the time children reached the age of 10, they were already deeply infected with the Nazi 'philosophy'.

Curiously, some of the changes the Nazis made in German education were improvements on the situation under the Weimar Republic. Both in schools and at university, there had been serious mistakes made. No attempt was made to instil moral values into children, and many 'non-practical' subjects vanished from the curriculum altogether. In most of the large cities, the majority of German teachers openly taught the children Communist ideas. The teaching of art, history, music and literature was particularly prone to being presented to German youth with a Marxist slant.

The situation was even worse in the universities. German students organised mass demonstrations on campus in support of their Marxist ideas. Professors who tried to stand up for liberal values were heckled, intimidated and often forced to resign. Before long, Communist students were openly rioting and engaging in violence on the streets as well as on campus. Challenged about their behaviour by German liberals, the students retorted contemptuously that the job of the universities was to be 'agents of revolution'. They rejected the very idea of 'free thinking'.

During the late 1920s, Nazi ideas began to find a following among German students. The result was, inevitably, a culture where Marxists and Nazis clashed repeatedly on and off campus. An American observer during this period described how bad the problems became in universities:

The idealistic youth broke up classrooms, invaded university campuses, broke shop windows. The liberals of Berlin and Vienna sprang to the defence of the youth. They labelled any police action against them as 'brutality.' One of the phrases used to describe the idealistic German youth by editorial writers and educators, believe it or not, was 'the culturally deprived.' When they broke windows of Jewish shops, the liberals — even intellectual Jews of Germany and Austria — said, 'how else shall they show their resentment? Most of the shops just happened to be owned by Jews'.[17]

The Nazis, contrary to myth, did not take over an education system that reflected independent thinking and a range of subjects. On the contrary, by the time Hitler came to power it was almost a case of substituting one form of biased education for another. In fact, even the hostile Roberts admits that, on the whole, except for the deliberate hero-worshipping of Hitler and the demonising of the Jews, German education was actually *better* under the Nazis than it had been under the Weimar Republic.[18]

At the age of 10, each boy received a brown shirt, and had to join the *Jungvolk*. Each girl would also join the *Bund Deutscher Mädel*, where she dressed in a uniform of a white blouse and blue skirt. Both boys and girls, even at this young age, were required to vow eternal loyalty to Hitler and sacrifice themselves willingly for him. He was the 'soul of the nation', and they, as individuals, were only a part of the 'organic whole'.

After four years of this, the boys moved on to the Hitler Youth, receiving brown trousers and a red swastika arm-band. From that point on, the boy was essentially an SA man in training. On reaching the age of 18, the boy then went to a camp for six months, as part of the compulsory labour scheme for young people. He worked, generally in the fields, with other youngsters. Following this, he was sent into the armed forces for two years.

In the camps for youngsters, great emphasis was placed on finding possible future leaders. Promising boys were sent on monthly training courses. The three main training centres were at Vogelsgang in the Eifel hills, Sonthofen in south Allgäu and Crossinsee in Pomerania. The primary focus of these training camps was on the physical development of the boys. They were then taught Nazi ideology and finally the principles of leadership and administration.

Even music was brought into the battle to indoctrinate the young. Before 1933 *Die Musik* had been a widely respected magazine in the field of musical criticism. After Hitler came to power, it was forced to adhere strictly to Nazi principles. In April 1934 it became the official music magazine of the Hitler Youth. Hitler Youth songbooks were drawn up, so that the youngsters sang Nazi songs from an early age. Von Schirach even wrote a few songs himself, though their quality was extremely poor. More ambitious works were also commissioned, such as compositions by Heinrich Spitta and Cesar Bresgen, who were also appointed musical organisers of the Hitler Youth. Their duties included arranging annual music festivals. In 1938, they held a Hitler Youth Festival devoted to the music of Beethoven at Bad Wildbrunn. The festival saw the composer's Eighth Symphony being performed by brown-shirted youngsters.[19]

Film was also used to convince youngsters to join the Hitler Youth. 1933 saw the remarkable *Hitlerjunge Quex* (The Hitler Youth named Quex), which was actually a genuinely impressive work of art. The story concerns a young boy with Communist parents, but who is attracted to the Hitler

Youth in spite of their influence. In the end he chooses them over his parents. The film is propagandist, but so well constructed that it has been compared with Brecht and Weill's *Threepenny Opera* and Fritz Lang's *M*. [20]

Von Schirach, in spite of his idolatry of Hitler, was never a passionate anti-Semite like his chief. He was guilty of the vaguely anti-Jewish attitudes so prevalent in Germany at that time, but was brave enough to express his hostility to acts of outright violence against Jews. Perhaps von Schirach's finest hour came on the day following the *Kristallnacht* atrocities, when thousands of Jews were attacked in the streets, had their homes and businesses looted or vandalised, and some were even murdered. Appalled by what he had seen, von Schirach called together the leaders of the Hitler Youth in Berlin and condemned the attacks as 'a disgrace to civilisation'. He went further than mere words, forbidding Hitler Youth members to take part in 'criminal actions', as he frankly described *Kristallnacht*. It is hard to believe that he was so detached from reality that he did not see that such behaviour was the logical outcome of demonising the Jews in the eyes of the people, but von Schirach, like many Nazis, seemed to have an infinite capacity for self-deception and splitting themselves almost into two different people. [21]

In spite of this rare display of independent thought, von Schirach continued to be one of the most loyal of all Nazis. Hitler had not been mistaken when he had singled out the shy, awkward student of 20 for future leadership roles. Even when he became Chancellor, Hitler allowed von Schirach far more autonomy than the majority of his Cabinet in the administration of his youth groups.

Hitler, however, conscious of the vital role that youth would play in the perpetuation of his fantasies, constantly put forward ideas to von Schirach, even though he left the implementation of his policies to the young man. Following a hint from Hitler, von Schirach designated 1934 as 'The Year of Inner Education and Orientation'. As he put it himself, 'The Hitler Youth seeks to embrace both the whole of youth and the whole sphere of life for the young German'. [22]

What followed was a sustained and systematic course of total indoctrination of young impressionable minds. Hitler was cunning enough to know that this process had to be carried out by degrees rather than with frontal assault. To describe the approach he wanted adopted, he used the expression 'the creeping revolution'. Many of the songs for the Hitler Youth were taken over wholesale from the *Bünde*; many of the uniforms were based on *Bünde* designs; many of the rituals were also borrowed from existing *Bünde* ceremonies.

It was not until the Hitler Youth Law of 1 December 1936 that Hitler officially proclaimed that the Hitler Youth and its related youth groups were the only permitted associations for young people in Germany. He had allowed a process of gradual assimilation to take place over the previous three years to minimise any possible friction or resentment from older, more established groups. In this matter, as in his approach to international relations, Hitler used the notorious 'salami' approach.

Again, Hitler did not immediately make it apparent that members of the youth organisations, at least in the case of the boys, were being groomed to become soldiers. It was not until the second of two subsequent laws that he formally declared that service in the Hitler Youth was to be equated with serving in the Labour Corps and even in the *Wehrmacht*.

By 1 December 1936, addressing a meeting of parents following the introduction of the new laws, von Schirach, after consultation with Hitler, felt confident enough about the changed attitudes within Germany to openly announce:

> Every Hitler Youth cub carries a marshal's baton in his knapsack. But it is not merely the leadership of youth that stands open to him; the gates of the state are also open for him. He who from his earliest youth, in this Germany of Adolf Hitler, does his duty and is competent, loyal and brave need have no worries about his future.[23]

Von Schirach, of course, was a young man in his twenties when he came to power in Germany. Hitler, by contrast, was in his early forties. However, apart from the inherent immaturity of the new Chancellor's own nature, he was also keenly aware that he needed to win the young for his cause or National Socialism would not survive for long. The young themselves, in spite of the reality of their situation, which was one of depersonalisation and indoctrination, felt empowered for the first time. One member of the Hitler Youth explained how he felt in the following words: 'To throw oneself into a cause, to take responsibility for one's contemporaries, to be able to work for an even stronger Fatherland in unison with equally enthusiastic comrades,' adding that another benefit of membership was 'public acknowledgment and promotion to positions which previously had been unthinkable lay open'.[24]

Von Schirach himself went even further, claiming at the Nuremberg trials that his intention had been to create 'a youth state within the state'. He made an even more extravagant declaration in his book, following an extraordinary attack on parents, teachers and church leaders, stating flatly 'in a higher sense the young are always right'.[25]

Such an extreme, not to say eccentric, claim may have been representative only of von Schirach's own views. However, Hitler too had very definite ideas on youth, which he certainly acted upon. His government contained probably the youngest Cabinet in the world. Hitler also made great play of the 'Immortal Band', the twenty-one youngsters who had fought and died for the Nazis during the 'years of struggle'. He stated firmly: 'Youth must be led by youth'. In a speech to German youth, Hitler informed them:

We must be dominated by one will, we must form one unity, we must be held together by one discipline; we must all be filled with one obedience, one subordination. For over us stands the nation. You must practise today the virtues that nations need when they wish to become great. You must be loyal, you must be courageous, you must be brave, and among yourselves you must form one great, splendid comradeship. Then all the sacrifices of the past that had to be made and were made for the life of our nation will not have been offered in vain.[26]

Following instructions from Hitler, von Schirach designated 1935 as the 'Year of Training'. He introduced the boys to physical, artistic, professional, racial and defence training. In the *Bund Deutscher Mädel*, physical, artistic, and racial training were also practised, along with 'domestic training', in accordance with Hitler's now well-known if absurd mantra, *Kinder, Kirche, Küche,* 'children, church, kitchen'.

By January 1937 Hitler and von Schirach felt confident enough to be blatantly militaristic in their training of the boys. That month saw an extraordinary speech delivered by Obergebietsführer Dr Hellmuth Stellrecht, in which he told his audience:

We wish in the course of the year to reach the point where the gun rests as securely in the hands of German boys as the pen. It is a curious state of mind for a nation when for years it spends many hours a day on calligraphy and orthography, but not one single hour on shooting. Liberalism wrote over the school doors that 'Knowledge is power.' But we have learnt during the war and the post-war years that the power of a nation ultimately rests exclusively on its weapons and those who know how to use them.[27]

Hitler made a number of speeches and pronouncements about the importance of 'ideological training' for the young. He stated, as early as 1933, that he intended 'to bring up that unspoilt generation which will consciously find its way back to primitive instinct'.[28]

As with Nazi ecological policy, the extent to which Hitler laid down broad principles for the indoctrination of youth has not been fully recognised. Perhaps in reaction against the old view of him as an autocrat who interfered in every aspect of policy, a recent trend has come to see him as a remote figure who hardly took a decision, preferring to leave everything to his ministers. This attitude is as misleading and inaccurate as the contrary view. We have already seen that Hitler was genuinely passionate about the environment and agriculture, and he was at least as much concerned with the direction of German youth. Even in *Mein Kampf*, he had expressed his desire 'one day to obtain the generation that is ripe for the last and greatest decisions on this globe'.[29] An even plainer statement was made by Hitler to Rauschning:

> My pedagogy is hard. The weak must be hammered away. In my castle of the Teutonic Order, a youth will grow up before which the world will tremble. I want a violent, domineering, undismayed, cruel youth. Youth must be all that. It must bear pain. There must be nothing weak and gentle about it. The free, splendid beast of prey must once more flash from its eyes. I want my youth strong and beautiful. In this way I can create the new.[30]

If the above quotation represents Hitler at his most removed from reality, another of his remarks makes equally clear the cynicism with which he also approached the task of indoctrinating German youth. He commented that he found a 'quiet special secret pleasure' in seeing 'how the people around us fail to realise what is really happening to them'.[31]

A young girl from a liberal family described how she joined the *Bund Deutscher Mädel* largely out of pressure from those around her. She was anything but sympathetic to Nazi ideas. As she related:

> At first I just made myself do it. The Nazi accounts were so fantastic — plots of world-Jewry, etc. — that I could hardly keep from laughing as I read them; but of course I had to be careful. It was somewhat of a shock to find how readily the children accepted these Nazi fabrications. But the most amazing thing of all was, that after a few years of going through the routine, I began to believe the stories myself and could no longer distinguish in my own mind between propaganda and truth.[32]

It is true that Hitler was a fanatic, and that his tenuous grip on reality grew worse as the situation deteriorated, but he was also a cunning and cynical manipulator. He deliberately took advantage of the idealism of youth and perverted their natural trust, turning them into ruthless killers who felt no pity when they saw or even carried out cold-blooded murder. In a notorious reply, one of the boys captured by the Allies replied: 'I saw women and children killed, but did not pay any attention to it. I have no opinion, I obey'. [33]

A horrified British soldier described German youth as being guilty of 'cruelty and bestiality practised for its own sake, the worst offenders being German boys between the ages of 16 and 18'. [34] A Swiss observer in Germany during 1943 described 'uncontrollable behaviour' by boys as young as 10.[35] These youngsters had become so brainwashed that they refused blood transfusions unless assured of the racial purity of the donor, preferring to die.[36] As a German teacher remarked after the end of the war,

'Never mind textbooks, the first job will be to teach these youngsters how to love'![37] There can be no greater indictment of the way in which Hitler perverted the minds of German youth than *that* statement.

Notes

1. Lanz himself, one of Hitler's early mentors in Vienna, was a passionate, not to say obsessive, advocate of 'nudism'. Several issues of his magazine *Ostara* were devoted to it.
2. Article reprinted in: Gregor Strasser, *Kampf um Deutschland*, Eher, 1932
3. Baldur von Schirach, *Die Hitlerjugend, Idee und Gestalt*, Berlin, 1934
4. Ludwig Stahl, 'Das Dritte Reich und die Sturmvögel des Nationalsozialismus', *Hochland*, No. 28, June 1931
5. 'Triumphant Youth', *Daily Mail*, 10 July 1933
6. Stephen Roberts, *The House that Hitler Built*.
7. Hitler, address to the Reich Party Congress in 1935
8. Most of the above from: Walter Laqueur, *Young Germany*, Transaction, 1984
9. Artur Dinter, *Die Sünde wider die Liebe*, Leipzig, 1922. Dinter's title literally means 'The sin against love', but 'The sin against the blood' gives a better idea of the thrust of his book.
10. E Y Hartshorne, *German Youth and the Nazi Dream of Victory*, Farrar and Rinehart, 1941. It is difficult to find an exact English equivalent for *Gemeinschaft*. It has overtones of 'family', 'community', 'nation' and 'people'. I have chosen 'society' as perhaps offering the closest fit in English.
11. Quoted in: Dusty Sklar, *The Nazis and the Occult*, Dorset Press, 1977
12. This aspect of the interface between members of the *Wandervögel* and similar groups has been well documented and discussed in: Karl O Paetel, *Jugendbewegung und Politik. Randbemerkungen*, Bad Godesberg, 1961
13. Quoted in Paetel, op. cit
14. *Der Weisse Ritter*, No. 6, 1921
15. This policy of working-class recruitment was quite deliberate. Hitler himself recommended it. See: Arno Klönne, *Hitlerjugend, Die Jugend und ihre Organisation im Dritten Reich*, Hanover, 1960
16. Hitler, speaking at Reichenburg on 2 December 1938
17. George Murray, 'New radicals a 1930 rerun', *Chicago Today*, 14 May 1969
18. Roberts, op. cit
19. Brandon Taylor and Wilfried van der Will, *The Nazification of Art*, Winchester Press, 1990
20 Ibid.
21. Von Schirach, Nuremberg Trials, *IMT*, XIV. On the other hand, when Himmler made his notorious speech on 6 October 1943, openly admitting to his role in the 'Final Solution', von Schirach and his colleagues 'sat

speechless at the tables avoiding one another's eyes', and made no protest of any kind against the appalling news of which he had just been informed. Baldur von Schirach, *Ich glaubte Hitler,* Hamburg, 1967

22. Hans Helmut Dietze, *Die Rechtsgestalt der HJ,* Berlin, 1939

23. Baldur von Schirach, *Revolution der Erziehung. Reden aus den Jahren des Aufbaus,* Munich, 1938

24. Werner Klose, 'Hitlerjugend. Die Geschichte einer irregeführten Generation. Nach Quellen und Erlesbnissen dargestellt', *Die Welt am Sonntag,* 10 March 1963

25. Von Schirach, *Die Hitlerjugend*

26. Speech by Hitler, quoted by: Cuno Horkenbach, *Das Deutsche Reich von 1918 bis Heute. Das Jahr 1933,* Berlin, 1935

27. Hellmuth Stellrecht, 'Die Wehrerziehung der deutschen Jugend', January 1937 lecture to the *Wehrmacht's* political education course. IMT, XXIX, 1992-PS

28. Speech by Hitler in Nuremberg, 1 September 1933

29. Adolf Hitler, *Mein Kampf*

30. Hermann Rauschning, *Hitler Speaks,* Thornton Butterworth, 1939

31. Hitler, quoted in Sklar, op. cit.

32. Account quoted in Sklar, op. cit

33. Captured Hitler Youth, quoted in Sklar, op. cit

34. Account quoted in Sklar, op. cit.

35. Ibid

36. Ibid

37. Ibid

CHAPTER XII

Hitler the Warlord

One of the most fascinating and hotly disputed questions about the Third Reich is the extent to which Hitler consciously planned for war. Some claim that the entire programme of Nazi aggression was mapped out at least as early as *Mein Kampf,* and that Hitler followed its detailed blueprint from start to finish. Others claim that there was no plan for war at all, only a series of almost accidental crises to which Hitler reacted as they happened. His growing belligerence was the result of the hesitancy of other countries in the face of his open threats of force. It was simply a game of brinkmanship in which the stakes got higher all the time until in the end they became too big. On the gambler theory, Hitler did not really want war, at least not on the global scale that he ended up facing.

In spite of his bloodcurdlingly militaristic speeches before his appointment as Chancellor, as soon as he was in power Hitler went out of his way to reassure foreign governments about his peaceful intentions. Nor was it simply a matter of words. In spite of the fact that *Anschluss,* or union with Austria, was one of Hitler's most cherished political ambitions, he promised Mussolini that he would respect Austrian independence. He also engaged in disarmament negotiations at Geneva. There was some illegal rearmament in spite of these facts, but to nothing like the extent that has been claimed. Goering was alleged to have said that 'guns will make us powerful; butter will only make us fat,' but in fact the Nazi government consistently put butter before guns at this period.[1] Indeed, it was not until Goebbels finally persuaded Hitler to agree to the policy of total war in 1943 that Germany's war effort began to come close to that of Britain and Russia, both of whom had adopted a total war policy from the very beginning of the conflict.

The first apparent signs of genuine belligerence in German foreign policy occurred in Austria. Only a month after Hitler had given his word to Mussolini that he would respect Austrian independence, Nazi activists in Vienna decided to launch a *putsch.* Disguising themselves as Austrian soldiers, one hundred and fifty conspirators stormed the Chancellery and tried to arrest the entire cabinet. All but two of them got away, but the

Chancellor himself, Dollfuss, was shot dead. The rebels then broadcast over the radio the 'news' of his resignation and their own takeover of the country.

Europe held its breath and waited to see what would happen next. Members of the German government could hardly conceal their delight. The dream of union with Austria seemed suddenly a real and imminent possibility. There was one notable member of the government who not only refused to share in the general excitement but who became increasingly nervous and angry as the day wore on. By the time he heard the news that Mussolini was mobilising the Italian army and air force on the Austrian border, Hitler was already too furious to talk to his colleagues. Later that evening he heard that the Austrian government had managed to suppress the coup and arrest the rebels. The German government was forced to endure more humiliation as the Austrians offered to let them negotiate the freedom of the Nazi conspirators. The furious Hitler told his State Secretary that he would put them all in concentration camps.

Mussolini not only mobilised his own troops against Germany but also formed what was known as the Stresa Front with Britain and France. He denounced the Germans as a nation of barbarians and claimed that any resemblances between Fascism and National Socialism were superficial. He also blamed Hitler for both the coup and the murder of Dollfuss. In general, this has been the line taken by most historians. However, it seems difficult to reconcile this theory with Hitler's own behaviour. Not only did he not welcome the news of the *putsch*, as other Nazi leaders unquestionably did, but he actually raged against the Austrian Nazis for 'having involved him in such an appalling situation.'[2] All in all, the evidence strongly suggests that the murder of Dollfuss, and the attempted *putsch* that accompanied it, far from having been carried out on the instructions of Hitler, was in fact a unilateral action by Austrian Nazis of which Hitler neither knew nor approved.

The next stage in Hitler's involvement in possible threats of war came soon after the return of the Saar to Germany after a referendum in which ninety per cent of the electorate had voted for union with Hitler's Nazi state. The British Government had become anxious to establish friendly relations with Germany and was not unduly concerned by the limited steps that had so far been taken in the direction of rearmament. It was at this very moment that Hitler chose to announce publicly that Germany now had a Luftwaffe, an air force, as an integral part of the armed forces. He followed this up by announcing the reintroduction of conscription and another increase in the size of the military. Both measures were forbidden under the terms of the Treaty of Versailles. The French made a formal protest about the matter but were assured that Germany's new military power was intended for use against (or rather as a counter to) the Soviet Union and not Western governments.

As well as trying to keep on good terms with France, primarily to avoid the possibility of a French alliance with Stalin, Hitler also tried to drive a wedge between Britain and France. At meetings with Eden and other top British government representatives, he stressed that the new increases in German naval strength which he was planning were not directed against Britain. He would be content with a ratio of only thirty-five per cent of the British fleet, but refused to accept inferiority to the French and Italian navies. His arguments eventually wore down British resistance, and at a subsequent meeting in London they agreed to his demands. Not only did he bring about dramatically improved relations with Britain, but he also signed a trade deal with Russia and a treaty of friendship with Poland. None of his foreign policy moves was aggressive in any way.

Indeed, his rapprochement with Russia and Poland led to uneasy murmurings among his closest supporters. Surely Bolshevist Russia was the natural enemy of the German people? Hitler had been telling them so for years. And an alliance with Poland was even more unbelievable, for the Poles had cut Germany off from Danzig and the Polish Corridor, territories which had belonged to the Germans before the Treaty of Versailles.

Hitler, of course, was trying to avoid the encirclement of Germany which had been one of its biggest problems during the First World War. All the same, even in private Hitler spoke constantly of his lack of desire to fight the British under any circumstances. He also showed quite remarkable restraint towards France after its conquest for a surprisingly long time. But to put his foreign policy during the pre-war years down entirely to a desire to avoid fighting a war on two fronts seems both naive and at variance with the facts. Hitler was always willing to accept a negotiated settlement rather than fight. One of the few consistent features of his foreign policy throughout the 1930s was his determination to remain friends with Italy and Poland, no matter how unpopular both these alliances were in Germany. Hitler genuinely thought that the Poles would surrender Danzig and then both countries could fight together against the Soviet Union.

His next aggressive move was to violate the Locarno Treaty by moving a symbolic presence of troops into the Rhineland. Under the terms of the treaty, that area of Germany had to be a demilitarised zone for an indefinite period. Hitler did not move troops into the Rhineland in an attempt to threaten France with war. What he was doing was declaring that he recognised no limitations on his sovereignty within Germany. Hitler had not planned to occupy the Rhineland in 1936, but two events which were outside his control led him to bring the occupation forward from its original date of 1937.

The first was the ominous news of the Franco–Soviet pact, which really alarmed Hitler. Suddenly the old fear of the encirclement of Germany was looking a possibility. Nervously he began to consider occupying the

Rhineland as a symbolic show of strength. For what it was worth, the French alliance with Russia was itself a direct violation of the Locarno Treaty, so from a strictly legal point of view Hitler was able to argue that he was only breaking it himself because of the French government's action. Much more important was the continuing international uproar over the Italian invasion and conquest of Ethiopia. This isolated Mussolini diplomatically and made him more willing to consider an alliance with Germany, which up to then he had always refused to contemplate. Behind these two fortunate smoke screens, Hitler sent his troops into the Rhineland.

The French Government wanted to go to war over the issue, but the combination of the British Government's refusal to become involved and the reluctance of their own military commanders to fight forced them to back down. Throughout the whole affair the Germans had contingency plans for withdrawal if the French army had moved against them. It was the first time that Hitler had used the threat of war, a threat which he knew very well he had no intention of carrying out, as an instrument of foreign policy. The gambler had taken an enormous risk and got away with it. From now on he was to gamble more and more outrageously.

The next international crisis was the Spanish Civil War. Contrary to the popular view, Hitler sent almost no help to Franco. He did allow a certain number of planes – mainly transport aircraft – to take part in the conflict, but refused to commit troops on anything but a purely symbolic scale. It was the Italians, not the Germans, who provided the meaningful foreign support to Franco.

In the same way it was not Hitler but the Austrian Chancellor, Schuschnigg, who precipitated the Austrian crisis that led to the *Anschluss*. The German strategy had not been to launch a full-scale invasion of Austria but to work slowly towards a policy of undermining Austrian independence from within. It was Schuschnigg's insistence on holding a referendum on the question of Austrian independence – a policy which, incidentally, was strongly supported by Seyss-Inquart, the Nazi choice for the leadership of Austria – that created the crisis in the first place. Even then, Hitler was ready to have a negotiated settlement. It was Goering, acting on his own initiative, who transformed the situation on to a war footing. Faced with his unequivocal threats of brutal force, the Austrian government resigned. Seyss-Inquart took over and the Germans marched into Austria, entirely peacefully.

Up to and including the time of the union with Austria, Hitler had been reacting to events and taking advantage of opportunities rather than following any coherent plan. Even the *Anschluss* had not been his original intention. Now, however, perhaps made overconfident by his continuing success in using the threat of force to achieve his objectives, he began to think seriously about waging a series of limited wars. From now on Hitler embarked upon a policy of sheer aggression. The first victim was

Czechoslovakia, a country which had alliances with both France and the Soviet Union. Neither country was willing to assist the Czechs, and in fact it was the British who were more prepared to risk a war on the issue. Eventually, of course, the Czechs were abandoned to their fate by all their allies. But it was the first time that the British Government had seriously considered fighting the Germans.

A year later Hitler was to find himself at war with Britain and France, following the German invasion of Poland. The actual course of the war is so well known that it is perhaps more profitable to look at Hitler's direct influence upon the conduct of the war. His first and most generally known contribution was to formulate what became known as the *Blitzkrieg* strategy. During the First World War Hitler had seen at first hand the waste and futility of trench warfare. He was determined that such horrors would never be repeated. He also knew that the German economy was in no state to withstand the rigours of a long war of attrition. Instead he proposed a series of lightning attacks, based on the element of surprise and also on heavily armed but mobile units, to outflank and cut off enemy armies. [3]

Such highly mobile warfare was completely novel to the German General Staff, who had serious misgivings about the idea. It was, however, to prove its worth in spectacular fashion. Even during the attack upon the Soviet Union it very nearly won the war for the Germans. Two factors conspired to make the Russian campaign the first failure of the new *Blitzkrieg* tactic. Both were entirely avoidable, and both were the result of bad judgement on the part of Hitler.

The first mistake was a military one. His insistence upon splitting the German forces led to smaller bodies of troops being forced to spread their resources too thinly, dissipating their strength in three separate attacks on Moscow, Leningrad and Stalingrad, when a single thrust against Moscow would almost certainly have led to the fall of the capital and the surrender of the Soviet Union.

The second folly was a political one. Hitler's refusal to listen to Rosenberg's advice on the treatment of the eastern peoples proved a disastrous blunder. As an Estonian himself, Rosenberg was well aware of the hatred and fear felt by millions of Soviet citizens for Stalin. When German troops first entered the country, they were welcomed as liberators from the tyranny of Communism. However, the arrival of the SS changed the feelings of the local population completely. Before long they were fighting the Germans to the death. If Hitler had listened to Rosenberg, he would probably have won the war in Russia. Instead he followed his own racist ideas and lost.[4]

Meanwhile 1939 saw an attempt to assassinate Hitler. A time bomb was placed in the Munich beer hall, designed to go off in the middle of a speech he was to make at the annual commemoration of the 1923 *putsch*. Unfortunately he left earlier than usual and the bomb killed other

Nazis present. The assassination attempt was the work of a disillusioned Communist named Elser. In spite of many speculations to the contrary, including some extraordinary claims by two former British intelligence officers that seem most plausibly explained as deliberate disinformation, there is no reasonable doubt that Elser acted alone. If he had any accomplices at all they can only have been from the anti-Nazi side.

It has been claimed that Heydrich faked the plot to increase Hitler's popularity, but Hitler already enjoyed the support of the overwhelming majority of his people. He did not need such a dangerous stunt to boost his reputation. What is more, no dummy bomb was used, but a real live and primed one with its timer running. Many loyal Nazis were killed as a result. It is difficult to imagine that Heydrich would have organised such an attempt without the knowledge of either Hitler or Himmler, yet there is no doubt at all that neither of them knew anything about the bomb plot, at least before it happened.

Who could have put Elser up to it, if it was a conspiracy? The usual suspects are Heydrich, Himmler, anti-Nazis within the armed forces, and Communists. It is just conceivable that the devious Heydrich might have intended to assassinate Hitler. However, he was still very young and inexperienced, and would have had almost no chance of taking over Hitler's position himself. As for Himmler, there is no doubt at all that the bomb plot took him completely by surprise. What is more, following the Gestapo interrogation of Elser, in which he stuck to his story under both torture and hypnosis, both Himmler and Heydrich ended up believing that he acted alone, hardly a normal reaction if either had been one of the plotters.

Anti-Nazis within the armed forces certainly acted in a peculiar way at this time. There is no reasonable doubt that they were engaged in treasonable contacts with members of British Intelligence In addition, on the very day of the bomb plot they had made plans for a military coup. Their role in the affair is, at the very least, deeply suspicious. In addition, not only was Elser a Communist but the Communists in Germany were in a position where only acts of sabotage and terrorism had any possibility of success. Elser, by his own admission, did have contacts with other Communists. It seems unlikely, though, that they were in any significant way involved in the planning of the assassination attempt. All the evidence points to Elser as having acted entirely alone, which is indeed what he claimed to have been doing.

The final possibility, and one that has never before been considered by any historian, is that Rudolf Hess was behind the attempted assassination. Hess, though formerly one of the most loyal of all the Nazi leadership, had become progressively disillusioned with Hitler since the party had come to power. The *Kristallnacht* pogrom of 1938, in which Jews had been beaten in the streets, murdered and plundered, deeply distressed him. By 1939 he had lost faith in Hitler to the point where he might well have considered murdering him to be the best hope for Germany, As Hitler's deputy, of course, Hess would have been in an ideal position to succeed him as the new Fuehrer. He had means, motive and opportunity.

Elser had contacts in Switzerland, and it was a quite extraordinary prophecy from a Swiss astrologer – sent to Hess – that predicted an attempt to blow up Hitler at the very dates between which it happened. All in all, the possibility that Hess, using his known contacts with anti-Nazi circles, got Elser to act as an unwitting tool of his own ambitions for the leadership is perhaps the most credible theory of all.[5]

Returning to military matters, the actual route for the invasion of France was also Hitler's idea. His generals had wanted to use the old Schlieffen Plan which had failed so narrowly in the First World War. Hitler's choice of route, and the clever way in which he bluffed the French into believing that he was following the old Schlieffen Plan, led the sudden appearance at their rear of the German army to panic the French troops. Encircled and bewildered, they surrendered almost out of sheer astonishment. In a brilliant series of lightning campaigns, Norway, Denmark, Holland, Belgium and Luxembourg were conquered. After a still more stunning campaign in France, at minimal cost, the mighty French army was brought to its knees. This achievement led to the German general Keitel referring to Hitler as 'the greatest Field Marshal of all time,' a tag which was soon abbreviated to *Grofatz*, and made much of in Nazi propaganda.

However, in spite of its overall success, the French campaign did show the first signs of Hitler's fallibility. Instead of cutting off the British army's retreat at Dunkirk, he allowed the Luftwaffe to try and smash the British on their own. They made such an appallingly inept job of it, almost the entire contingent of British troops escaping safely, that some people actually wondered if Hitler had wanted to let them get away as a gesture of peace. This seems highly unlikely, and in fact the general track record of Goering as a military strategist was so abysmal that blaming the Dunkirk fiasco on his incompetence seems far more sensible.[6] The Battle of Britain was another disaster for the Luftwaffe. Hitler knew that without superiority in the air his outnumbered navy could not hope to land the numbers of troops necessary to successfully invade the British mainland. Again, Hitler's excessive confidence in Goering's judgement led to his second military fiasco.[7]

The next problem he had to deal with was not of his own making. Mussolini's jealousy of Hitler's military success led him to engage in a disastrous invasion of Greece. The Greek army fought like tigers and drove the Italians back in total disarray. As a result of Mussolini's failure to conquer the Greeks, Hitler was forced to deploy German troops in a full-scale war which cost German lives and involved the commitment of vast quantities of weapons and manpower in a war which Hitler had not even wanted to engage in. As if this was not bad enough, a sudden crisis blew up in the Balkans.

Hitler had been putting pressure on the king of Yugoslavia to join the Axis forces. At last he had been successful in extracting from him a commitment to join his side in the struggle. The reaction within the country was explosive. The king was deposed in favour of his infant nephew and the new Yugoslav Government declared firmly that it would do nothing that might involve it in war with Britain and America. Although Hungary, Romania and Bulgaria were virtual satellites of Germany by now, a hostile Yugoslavia would make the conquest of Greece far more difficult. Bribing his various allies to support him, Hitler made his plans to invade Yugoslavia. He became positively irrational as he took the Yugoslavian decision as a personal insult. Even the advice of his generals, that the timetable for the invasion of Russia did not leave the scope for such an ambitious undertaking as a Balkan adventure, had no influence upon him. He spoke instead of how he would smash the 'mad' Yugoslavs and destroy their country forever.

The result of the combination of Mussolini's military incompetence and Hitler's wounded vanity was to be disastrous. In the first place, the British felt sufficiently confident to launch an attack upon Italian forces in Libya, which was a resounding success and forced Hitler into overextending his forces still further by sending German troops to Mussolini's rescue in North Africa. Even more disastrously, it forced the Russian campaign to be postponed for a whole month. The result was that the German army found itself faced with the rigours of a Russian winter a whole month earlier than originally planned. This miscalculation was one of the most decisive factors in slowing the German advance. Ultimately, it probably cost Hitler the war.[8]

There is no doubt at all that Hitler wanted Germany to be the most powerful country in the world. Nor is there any question that he was willing to use force and engage in war to achieve his ambitions. On the other hand, he always preferred to get his way without fighting, whenever possible. Nor is there any doubt that he devised the concept of the *Blitzkrieg* as a result of the horrors of the trench warfare which he had experienced at first hand during the First World War. In no sense did he either plan for or desire a world war, only a series of local conflicts with minimal casualties. It was a combination of bad political judgement on the part of Hitler and, to some extent, Mussolini, together with some rash military decisions and unexpected circumstances which led him, almost by accident, to become slowly embroiled in a global conflict.

Notes

1. This remark was actually made by Rudolf Hess, perhaps more appropriately in the light of Goering's own notorious corpulence. See: R J Overy, *Goering the 'Iron Man,'* Routledge, 1984
2. Franz von Papen, *Memoirs*, Andre Deutsch, 1952
3. William L Shirer, *End of a Berlin Diary,* Alfred A Knopf, 1947
4. Alfred Rosenberg, *Memoirs*
5. J P Stern, *The Führer and the People,* is particularly critical of the various attempts that have been made to paint Elser as a fraud acting on behalf of Himmler and Heydrich.
6. See, for instance, the scathing comments on Goering's military capabilities in: Overy, op cit
7. Ibid
8. On the Yugoslavian debacle, see: a) Wilhelm Keitel, *Memoirs*, William Kimber, 1965 b) Ernst von Weizsäcker, *Memoirs*, Gollancz, 1951

CHAPTER XIII

Hitler as Murderer

The darkest aspect of the National Socialist episode of German history remains its policy of mass extermination under the euphemism of the Final Solution. It is also known as the Holocaust, although the name is something of a misnomer, as there were in fact several holocausts during the Third Reich.

Violence had been one of the leading weapons of the Nazi party from its earliest beginnings. The SA, the party's paramilitary wing, had engaged in street brawling and even the occasional murder from the early 1920s. The notorious Potempa killings in 1932, when five drunken SA men trampled a Communist to death in front of his mother, and the immediate and unconditional support for his murderers by Hitler, shocked the German people. It cost the Nazis numerous votes in the general election that followed, offering people who had formerly failed to notice the sheer brutality that so often accompanied the Nazis an example that could hardly be ignored.

Further evidence of the violence that lay barely under the surface of the Nazis was demonstrated by the 'Night of the Long Knives'. The new and sweeping powers of arbitrary arrest, imprisonment and torture which the Gestapo possessed under the Nazi regime were a further sign that the resort to violence was never far from the minds of Germany's rulers. Further instruments of repression were the labour camps and, of course, the concentration camps.

Even when no overt violence was being inflicted by the regime on its own citizens, its implicit glorification was a fact of everyday life. The cult of athleticism and physical fitness, the Strength through Joy movement, the Hitler Youth propaganda and above all the emphasis on heroism in battle kept a militaristic ethos firmly fixed in the minds of the German people as representing the highest moral values. Instead of taking the normal view that violence was an unpleasant part of life that was nevertheless sometimes regrettably necessary, they made violence and conflict into positives. The values of 'strength', 'physical fitness' and 'hardness' were seen as the truest and most complete expression of a nation's civilisation. Intellectuals, humanitarians and weak people were despised.

Before long all forms of 'deviation' from Nazi orthodoxy were being put down to racial degeneracy, either as a result of the possession of 'non-Aryan blood' or else to congenital defects. The idea that mental illness could be purely psychological in origin, and therefore treated, became largely rejected almost overnight. Nazi 'psychologists' were soon ascribing all mental illness to racial or congenital deficiency, in the same way that Soviet 'psychologists' vouched for the 'mentally unbalanced' state of political dissidents in the Soviet Union.

From 1933 onwards the compulsory sterilisation of 'congenital mental defects, schizophrenia, manic-depressive psychosis, hereditary epilepsy and severe alcoholism' was practised throughout Germany. The sheer absurdity of treating all these illnesses as resulting from the same basic cause did not deter the Nazi psychologists. Throughout the lifetime of the regime, their only complaint seemed to be that the Nazis were not as brutal as they wished them to be. As it was, mental hospitals were turned into virtual concentration camps. The only 'treatments' given to the unfortunate patients were ECT (electric shock treatment) or two drugs, which produced similar results. It was very common for patients to receive *sixty or more* courses of ECT, and broken bones and death became an everyday occurrence in German mental hospitals. They were also compelled to perform forced labour, regardless of their physical or mental state, on the grounds that 'work gives health'.[1]

As if these facts were not horrifying enough, the patients who endured the dubious medical 'care' detailed above were the lucky ones. In numerous other mental hospitals, patients were deliberately left to die of illness and starvation. In 1938 one particular case became such a scandal that Professor X Kleist declared that in the absence of a law permitting euthanasia, such patients had the right to 'humane treatment which assures their continued existence.'[2]

Instead of producing a humanitarian reaction, Kleist's comments led to various 'experts' putting their heads together and drafting a new law legalising compulsory euthanasia – a law which was kept strictly secret. In a single sentence letter dated 1 September 1939, Hitler gave a free hand to two men to carry out a programme of mass, compulsory euthanasia. Perhaps the most sinister thing of all about this letter from Hitler is that it was unquestionably backdated to legitimise an unauthorised programme of euthanasia which was already in full swing. The fact that Hitler gave it his approval in no way absolves the doctors from their own disgraceful behaviour.[3]

The euthanasia programme was carried out between 1939 and 1944. It led to the murders of at least ninety-four thousand people by shooting or gassing. On its suspension, the old policy of allowing patients to die as the result of starvation and neglect was restored. This led to the deaths of one hundred thousand further patients, as well as some forty thousand in French hospitals.[4]

The fate of the Jews is more controversial. Only the most blinkered person could possibly believe that, as the neo-Nazis maintain, the Holocaust never happened. There are, however, serious differences of opinion among historians on three key questions. The first concerns the actual numbers of Jews killed as a result of the extermination plans. The second is the degree to which a specific order for mass murder can be said to have existed. Finally, the question of how far, if at all, Hitler knew of and approved the Final Solution is still in dispute.

With regard to the question of numbers, figures range from as high as seven million to as low as one million. The generally accepted figure has long been set at six million. Before he began to deny that the Holocaust had ever taken place, the British historian David Irving suggested that the true figure was probably around one million.[5] By contrast, the account given by Adolf Eichmann at his trial would suggest that the accepted figure of six million is too low.[6] The testimony of the commandant of Auschwitz, Rudolf Hoess, also implies that far greater numbers were killed. [7] Gerald Fleming's figure is just under five million deaths.[8]

Even Himmler seems to have been unsure as to how many people had been killed. In 1943 he claimed that six million Jews had already been put to death; a year later he was still quoting the same figure. This can only mean that either no Jews had been killed between 1943 and 1944, which we know to be untrue, or that his original estimate had been too high. The former is obviously the case.[9]

Why is there so much dispute over the true figures? In the first place, men like Eichmann and Hoess, either deliberately or otherwise, unquestionably claimed to have killed more people than they really had. Hoess's figures in particular have been shown to be wildly inaccurate, claiming 'credit' for three million deaths in Auschwitz alone when the true figure is around one million. Secondly, the Allies kept no separate record of Jewish victims, listing them simply as Poles, Russians, French, Germans or whatever other nationality they were. Finally, although there were numerous concentration camps throughout the Greater Reich, there were never more than six extermination centres, and only four of them were large-scale murder factories. From a purely technical point of view, it would have been difficult for only six centres to exterminate six million or more Jews. Nor does this take account of the massive number of non-Jewish victims.

However, the story of the Holocaust is not only a question of the murders in the extermination centres. Many died on their way to the camps, and many also died as a result of the forced labour programmes. It was, however, the unsystematic massacres carried out by the SS and regular troops which account for the bulk of the killings, and during this series of random shootings an unknown number of people died. Not all of them, nor even a majority of them, were Jewish. The number of Russians and Poles murdered in cold blood is particularly appalling.

For the reasons which have already been discussed, no one will ever be able to give a precise account of the number of victims of the Final Solution, Jewish or otherwise. However, in terms of the Jews alone a figure of between four and five million deaths seems the most plausible. According to a secret report by the official SS statistician, Dr Korherr, 2,400,000 Jews had been exterminated by March 1943.[10] Given a similar projection for the two remaining years of the Holocaust – and we know that its pace slowed dramatically in the last two years of the war, particularly in the last few months – somewhere between four and five million deaths seems the likeliest figure. Probably nearer to four than five million, but almost certainly at least four million. Even if the traditional figure of six million may be too high, that in no way excuses the Holocaust and its perpetrators. Mass murder is not made any less contemptible because slightly fewer lives may have been lost than once thought. In the words of the German poet Erich Fried: 'Who bids lower?'[11]

A very controversial question indeed is the degree to which the policy of extermination was consciously planned and ordered. There are two main schools of thought on the matter, one known as the intentionalists and the other as the functionalists. The intentionalists maintain that the Final Solution was always planned at some indefinite point in the future and that a conscious order to implement the policy was given. The functionalists believe that the Holocaust began as a random series of unplanned massacres and that the continual deportations to the eastern territories forced the policy of murder upon the local Nazi authorities. In its most extreme form, the functionalist position claims that no specific order for the extermination programme was ever given and that it simply arose out of a series of local responses to a crisis.[12]

It would be tedious to try to unravel the question of how far a definite order for extermination was actually given. However, it does not seem that the intentionalists and functionalists are necessarily opposed. There is much truth in the arguments on both sides. If the intentionalists attach too much weight to the autocratic position of Hitler – with his known viciously anti-Semitic views – so too the functionalists place too much stress on the chaotic and shambolic nature of the Nazi state. The truth probably lies between the two extreme positions. There is no doubt, for example, that Heydrich's instructions to shoot 'Bolshevist commissars' and 'Jews in the service of the state' were not a licence for indiscriminate slaughter. When such random killings nevertheless took place after the German invasion of Russia, apparently on the authority of an SS officer named Koch, Heydrich exploded. However, Himmler gave his approval to the actions and such acts of instant murder when Jews were discovered became normal practice.

The way in which the euthanasia campaign began is certainly a clear case where the functionalist viewpoint appears to be the only correct one.

A father with a deformed child had asked Hitler for permission to end his life. Hitler agreed to his request and remarked casually to Bormann that similar cases could perhaps be dealt with in the same way. Needing no further encouragement for his murderous urges, Bormann hastened to authorise this disgraceful action – aided and abetted by the very doctors who had not only been urging euthanasia upon the state but also illegally starving and torturing patients to death themselves already. As we have seen, Hitler's later written authorisation for the programme was back-dated to the beginning of the war, in order to 'legitimise' an unauthorised and illegal act.

Is it possible that the policy of mass extermination could also have been an unauthorised action, carried out without the knowledge or even against the wishes of Hitler? Certainly no written order for the Final Solution appears ever to have been given. It might just be possible for the random shootings in Russia to be dismissed as aberrations. However, there is no way in which the extermination centres could be considered as a purely local initiative. Such a policy, requiring vast building work, equipment installation and administration to keep it going, could only have been authorised at the highest level. This means, and can only mean, that a direct order for the Final Solution *must have been given* at some stage, probably either in July 1941 or else in November of the same year.

Did the order for the policy of mass extermination come from Hitler? It is difficult to see who else could have given such orders. Even though they were to implement its proposals ruthlessly, both Himmler and Heydrich were opposed to the policy of genocide. When challenged by doubters in his ranks about the mass killings, Himmler retorted that his instructions had come from Hitler himself. Heydrich made the same statement, in an extremely angry and upset fashion, when the policy was raised with him. As all witnesses agree about the strong opposition to the Final Solution by both Himmler and Heydrich, the idea that either man could have carried it out on their own initiative and without Hitler's knowledge and consent is doubly implausible.

The same is true of Goering. As for Goebbels, who was admittedly a strong supporter of the genocide programme, he was out of favour with Hitler at this time (1941–2). He did not even find out about the Final Solution until it had been in operation already for over a year.[13] The only possible remaining candidates are Martin Bormann and Hitler. Bormann certainly 'improved' upon Hitler's orders and even gave his own purporting to be from Hitler. But the evidence from all the participants, including Bormann and Hitler themselves, is quite clear and unequivocal. The idea for the Final Solution was Hitler's, and it was his orders that were carried out with regard to the Jews and the Slavs.[14]

As we have seen already, the notion of 'The Holocaust' is rather a mistaken one. There were in fact several separate holocausts. Some of them were directly authorised and ordered by Hitler himself. Others were unquestionably undertaken by subordinates without any such direct order from Hitler having been given. The first of these holocausts was the mass extermination of mental patients, which began in 1939 and went on in a surreptitious way until the end of the war. This was only authorised by Hitler retrospectively, to legitimise an existing practice which claimed over 100,000 lives. The second was the mass shooting of Poles, Russians and Jews, which began in 1939 in a small way with regard to the Poles and was extended to the Russians and Jews from 1941 to about 1943. These mass shootings almost certainly began without any direct authorisation or order, from Hitler or anyone else, but Himmler, unquestionably after discussing the matter with Hitler, declared them legitimate retrospectively.

The third was the decision to set up extermination centres for Jews, gypsies and homosexuals. Jews were being killed in these camps from 1941 onwards. Although some gypsies were also killed at this time, it was 1942 before they were finally subjected to the full horrors of the extermination programme. In 1941 two Nazi 'race experts' put the gypsy population – which they euphemistically referred to as 'social misfits' – at over one million. This was a gross overestimate of the number of Romanies within Germany and Austria at that time.

The true number of gypsy deaths remains unknown. Official figures give a total of between twenty and twenty-five thousand Romanies murdered. However, these statistics apply only to those already registered as gypsies and then transported to the death camps. It was really possible only to register the gypsy population within Germany and Austria. In the occupied territories, the process was hardly carried out at all. Certainly the number of gypsies who were put to death in Eastern Europe and Russia was enormous, far in excess of the twenty to twenty-five thousand who died in Auschwitz and Bialistock At the most conservative estimate, well over two hundred thousand gypsies were murdered. The true figures are most certainly higher, perhaps as many as a million. In all probability the numbers of Romanies killed was at least close to the million mark, the most likely estimate being around three-quarters of a million.

Partly because the numbers were lower, partly because of the racism from which they have always suffered and continue to suffer, the gypsy holocaust has never caught the headlines or stirred the heart in the same way that the sufferings of the Jews undoubtedly have. The Romanies have no powerful voice to speak on their behalf, no nation to fight for them. Yet in proportion to the gypsy population of Europe within the occupied territories, their losses were at least as great as the other victims of the Holocaust. It would be nothing less than a crime for their tragedy to be forgotten or minimised.[15]

The murder of the gypsies also seems to have been different from the exterminations of the Jews, Poles and Russians. While there is no doubt at all that Hitler hated and despised Jews and Slavs, nor any reasonable doubt that he was behind the orders to exterminate the Jews, the same does not seem to be true of the fate of the gypsies. As with the euthanasia programme against mental patients, it seems to have been a policy pressed upon the regime by its so-called racial experts. Heydrich included the gypsies in the Final Solution almost by way of afterthought, and at the prompting of Dr Ritter, a fanatic who had been calling for the compulsory sterilisation and extermination of the gypsies since 1935.[16] Although he never attempted to stop the genocide programme against the gypsies, there is no evidence that the *idea* of exterminating the Romanies came from Hitler. Rather, Ritter seems to be the main criminal responsible for this particular atrocity.[17]

The truth about the various extermination programmes is unquestionable. The evidence is so overwhelming that no honest person could possibly deny its reality. The extermination programme was and will remain for all time the darkest blot on the Nazi record. Nor is there any reasonable doubt that Hitler's direct orders led to the death of millions of people on the basis of racial mythology.

The question that still remains to be answered is why? What dark forces within Hitler drove him so relentlessly to a policy of mass murder when even a man as irrational as Himmler could see that it was both morally wrong and politically insane? And had the idea of the annihilation of the Jews always been his ultimate goal? These are all questions to which it is almost impossible to give definite answers. Hitler himself gave conflicting reasons for his gradual turn towards anti-Semitism. One was his discovery in Vienna of Orthodox Jews from Russia and Eastern Europe; another was his encounter with a Jewish pimp. Among his close associates he only remarked that it was 'a personal thing.'

What could this 'personal thing' have been? It has been suggested that Hitler harboured deep resentment towards Dr Bloch, the physician who had treated his mother during her terminal cancer. Yet he never spoke a word against Bloch, only praised him for his kindness and never molested him when the doctor was within his power. Francis King's suggestion of syphilis caught from a Jewish prostitute seems very plausible, especially when we remember how Hitler referred to his anti-Semitism as being connected with his discovery of a Jewish pimp. It is, however, Hans Frank's suggestion of Jewish blood in Hitler's own family that seems to me to offer the most likely explanation. Frank's theory is not enough in itself, in my opinion, but when taken in conjunction with the work of a Jewish melancholic, Otto Weininger, it suddenly assumes a new significance.

Weininger was a Jewish psychologist who converted to Christianity a year before his death in 1903. Like a surprisingly large number of Jews, especially in the 19th and early 20th centuries, he felt a deep sense of shame and guilt about his Jewishness. Adopting the then fashionable idea that there were inherent differences between the various nations and racial groups, he divided these groups into what he called 'masculine' and 'feminine' nations. The Mediterranean people were seen as female, the Northern Europeans as male. Needless to say, women were seen as inferior to men, as expressed by Weininger himself in his notorious formulation 'The best woman is inferior to the worst man.'[18] In the same muddle-headed way, Weininger saw certain nations and racial groups as being active or passive. Masculine nations were active, feminine ones passive. The Germans, of course, were masculine and active, the Jews feminine and passive. In a complete reversal of traditional ideas on the subject, women were also seen as materialistic and men as spiritual.

On the basis of these half-baked notions, the guilt-ridden Weininger, deeply ashamed of his Jewishness, declared that neither women nor Jews were fully human at all. Indeed, in one sense the Jews were inferior even to women, since at least women believed in something, while Jews, the incarnation of the spirit of materialism, believed in nothing at all. Weininger loved Wagner and was a firm believer in *völkisch* racist ideology. Two years before Weininger's death, Freud read a copy of his book in manuscript. One wonders what the founder of psychoanalysis made of the mental state of its author.

Weininger, perhaps not surprisingly, committed suicide. We do not know whether or not Hitler read his book in Vienna, but it is possible. The work ran into a number of editions. We do, however, know that the early mentor of Hitler, Dietrich Eckart, was a great admirer of Weininger. Another admirer was Rosenberg, particularly in his earlier writings. Rosenberg's bizarre 'The Earth-centred Jew lacks a soul' is awash with the spirit of Weininger and might almost have been written by him. Finally, we know from his conversations that Hitler himself was also familiar with Weininger's work, describing him as 'the only Jew fit to live.'[19]

If we assume that Hitler, already familiar with Weininger's work, suddenly discovered his own possible Jewish ancestry in the 1920s, at a time when he had already made anti-Semitism one of the principal planks of his political programme, we can understand perhaps how even Hitler became consumed with anger and self-hatred. In a sense he was acting out his own fantasies of guilt and shame by punishing the race whose possible admixture of their own genetic heritage with his own had 'polluted' him.

In this context it is perhaps worth considering the following quote from Weininger's book:

> The most genuine Aryans, those who are most Aryan and most sure of their Aryanism are not anti-Semites. On the other hand, in the aggressive anti-Semite one can always detect certain Jewish traits even when his blood is free from any Semitic strain. That is why the most violent anti-Semites are Jews.[20]

Psychologically speaking, this analysis is particularly interesting when considering some of the leading protagonists in the Nazi movement. Hitler himself, tormented by the thought of his Jewish blood; Heydrich, at least partly Jewish; Rosenberg, with a Jewish mistress and probable Jewish ancestors; Himmler, with Jewish relatives; Goebbels, formerly engaged to a Jewish girl and nicknamed 'the Rabbi' by his staff, whose own racial ancestry is altogether obscure; Haushofer, with his Jewish wife; Princess Stefanie Hohenlohe, partly Jewish, and a frequent go-between for Hitler in his first years of power; Hanussen the psychic, really a Jewish vaudeville entertainer named Herschel Steinschneider; Milch, deputy head of the Luftwaffe; and this is to name only the most prominent.

In the SS, for instance, whose members were supposed to be able to produce a 'Jew-free' family tree going back to 1750, this rule proved so difficult to enforce that numerous exceptions had to be made for SS members who had at least some Jewish ancestry. We come back again to Weininger's phrase 'the most violent anti-Semites are Jews'.

If we assume that Hitler, who knew and admired Weininger's work, also shared some of his Jewish ancestry, perhaps the degree of shame and self-hatred which this might have induced in him could explain the extraordinary virulence of Hitler's anti-Semitism. His racism far surpassed that of any of his fellow-Nazis, even the repulsive Streicher, of whom Hitler once complained that 'he idealised the Jew.'[21]

Like Weininger, whom he admired so much and in some ways even resembled, Hitler committed suicide. If one of the greatest ironies of Weininger's life was to plant the seeds of the Final Solution in the warped brain of Hitler, so too Hitler's own legacy was the exact opposite of all that he had intended. Hitler had devoted much of his life to a vicious and bloody campaign against the Jews and Communists, yet the net result of his activities was to leave Stalin in possession of the whole of eastern Europe and half of Germany, as well as finally persuading the western nations that a Jewish national home in Israel had to be set up. There could hardly be a greater irony than the way in which Hitler's anti-Semitism made the triumph of Zionism inevitable.

Notes

1. Benno Müller-Hill, *Murderous Science: Elimination by scientific selection of Jews, Gypsies and others, Germany 1933–1945*, OUP, 1988
2. Kleist's comments quoted in Müller-Hill, op cit
3. There is absolutely no question of this. The euthanasia programme had been going on for years before Hitler was finally asked to give a formal, written authorisation.

4. Müller-Hill, op cit

5. Television interview with Irving.

6. See: Hannah Arendt, *Eichmann in Jerusalem: The Banality of Evil*, Viking, 1965

7. Rudolf Hoess, *Commandant of Auschwitz*, Orion, 2000

8. Gerald Fleming, *Hitler and the Final Solution*, Hamish Hamilton, 1985

9. On Himmler's two speeches, see: a) Erich Goldhagen, 'Albert Speer, Himmler, and the Secrecy of the Final Solution,' *Midstream*, October 1971; b) Bradley Smith, Agnes F Peterson, *Heinrich Himmler Geheimreden 1933 bis 1945*, Propylaen, 1974

10. Korherr's report is quoted in Müller-Hill, op cit. Its title is: '*The final solution of the Jewish question in Europe. A statistical analysis.*' Its date is 23 March 1943.

11. Erich Fried, *The Hagglers*, from, *On Pain of Seeing*, Rapp & Whiting, 1969

12. Fleming, op cit., takes the most extreme position among the intentionalists. A moderate functionalist position is taken by: Uwe Dietrich Adam, *Judenpolitik im Dritten Reich*, Dusseldorf, 1972. A more radical analysis is found in: Martin Broszat, *Studie zur Geschichte der Konzentrationslager*, Stuttgart, 1970. The most extreme functionalist position is taken by Hans Mommsen. See: Walter Laqueur (editor), *Fascism: A Reader's Guide*, Wildwood, 1976

13. See: Josef Goebbels, *The Goebbels Diaries*, Hamish Hamilton, 1949

14. See, for example; a) *Hitler's Table-Talk*; b) *Hitler's Secret Conversations*

15. Sadly, even disgracefully, almost no research has been done on the Romany genocide programme. Even now one still reads constantly that the Jews were the only victims of the Nazis who suffered because of their race. This is quite simply not true. The Gypsies were also persecuted on racial grounds alone. There are a few pages on the Romany genocide programme in Müller-Hill, op cit. The best book, and almost the only one, on the subject is Donald Kenrick and Grattan Puxon, *The Destiny of Europe's Gypsies*, Chatto/Heinemann, 1972

16. Müller-Hill, op cit

17. Ibid

18. Otto Weininger, *Sex & Character*, Heinemann, 1906

19. Hitler, *Table-Talk*

20. Weininger, op cit

21. Hitler, *Secret Conversations*

Conclusion

One question that has often been asked is how and why a man like Hitler ever came to power. How could Germany, a country which had produced some of the most enlightened thinkers of the 18th and 19th centuries, turn to a leader who represented a total and defiant rejection of those values?

It is not easy to account for his rise to power, although many explanations have been offered. Between the 1930s and 1980s, conspiracy theories were widely put forward and even believed, frequently supported with an array of bogus 'facts'. From the 1970s onwards, 'functional' explanations, particularly in terms of the impact of unemployment, came into fashion. The 1980s saw the beginnings of the process of re-evaluating Hitler and the Third Reich, and political and psychological analyses of Hitler, Germany and the Nazi regime began drawing attention to important aspects of National Socialism that had been neglected previously.

The oldest and most widely believed of the conspiracy theories is the Marxist 'analysis' of Nazism. This claims that Hitler and his movement represented a last despairing attempt by German capitalists to cling on to power in the face of the threat from Communism. As one commentator expressed it in the 1930s:

> 'Fascism [in which the writer also included Nazism] is little more than a reactionary countermove against Communism. It has come into power only where and when there has been a real possibility of a Communist revolution'.[1]

The writer just quoted, Malcolm McAlpine, supports his claims with a variety of arguments, beginning with the old standby, inaccurate statistics. He makes the entirely untrue claim that wages in Germany fell after Hitler came to power, whereas the true statistics show an increase of 15%. He also makes much of a statement by Robert Ley, leader of the German Labour Front:

> Corporate organisation will as its first work restore absolute leadership to the natural leader of a factory. That is, the employer; and will

at the same time place full responsibility on him. Only the employer can decide.[2]

McAlpine regards this as incontrovertible proof that Hitler and the Nazis were simply acting as a kind of police force for German capitalism. Apart from his use of inaccurate statistics, and that Ley was probably the least intelligent of all the leading Nazi inner circle, it is also far from clear that his words bear the interpretation that McAlpine puts upon them. He is confusing the undoubted *authoritarianism* of National Socialism with its *economic* policies. One could just as easily use comparable quotes from Stalin's ideologists to support Hitler's equally untrue claim that the Soviet Union was a *capitalist* society.

Even more damagingly for McAlpine's argument, the reality of life for German employers under Hitler was quite different from Ley's statement, obviously designed to reassure and mollify them over the indignity of State control. Employers were told what to produce, the quantities they were permitted to manufacture, and the price at which they were allowed to sell their goods. They were virtually forbidden to dismiss their employees, compelled to make donations to help the poor, and subjected to an excess profits tax. Hitler also nationalised various enterprises and ensured that the government, *not* the employer, dictated policy and organisation. In addition, when Darré raised the hostility of industrial giants like Krupp, Hitler sided with his Agriculture Minister and dismissed the protests of the employers. Throughout his rule in Germany, employers were always complaining that Hitler and his government interfered too much with the way they ran their companies. The extent of central economic planning in Germany was rivalled only by the Soviet Union.

The above facts demonstrate clearly that if German capitalists really *had* been keen supporters of Hitler, they would have made a very bad choice. Furthermore, the idea that the bulk of the funding for Hitler's party came from big business is, quite simply, a blatant lie, put about cynically by the Communist Party during the 1930s. Throughout the period 1918-1933, German capitalists spread their political donations across a very wide range of parties. Until 1929, the Nazis actually received *less* funding from employers than any other political party except the Communists. Even as late as 1932, the *majority* of German capitalists gave little or no money to Hitler. In the 1933 election, that changed, but by then the Nazis were already in power and they were simply putting their money on the winning horse.

What is more, at *no* time during the Nazi rise to power did the donations from companies ever amount to more than a small percentage of the party's revenue. By far the greatest part of Nazi income came from membership subscriptions, the sale of *Mein Kampf* and the party newspaper, the *Völkischer Beobachter*.

Nor is it true that the majority of party members were middle or even lower middle class, The Nazis remained what they had always been, an overwhelmingly working class organisation. All in all, the notion that the Nazis were shuffled into power by a conspiracy of German capitalists is absurd, paranoid and dishonest.

Another group that has been blamed for helping Hitler into power is what has been referred to as the 'military-industrial complex'. Hitler certainly placed great emphasis on German rearmament, on regaining territory lost after the First World War, and on the nation's ability to wage war successfully. It is also true that throughout the Weimar Republic, the German army deeply distrusted democracy, turned a blind eye to illegal activities by paramilitaries and connived at the attempted coup in Berlin by Kapp. They even formally invited the Social Democratic politician Gustav Noske to become the dictator of Germany, an offer he declined.

Nevertheless, of all the ruling elites in Germany under Weimar, the Army was always the *least* receptive to Nazi propaganda. Individual generals, such as Keitel, did become 'converts' but the bulk of the officer corps regarded Hitler as at best a useful 'drummer' for Germany and at worst a dangerous madman with radical ideas. To begin with, the Army, before Hitler purged it, contained a number of high-ranking and able Jewish officers. Its leadership also tended to come from the aristocratic *Junkers*, who despised Hitler and his followers as a bunch of uncouth roughnecks. It was also genuinely frightened of fighting another World War, and sections of it contemplated a coup against Hitler on more than one occasion. They also engaged in treasonable activities with British intelligence both before and during the war. It was even the Army 'resistance' that almost succeeded in assassinating Hitler in 1944. Though the Army tolerated Hitler, they certainly neither liked nor respected him.

The remaining conspiracy theories are too absurd to dignify with serious analysis. The notion that Hitler was the tool of the German aristocracy is refuted by the mutual contempt both he and the *Junkers* displayed towards each other. It is also shown by the aristocratic Hindenburg's extreme reluctance to appoint Hitler as Chancellor, which was almost entirely on the grounds of snobbery rather than of ideological objections to his views. It was also demonstrated by Hitler's ruthless suppression of their privileged position once he came to power. He made sure that merit rather than birth was the passport to success in 'his' Germany; he confiscated money and lands from some aristocratic families; and he forced their sons to work on the land and their daughters to become domestic servants. Hitler would have executed the aristocratic Papen in 1934 if Hindenburg had not pleaded for his life to be spared.

At the extreme lunatic fringe even of conspiracy theories is the idea that Hitler was a tool of the Jews. The most convincing 'evidence' for this claim comes from a British journalist who was told by a Czech

Jew that his rabbi had been preaching in the synagogue at Prague in early 1939 that 'Hitler is the Jewish Messiah, because he will cause all those countries of the world to be opened to the Jews, which are now closed to them'. [3] It is not only absurd, but deeply offensive, that such theories are still occasionally put forward by certain neo-Nazi groups who wish (understandably perhaps) to distance themselves from Hitler.

Almost as laughable, though less obscene, is the claim that Hitler was really a tool of the Communists. Certainly Hitler *had* been an active and enthusiastic Communist in his youth; certainly there were frequent 'defections' from Nazi to Communist and vice versa; certainly there was little difference between the public ideologies of the two parties; Gregor Strasser advocated a coalition between the Nazis, Communists and Social Democrats; and it is curious that those Nazis who went to Russia to sign the non-aggression pact with Stalin in 1939 described themselves as feeling like being 'among old party comrades'. Nevertheless, Hitler's socialism was specifically German, not international, and there is no credible way in which his behaviour can be regarded as an attempt to impose a Communist regime on Germany by stealth.

The functional explanations have far greater plausibility than the conspiracy theories. The most popular one, and the one with the greatest connection with the truth, is the level of German unemployment. This undoubtedly stood at an enormous figure between 1929 and 1933. On the other hand, Britain, France and the United States also had massive unemployment with far less 'welfare' measures available to help tide the jobless through their ordeal, yet none of those countries even came close to abandoning democracy for an authoritarian regime.

In Britain, the National Government under Ramsay Macdonald may have been weak, ineffective, wrong in its diagnosis of the problem and outdated in terms of the remedies it proposed, but it was their failed solutions, not the radical and effective proposals put forward by Mosley, which captured the votes of the British people. In America, the new Democratic government put in place a raft of measures aimed at correcting the problems, with considerable success (though much less than is sometimes claimed). France, it is true, saw a succession of weak governments that failed to grasp any kind of solution that involved political risk, but it never produced a home-grown Fascist party of any significance. The *Action Française* was almost entirely a movement of literary figures with no political following among the French people. Why, then, when the state of the German economy was no worse relatively than it was in Britain, France and the United States, did Germany alone turn to the Nazis?

Another explanation that was often put forward during the 1930s, though mercifully less often now, is that the German economy and in particular the highly paid professional jobs were disproportionately held or controlled by Jews. This is simply not true in terms of German businesses, the reality being that Jewish firms controlled no more than a proportionate share of the market. It is true that Jews may have bulked bigger than their percentage of the population among dentists, doctors, psychoanalysts, and the like, but they were actually *underrepresented* in the fields of education, social work and nursing. The *perception* that they owned a greater share of German business than was in reality the case was, of course, deliberately put forward to the people of Germany by the Nazis, who knew perfectly well that they were lying to win votes by appealing to prejudice.

Another explanation offered for Hitler's rise to power is the gradual collapse of German democracy under the Weimar Republic. To begin with, it is by no means clear that this is the 'fact' it is so often assumed to be. Until 1930, there had been a period of political stability in the country, with the Social Democrats, the Centre Party and the Democrats running the country in a stable coalition.

Although the 1930 election produced a state in which no combination of parties that excluded either the Nazis or the Communists could possibly obtain a working majority in the Reichstag, that was a conscious *choice* by German voters. They were tired of the small parties exerting disproportionate power and chose to move towards four main parties. Both the Social Democrats and the Centre Party maintained their vote almost up to the 1933 election, so it was really only the small parties – the Democrats, the National Democrats and the Nationalists – who lost ground during this time. The majority of the electorate had no particular brief for *any* of the parties presented to them, and certainly the 1932 election showed a fall in the Nazi vote and a marked swing to the Communists. Hitler's unashamed defence of a cold-blooded murder of a Communist by the SA was largely responsible for the drop in support for the Nazis, a contradictory reaction for such writers as Ben Hecht, who claim that somehow the German people are inherently attracted to brutality and an authoritarian leadership. The reality is that Germany is now perhaps the *least* likely country in Europe to go Fascist or Nazi.[4]

It is difficult to have much respect for Hindenburg, who was almost certainly senile for at least the greater part of his second term in office as President. On the other hand, his extreme reluctance to make Hitler his Chancellor stands in his favour, as does his dogged attempt to make the Weimar Constitution work in circumstances that would have challenged a more sophisticated politician than him. In the end, Hindenburg's appointment of Hitler as Chancellor, in a coalition with Hugenberg's Nationalist Party, was at least a genuine attempt to find a democratic solution to the problems that faced Germany, *not* some aristocratic manoeuvre to foist a puppet of capitalism or the *Junkers* on an unwilling people.

What alternative did Hindenburg have? He could have asked the Centre Party, the Social Democrats and what small parties remained to form another minority government. He could have brought the Nazis into a coalition with the Centre Party and the Nationalists, which might well have been the best solution of all. None of these scenarios in any sense would have represented either the collapse or even the suspension of democratic government in Germany.

If the Nazis only had gained votes out of the depression, there would have been enough small parties remaining to enable a democratic alliance to be formed from among the Reichstag members. It was the fact that the Communists *also* increased their support, and in the 1932 election, more strongly than the Nazis, which made parliamentary government in Germany without either of the two extreme parties impossible. If Hindenburg had continued in his refusal to appoint Hitler as Chancellor, the likelihood is that the party would slowly have lost support and shrunk to a more manageable size. It would still have been an extremist party, but would have lost the ability to be dangerous. The lives of millions of people would have been saved. The treachery of Papen, victim of his own wounded vanity, was largely responsible for Hindenburg failing to follow his instincts and refuse to appoint Hitler to the top position in Germany. If anyone was a war criminal, it was Papen.

It is also true that the reaction of millions of Germans to the appointment of Hitler as Chancellor was *not* one of despair, hostility or even anxiety. The Social Democrats were certainly concerned about his programme, but they had no idea of the lengths to which he was prepared to go. The Communists positively welcomed his appointment, seeing it as the final act in a drama that would inevitably lead to their own emergence as the new leaders of Germany following a people's revolution. To most Germans, though, Hitler was simply the man who offered a chance of escape from the turmoil and chaos of the past three years. He was regarded as an experiment that was worth the risk, not as the assassin of the parliamentary process. Except among his hard-core supporters, there was little *positive* enthusiasm for Hitler. It was his performance as Chancellor that rallied neutral Germans around him.

At the time, Hitler could even be seen as offering the best chance of a democratic solution to the country's problems. German democracy was certainly in crisis by 1933, but it was in no danger at all of collapsing under the weight of the economic difficulties that beset it. It was instead brutally terminated by Hitler in 1934, and under severe protests by many brave Germans, particularly from the Social Democratic Party.

We now come to the psychological explanations offered for Hitler's accession to power. The most obvious one is his personal charisma and skill as an orator. His style and delivery are not perhaps to a modern taste; the content is definitely far from appealing. On the other hand, to the people who witnessed his oratory he was an electrifying speaker. At a time when the radio, the press and cinema were the chief means of communicating with the masses, Hitler made brilliant use of all three media. In an age when most German politicians were colourless and old-fashioned in their attempts to attract voters, he behaved like a rock star.

His charisma too was so strong that even men who were ordinarily powerful characters were overwhelmed by the force of his personality. On crowds his magic was almost irresistible. An English visitor to Germany once found himself at a Nazi meeting and, after a few minutes of listening, stood up and shouted 'Heil Hitler!' along with the rest of the audience. The somewhat staid German politicians from the mainstream parties had no answer to his electrifying appeal, and no member of their ranks who could step forward on their behalf and win comparable support and adoration. Even the Communists had no one of Hitler's calibre as a speaker or symbol.

On the other hand, as must never be forgotten, the 1932 election had seen the Nazis, in spite of Hitler's undoubted magnetism and oratorical skills, lose ground and appear to be no longer capable of winning power. It is also worth remembering that even in the 1933 election, he was unable to win more than 44% of the vote. The *majority* of the German electorate *never* voted for Hitler. Without the collaboration of Hugenberg and Papen, he would have remained an outsider, still unable to enter the highest position in the land. Charisma and oratorical skill alone were not enough to bring Hitler to power and, though they undoubtedly help to explain his popularity to an extent, they are not enough in themselves to account for his ultimate success.

Another reason that has sometimes been put forward is the alleged greater skill at propaganda displayed by the Nazis. It is difficult for us today to take seriously the frequently vacuous and even repulsive *content* of much of the 'message', and it is also doubtful whether it was actually better than the rival propaganda put out by the Communists, who had been using its power brilliantly for twenty years. Even the Social Democrats produced some pretty impressive propaganda efforts. Although the Nazis undoubtedly *were* skilled propagandists, particularly Goebbels, they were not significantly better than their two principal rivals for the working class vote. The propaganda theory therefore fails completely to explain the astonishing rise to power of Adolf Hitler.

The two remaining psychological theories, despite their relative vagueness, are in fact among the most plausible explanations for Hitler's success. The first is the German longing for 'strong' government. Abraham Lincoln might have said once, 'Strong government is no substitute for good government', but millions of Germans found the impossibility of taking radical measures to end the economic crisis harder to understand than the depression itself. For three years they watched a succession of leaders try and fail to build a stable government, and at least the Nazis offered them that. The Communists also held the same appeal for a number of people, well aware that both parties were profoundly anti-democratic and would certainly introduce an authoritarian government if they were successful.

Some commentators have claimed that the Germans, at least during this period of their history, longed for deference and subordination to authority. The curious story of the 'Captain of Köpenick' is often adduced as proof of this. This remarkable man dressed up in an officer's uniform under the Kaiser and marched the townsfolk around, giving them ridiculous orders, before his imposture was finally detected and he was arrested. Certainly there were people in Germany who genuinely longed for an authoritarian state, but the mass of the population felt quite differently. It was not order, but stability, that they craved. They would have preferred a democratic regime to succeed and passively accepted Hitler's rise to power rather than showing any great enthusiasm for the man or his ideas. Such genuine cross-party appeal did not come until later, around 1935. The Germans might have wanted 'strong' government but that was certainly anything but an approval of brutal, repressive policies. To the ordinary German, strong government meant simply sorting out the chaos in the economy and putting people back to work again. They most certainly did *not* want the totalitarian state with which they were finally burdened.

The final psychological theory is the desire for greater national self-esteem by the German people. Defeated in 1918, stripped of large sections of land, victims of an Allied war crime in the deliberate maintenance of an illegal blockade long after the Armistice had been signed – a crime that led to the death of thousands of Germans by starvation – and treated as the outcast of Europe, they certainly did feel resentment and wanted to be once more the proud and confident nation they had been before the First World War. On the other hand, from 1924 onwards, Stresemann in particular had managed to lift them up again to the point where they were full of pride and anything but anxious to engage in wars of revenge. It was only the economic collapse in 1929 that forced them once more to lose self-respect.

Hitler certainly appealed to that particular desire of the German people more successfully than any of his rivals. To some extent, the desire for German self-esteem really did play a part in his rise to power, though even that did not stop them from turning away from him at the 1932 general election. A sympathetic British observer quoted a German woman who told him in 1933 'I assure you this is the first time we have felt safe for fourteen years'.[5] Another witness, described by the same author as 'a cultured German high up in the Nazi councils' remarked that 'Hitler has given us back the feeling that there are more things than trying to make money; he has given us a new faith in ourselves and in our destiny. A new faith in the power of each one of us to act as a unit in the nation'.[6] Another young German told the same writer 'I was fourteen when war broke out. I have never known a stable society. I have lived all my life in a world of chaos'.[7]

Stefan George, certainly not a Nazi sympathiser, gives a graphic picture of the national mood in Germany in the 1920 and 1930s, and the longing for a 'leader':

'He breaks the chains, sweeps order on the rubbish heaps,
Flails the dispersed and scattered back to their home
To the everlasting right where greatness is great once more.
Master again more master, discipline again more discipline.
He fixes
The true symbol on the banner of the people
And leads through the storm and fearful omens
Of the early dawn his loyal troops to the work
Of the awakening day and planting the New Reich'[8]

Our final analysis is of the various 'political' explanations of Hitler's success. The first is the theory that the classless nature of National Socialism contrasted with the class-based politics of their rivals. This is undoubtedly true, but the bulk of the voters who chose Hitler remained working class. The party's disproportionate appeal to youth has also been suggested as a reason, but that fails to explain why older voters also found it an attractive electoral option. The same might be said of its once again disproportionate appeal to women.

Ultimately, Hitler came to power because Germany was in economic crisis and most voters believed that he was the most likely man to remedy the situation effectively. They also saw him as the lesser of two evils, which is why there was also a vast increase in the Communist share of the vote. Germany chose Hitler, and for a while it seemed as if most Germans had no reason to regret their choice.

What constructive achievements can Hitler be held responsible for? He has been accused of being a purely destructive figure, imprisoning and murdering people, starting unnecessary wars, and having no items that can be entered in his favour on the credit side of the balance sheet. This picture of him, though understandable, is a gross caricature. At best, it is naïve and at worst, dishonest.

Perhaps the most lasting aspect of Hitler's rule in Germany is the impact of his 'Green' policies on subsequent thinkers and, eventually, governments. Every major ecological activist from Schumacher onwards was profoundly influenced by what had taken place in Germany. It is perhaps ironic to think of Hitler as the father of the modern environmental movement, yet that is the strange truth of the situation.

Another achievement for which he has also not been given sufficient credit is his economic policies. The effect of Hitler's total rejection of 'classical economics' in favour of a policy of reflation, not deflation; increasing rather than reducing public expenditure; encouraging domestic production of products by subsidising the home manufacturers, rather than allowing them to collapse; refusing to accept the idea that unemployment was unavoidable, still less desirable; choosing to open German borders to imports at a time when every other country was trying to stop foreign goods from entering their country – all these radical measures flew right in the face of conventional economic wisdom. They were not entirely new, and Lloyd George had put forward a less radical version of them at the 1929 British election, but, with the sole exception of the United States, where Roosevelt was also trying new remedies for a desperate situation, no other country in the world was so defiantly experimenting in the economic sphere.

The effect of Hitler's example was not lost on democratic politicians. George Lansbury, leader of the Labour Party until 1935, went to Germany and returned home full of enthusiasm for the Chancellor's proposals. His open praise of Hitler cost him his job, but his successor Clement Attlee, while having the political sense not to give open acknowledgment to the tainted source, quietly adopted many of Hitler's own economic ideas into the new Labour programme.

Oswald Mosley's British Union of Fascists modified their own economic policies in the light of Hitler's outstanding success. They continued to be more akin to Mussolini's movement than Hitler's, but on the economic front at least, it was the German rather than the Italian example that now inspired them.[9]

As well as giving the death blow to classical economics, on the practical level Hitler restored full employment to Germany. At a time when the rest of Europe and most of the world continued to undergo a depression, Germany, under Hitler's new measures, prospered, in defiance of all the economic orthodoxies.

Nor must the effect of such measures as *Kraft durch Freude* upon the people be underestimated. When Hitler came to power, malnutrition was rife, and even actual starvation was not uncommon. Within three years he had turned the situation round to the point where the Germans had the healthiest population in Europe. The outbreak of the Second World War found numerous British men either being rejected altogether for service on the grounds of their health or else having to be fed up for months before it was possible to send them out on active service. The raising of the physical fitness of a whole nation is also not a negligible achievement.

Again, Hitler's ruthless destruction of the old hidebound class structure in Germany is something for which he can only be praised. The power of the German aristocracy was broken for good under Hitler. For the first time in the history of the country, ordinary Germans found themselves in positions of power. It is true that Ebert, the first leader of the Weimar Republic, had previously been a saddler of horses, but he was a rare exception to the rule. Until Hitler, the upper and middle classes were in privileged and even dominant positions. After his arrival, the time of the working classes finally arrived.

Perhaps the most enduring symbol of Hitler is the Volkswagen. This vehicle, whose name means 'the people's car', was deliberately aimed at the working class market. It was originally christened by Hitler the *Kraft durch Freude Auto*, but this cumbersome title never found favour. Instead it became known as the *Volksauto*, and was renamed the Volkswagen after the end of the war. Hitler's involvement in the project was considerable. He reduced car taxes and ordered the construction of a network of motorways, of which 1,500 miles had been completed by 1938. Hitler also came up with the idea for the *Volksauto*, promoted it at every German motor show from 1933 onwards, laid down the basic principles for its construction and even made a number of preliminary sketches. Hitler loved cars and particularly enjoyed driving at speed, occasionally with himself at the wheel. The *Volksauto* was a project that was very dear to his heart.

In spite of Hitler's enthusiasm, the German manufacturers declared that they were unable to produce the car at the price the government wanted. The idea of producing a car for the masses rather than the rich was a revolutionary one in Germany at that time. Hitler simply told the German Labour Front to produce the vehicle. They introduced a finance package for employees to pay in instalments, revolutionary in Germany at that time, which involved a cost of 5 marks a week, including insurance, payable over 5 years. The first Volkswagens rolled off the production line in 1938, and but for the outbreak of war in 1939, Germany might have been the first country in Europe to enjoy mass car ownership among the people. (Though whether the cars would really have been delivered at such a price in large numbers is debatable.) The Volkswagen, of course, continues to be a powerful symbol of German design and the postwar economic success of the country.[10]

Finally, Hitler presided over some of the most stunning examples of German art and architecture. Nazi art is admittedly repulsive and infantile to many, although in the last few years attempts have finally been made to rehabilitate it to an extent. It is, actually, remarkably similar to Art Deco, and was essentially modernistic in its broad thrust. The sculptural work by Thorak and Breker has been unjustly criticised, but the power of Kolbe's work is at long last being rescued from its neglect. The various architectural projects, of which those carried out by Speer and Troost were among the most impressive, are also beginning to be recognised for what they are, superb examples of architecture in the modern style.

Hitler does after all, then, have *some* genuinely constructive achievements to his credit, no matter how much the deficit side of the balance sheet outweighs it. It is now time to turn to his philosophy. We have already seen the extent to which he was influenced by the ideas of Social Darwinism and the eugenics movement. Hitler was certainly not alone in subscribing to these notions, but he implemented them with a ruthlessness never seen before or since. Under Hitler's rule, and with his full approval, a series of measures were taken that increased steadily in their barbarity. Beginning with the compulsory sterilisation of 'racially inferior elements', continuing with the policy of torture and starvation of mental patients, and culminating in the horror of the 'medical experiments' and mass extermination programmes, it can only be said that the effect of these ideas was to bring out the worst possible aspects of human nature, Hitler's own and those who willingly assisted him in his obscene programme.

Hitler's admiration for Nietzsche led him to adopt the philosopher's concept of the *Übermensch*, the 'Superman'. This idea, which Nietzsche had not at all intended in the way the Nazis misused it, led in Hitler's twisted mind to an inexorable connection with 'racial improvement' and the 'survival of the fittest'. It also meshed in with some of his bizarre occult ideas. In a conversation with some of his 'disciples', Hitler remarked: 'Gods and beasts, that is what our world is made of'. [11]

Rosenberg, echoing Hitler's own views, went even further, publicly claiming that the 'creation of a new human type' was 'the task of the twentieth century'.[12] In numerous speeches Hitler himself called for the creation of 'the new man'. One of the most remarkable examples of how far this tendency went is shown most graphically by an extraordinary pamphlet published by the SS. An extract from it reads:

'Just as the night rises against the day, as light and shadow are eternally hostile to each other – so is the greatest enemy of man dominating the earth man himself. Suburban man – that biologically apparently completely identical creation of nature with hands, feet and a sort of brain, with eyes and mouth – is something entirely different, a terrifying creature, more than a stone's throw in the direction of man with features that resemble a human face – but mentally, spiritually lower than any beast ... subhuman – nothing more! For all is not equal which wears a human face! Woe to him who forgets this!'[13]

Hitler, again, remarked that 'those who see in National Socialism nothing more than a political movement know scarcely anything about it. It is more even than a religion: it is the will to create mankind anew'.[14] He also stated:

> The selection of the new Führer class is what my struggle for power means. Whoever proclaims his allegiance to me is, by this very proclamation and by the manner in which it is made, one of the chosen. This is the great significance of our long, dogged struggle for power, that in it will be born a new master class, chosen to guide the fortunes not only of the German people but of the world.[15]

From the moment of his accession to power in 1933, Hitler tried to create his *Übermensch* through a variety of methods. Compulsory sterilisation of people with mental conditions, the prohibition of marriage or sexual relations between Germans and 'non-Aryans', the *Lebensborn* programme for selective breeding, and even the genocide programmes were all designed to raise the 'racial stock' of the country. A longer-term solution was also attempted through the education programme, and in particular through the use of the Napolas, the Women's Universities, and the strange political education establishments known as the 'Order Castles', designed to create the next generation of Nazi leaders. Robert Ley described the type of person these 'Order Castles' were designed to create:

> We want to know whether these men carry in them the will to lead, to be master, in a word to rule. The NSDAP [Nazi Party] and its leaders must want to rule. He who does not take up a total claim to leadership of the people, or is even willing to share it with others, can never become a leader in the NSDAP. We want to rule, to take pleasure in ruling, not in order to become a despot or to pay homage to a sadistic tyranny, but because we unshakably believe that in all things only one man can lead and only one can bear the responsibility. To this one man power also belongs. These men, whom the Order of the NSDAP is thereby bringing honour and power and giving everything which a real man can hope for from life, must on the other hand recognise and preserve in the depths of their hearts that they belong to this Order for better or for worse and must obey it utterly. He who fails or actually betrays the party and its Führer, he who is unable to master the baseness in himself, the Order will destroy. These are the harsh and implacable laws of an Order. On the one hand men may reach to the skies and grasp whatever a man can desire. On the other hand lies the deep abyss of annihilation.[16]

One of the principal reasons that Hitler introduced the Napolas and Order Castles was because of the poor quality of many of the Nazi leaders. Goebbels, Himmler and a few others were relatively able, but far too many were incompetent, particularly Ley, Streicher and even Goering. Privately, Hitler was contemptuous of many of his colleagues, though he had a tendency to support old comrades from the 'period of struggle' even when he knew that they were incapable of carrying out their duties effectively. Hitler's loyalty to his friends was one of his most surprising qualities.

It is too often forgotten that Hitler regarded himself as a revolutionary, *not* a conservative. The fact that he made compromises for tactical reasons he saw always as simply a temporary postponement of his programme, *never* its abandonment. It is largely because of the dominance of the Marxist interpretation of Hitler and National Socialism until recent years that this fact has been overlooked or even suppressed.

His philosophy was based primarily on the Social Darwinist ideas fashionable in his day. However, he also broke genuinely new ground in a number of areas. The popular image of Hitler, to say nothing of many of his public pronouncements on the issue, is that of a conservative who believed in *Kinder, Kirche, Küche*. The reality is altogether more complex, and in many respects it would not be wrong to see him as something of a feminist.

To begin with, Hitler created the largest ever organisation of women, with *real* power and influence. Its leaders, particularly Gottschewski, Diehl and Scholtz-Klink, though loyal Nazis, were in no sense figureheads. All of them showed surprising signs of independent thinking and certainly all three frequently rode roughshod over the opposition of local men. It was their influence on Hitler that led him to prevent the ludicrous attempts to control 'unfeminine' behaviour which the conservative forces in Germany tried to impose after the Nazi victory. Hitler was also fiercely committed to women's education, which improved dramatically under the aggressive, almost confrontational leadership of Hedwig Foerster. The Napolas too, designed to train the future leaders of the Reich, were expressly designed to be as open to women as they were to men. The 'High Women' programme was an even more surprising instance of Hitler's determination to groom women as well as men for the exercise of power. The *Bund Deutscher Mädel* was called 'the great school of a new people's culture'. [17] Hitler encouraged the women of Germany to be physically active, to strive for leadership in their community, and openly called for all positions to be filled on the basis of merit (subject of course to the usual racial criteria and loyalty to National Socialist ideas). He admitted, in private conversations with Himmler, that most of the women in posts of power within the Nazi Party were of a higher calibre than most of their male counterparts.[18] The popular idea of Hitler as a male chauvinist is shown, like so many misconceptions about him, to be untrue.

Hitler and his inner circle regarded themselves, not as conservatives, but radicals. The depth and genuineness of his commitment to modernity has been consistently underrated, or even denied, in spite of the evidence. There is a picture of Hitler sitting in a Bauhaus chair, for instance, in spite of his official disapproval of the movement that had produced it. He was always trying to reach forward in his policies, however much he may have used the appeal of a mythical past as a propaganda tool. His enthusiasm for innovation, his interest in the spread of more efficient technology, his massive building programmes that were to produce some of the most spectacular examples of 20th century architecture – all these are aspects of his personality and his rule that have too often been overlooked. Hitler was a man who looked constantly forwards to an imagined future, not back to a fictitious past. He was, like so many of the thinkers who inspired him, a Utopian dreamer.

Hitler has often been compared with Stalin, but in reality he was much more like Trotsky. Both Hitler and Stalin were opportunists, but whereas with Hitler there was a certain point beyond which he could not or would not compromise his principles, Stalin had no principles at all.[19] Stalin would never have allowed the madness of the Final Solution to take priority over political and, military realities, as Hitler did. Trotsky was a fanatic who put the cause of world revolution above all else.

Since Stalin's own rule in the Soviet Union was as vicious and bloody as Hitler's parallel regime in Germany, it has often been thought that if Trotsky had won the power struggle on Lenin's death, events in Russia would have taken a more liberal and humane course. This is an entirely false impression of Trotsky. If he had won, he would almost certainly have been just as ruthless as Stalin when it came to the repression of enemies at home. The only real difference is that Trotsky would also have brought chaos to the whole of Europe as well by his determination to export the Russian Revolution. This might possibly have led the West to allow Hitler to destroy the Soviet Union, seeing him as the lesser of two evils.

The extent to which the fear of Communism played a significant part in Hitler's rise to power has normally been examined from a Marxist point of view rather than from an objective one. Wrench, for instance, a man who made repeated visits to Germany and was deeply hostile to Nazism, nevertheless felt, following his visit to the Soviet Union, that life in Stalin's Russia was actually *worse* than life under Hitler. He pointed out the absence of poverty in Germany, the lack for the most part of obvious examples of brutal repression, and the *comparative* willingness of Germans to express doubts about the regime as opposed to the total inability of Russians to risk any comment that might be construed as subversive. Germans would at least talk to him whereas Russians were frightened even to be seen with him.[20]

What of Hitler the man, the individual person Adolf Hitler? We have seen already how his whole life was dominated from start to finish by his vision of himself as a great artist. He was perhaps the most bohemian character ever to have been elected to the highest office in any democratic country, and certainly the most bohemian and eccentric Chancellor ever to have ruled Germany, His habits of work were bizarre and dilettante in the extreme, and he had no interest in details at all, preferring to lay down a broad vision and let others get on with the job of carrying it out on his behalf. His character showed a bewildering mixture, with its violent mood swings, choking hatred, simmering resentment against his real and imagined enemies, together with a staggering lack of compassion towards those who became victims of his hostility. He certainly showed a surprising combination of low cunning with lack of grasp on reality. On the other hand, he genuinely loved art and was capable of great tenderness towards those few people who became close to him. To state the obvious (ad absurdum) the negative aspects of his character far outweighed the positive.

What genuine political beliefs, as opposed to purely cynical and opportunistic slogans, did Hitler have? His anti-Semitism, however repulsive and paranoid, was maintained even when it flew in the face of German national interests. Contrary to popular belief, Hitler's socialism, however individual it might have been, was also quite genuine. He certainly hated and despised the upper and middle classes, and commentators during the period when the party was still campaigning for power often noted how little difference there was in the speeches made by Hitler and other Nazis and those made by the German Communists.

Hitler's attitude to the economic aspects of his socialism was essentially that he had created full employment, given Germany job security, built houses, given land rights to the peasants, and opened up the prospect of car ownership to the ordinary people. The more refined process of economic structures could wait until after the war. In the meantime, everyone had a home, a job and enough to eat. None of these things had been true under the Weimar Republic. It is also true that, although the cost was staggeringly high in proportion to the achievement, Hitler destroyed the old class basis of German society for ever. After the Nazis, Germany really was a classless society.

He was also the first major politician to seriously instigate town planning policies and to take "green" measures with regard to the environment and pollution control. He gave the Germans back a sense of pride and national identity, even if this was at the quite unacceptable cost of demonising and then eventually killing large sections of the population who had the misfortune to possess Jewish or other non-Aryan racial characteristics. [21]

No matter how hard one tries to be fair-minded and stress the positive aspects of Hitler's rule, it remains a fact that his regime installed and operated a vast machinery of discrimination, denial of political and civil rights, brutal torture and slave labour, culminating at last in the final horror of the deliberate mass murder of millions. As well as the systematic genocide practised against the Romanies and the Jews, such acts as the medical experiments on not only concentration camp inmates but also, in clear violation of all agreed conventions, on captured prisoners of war as well, put the Nazi regime altogether beyond the pale. The slaughter in cold blood of numerous Russian soldiers and civilians is yet another blot on Hitler's record.

If his political success is unparalleled in German history, and his military success almost unequalled at the height of his power, so too was the spectacular nature of his collapse. On Hitler's suicide, the new German government hastened to surrender as quickly as possible. The legacy of Hitler to his own country was occupation of its eastern half for forty-four years and the complete failure and discrediting of National Socialism as a political creed. Only on the very farthest lunatic fringe of politics are Nazi ideas still taken seriously. Yet, for a brief and astonishing time in human history, they had the power to grip the world.

Notes

1   Malcolm McAlpine, 'Capitalism at the Cross-Roads – II', *Economics and Law: The Machinery of Social Life*, Odhams, 1936

2   Robert Ley, *Fundamental Ideas on Corporate Organisation*, 1935, quoted in McAlpine, op. cit.

3   Dr Faristy, a Czech Jew, talking to Douglas Reed in February 1939. Reed, *Lest We Regret*, Cape, 1943

4   Ben Hecht, 'The Sickness Called Germany', *The Fourth Reich*, Argonaut, New Series No. Two, vol. 138, No. 4213, 1993. This article is perhaps the most distasteful of a series of racist ramblings in this sorry collection.

5   Evelyn Wrench, *I Loved Germany*, Michael Joseph, 1940

6   Ibid.

7   Ibid. Perhaps the most interesting of the series of quotes that Wrench gives from the young man he interviewed was the following remark: 'The Communists missed their great chance. If they had had as good leadership as the National Socialists they would be in power today'.

8   Stefan George, *Das Neue Reich*

9   See, for example, Arthur Raven Thompson, *The Coming Corporate State*, London, 1937

10 Otto Tolischus, *They Wanted War, has* a whole chapter on the Volkswagen, which clearly impressed him deeply.

11 Rauschning, *Hitler Speaks*

12 Alfred Rosenberg, *Der Mythus der 20. Jahrhunderts. Eine Wertung der seelisch-geistigen Gestaltungskämpe unserer Zeit*, Munich, 1934

13 SS, *Der Untermensch*, 1935

14 Rauschning, op. cit.

15 Ibid

16 Robert Ley, *Der Weg zur Ordensburg*, 1936

17 Hans Retzlaff, *Arbeitsmaiden am Werk*, Leipzig, 1940

18 Felix Kersten, *The Kersten Memoirs*, Odhams, 1956

19 This is seen most clearly by Stalin's persistent attempts to conclude a separate peace with Germany, as late as 1943, when Mussolini had fallen from power and the Allies were liberating Italy. Even Ribbentrop, Hitler's Foreign Minister, wanted to sign an agreement with the Soviet leader. It was Hitler, and Hitler alone, who refused for a moment to consider the idea. See: Peter Kleist, *European Tragedy*, Gibbs & Phillips, 1965

20 Wrench, op. cit.

21 See, for instance: a) Ernst Nolte, *Three Faces of Fascism*, Holt, Rinehart & Winston, 1966; b) J M Stern, *The Führer and the People*; c) Martin Broszat, *The Hitler State*, Longmans, 1981; d) D Schoenbaum, *Hitler's Social Revolution*, Doubleday, 1967

Sources and Bibliography

Primary Sources

Archives
Bundesarchiv, Koblenz
Bayerisches Hauptstaatsarchiv, Munich
Hauptarchiv der NSDAP
Imperial War Museum
Wandsworth Libraries, West Hill Branch Special Collection
Wiener Library

Trial Records
Der Hitler-Prozess, Deutscher Volksverlag, 1924
International Military Tribunal, *Trial of the Major War Criminals before the International Military Tribunal, 14 November 1945 to 1 October 1946*

Official Documents
The Cabinet Minutes & Memoranda, 1937–1939
Jane Degras (ed.), *Calendar of Soviet Documents*, Hyperion, 1983
Documents on British Foreign Policy 1919–1939, HMSO, 1950–3
Documents on German Foreign Policy, Series C, The Third Reich, HMSO, 1953–6
M Domarus (ed.), *Hitler, Reden und Proklamationen*, Wurzburg, 1962
Foreign Office, 1937–9
The French Yellow Book, 1938–9, Hutchinson, 1940
Hitler's War Directives, Sidgwick & Jackson, 1964
W Hofer (ed.), *Der nationalsocialismus, Dokumente*, Frankfurt, 1957
Nazi-Soviet Relations, 1939–41, US Department of State, 1948
Jeremy Noakes and Geoffrey Pridham (eds), *Documents on Nazism*, Cape, 1974
Otto Neuburger, *Official Publications of Present-Day Germany*, Washington, 1942
Papers of the Prime Minister's Office, 1937–9
Arnold Toynbee (ed.), *Documents on International Affairs*, OUP, 1939–54

Memoirs, diaries & correspondence of Hitler & his associates
Martin & Gerda Bormann, *The Bormann Letters*, Weidenfeld & Nicolson, 1954
Count Galeazzo Ciano, *Ciano's Diary, 1937–1938*, Methuen, 1952

Ciano's Diary, 1939–1943, Heinemann, 1947

Rudolf Diels, *Lucifer ante Portas*, Deutsche Verlags Anstalt, 1950

Otto Dietrich, *The Hitler I Knew*, Harper Torchbooks, 1967
    Mit Hitler in die Macht, Eher, 1934

Admiral Karl Doenitz, *Memoirs*, Weidenfeld, 1956

Anton Drexler, *Mein politisches Erwachen*, Deutsches Volksverlag, 1923

Hans Frank, *Im Angesicht des Galgens*, Beck, 1953

Hans Frank's Diary, Panstwowe Wydawnictwo Naukowe, 1961

Hans-Bernd Gisevius, *To the Bitter End*, Jonathan Cape, 1948

Joseph Goebbels, *My Part in Germany's Fight*, Hurst & Blackett, 1935
    The Early Goebbels Diaries, Weidenfeld, 1952
    The Goebbels Diaries, Hamish Hamilton, 1949
    The Goebbels Diaries: The Last Days, Secker and Warburg, 1978

Joseph Greiner, *Das Ende des Hitler-Mythos*, Amalthea, 1947

Ernst Hanfstaengl, *Hitler: The Missing Years*, Eyre & Spottiswoode, 1957
    Zwischen Weissem und Braunen Haus, R Piper Verlag, 1970

Ulrich von Hassell, *The Von Hassell Diaries*, Hamish Hamilton, 1948

Rudolf and Ilse Hess, *Prisoner of Peace*, Britons Publishing, 1954

Adolf Hitler, *Mein Kampf*, Hurst & Blackett, 1939
    Hitler's Secret Book, Grove Press, 1961
    The Testament of Adolf Hitler, Cassell, 1961
    Hitler's Table-Talk, Phoenix, 2000
    Hitler's Secret Conversations, Signet, 1961

Brigid Hitler, *The Memoirs of Brigid Hitler*, Duckworth, 1970

Heinrich Hoffmann, *Hitler Was My Friend*, Burke, 1955

Hans Kallenbach, *Mit Adolf Hitler auf Festung Landsberg*, Kress & Horning, 1943

Field Marshal Wilhelm Keitel, *Memoirs*, William Kimber, 1965

Felix Kersten, *The Kersten Memoirs*, Hutchinson, 1956

August Kubizek, *Young Hitler, The Story of Our Friendship*, Allen Wingate, 1954

Kurt Lüdecke, *I Knew Hitler*, Jarrolds, 1938

Benito Mussolini, *Memoirs 1942–1943*, Weidenfeld, 1949

Franz von Papen, *Memoirs*, Andre Deutsch, 1952

Hermann Rauschning, *Hitler Speaks*, Thornton Butterworth, 1939
    Germany's Revolution of Destruction, Heinemann, 1939
    Makers of Destruction, Eyre & Spottiswoode, 1942

Joachim von Ribbentrop, *The Ribbentrop Memoirs*, Weidenfeld, 1962

Ernst Roehm, *Die Memoiren des Stabschefs Roehm*, Uranus Verlag, 1934

Alfred Rosenberg, *Memoirs*, Ziff-Davis, 1949
    Das politisches Tagebuch Alfred Rosenberg, Hans-Gunther Seraphim, 1956

Hjalmar Schacht, *Account Settled*, Weidenfeld, 1948
    Confessions of the 'Old Wizard,' Houghton Mifflin, 1956

Walther Schellenberg, *The Schellenberg Memoirs*, Da Capo, 2000,

Henriette von Schirach, *The Price of Glory*, Frederick Muller, 1960
Albert Speer, *Inside the Third Reich*, Weidenfeld, 1970
  Spandau: The Secret Diaries, Collins, 1976
Otto Strasser, *Hitler & I*, Jonathan Cape, 1940
  Mein Kampf, Heinrich Heine, 1969
Fritz Wiedemann, *Der Mann, der Feldherr werden wollte*, Velbert, 1964

Speeches & Writings of Nazi leaders
Walther Darré, *Das Bauerntum als Urquell der nordischen Rasse*, Eher, 1929
  Um Blut und Boden, Eher, 1940
  *80 Merksütze und Leitspräche über Zucht und Sitte aus Schriften und Reden
  von R Walther Darré*, Goslar, 1940
Gottfried Feder, *Kampf gegen die Hochfinanz*, Eher, 1933
  Die Juden, Eher, 1933
  Das neue Deutschland und die Judenfrage, Leipzig, 1933
  The Programme of the NSDAP, Allen & Unwin, 1934
Joseph Goebbels, *Der Angriff, Aufsätze aus der Kampfzeit*, Eher 1935
  Wetterleuchten, ('*Der Angriff*', volume 2), Eher, 1938
  Kampf um Berlin, Eher, 1933
  Revolution der Deutschen, Stalling, 1933
  Das eherne Herz, Eher, 1943
  Michael, Eher, 1933
Hermann Goering, *Germany Reborn*, Elkin Matthews, 1934
  Reden und Aufsätze, Eher, 1942
Rudolf Hess, *Reden*, Eher, 1938
Heinrich Himmler, *Die SS als antibolschewistiche kampforganisation*, Eher,
  1938
Adolf Hitler, *The speeches of Adolf Hitler, April 1922 – August 1939*, Oxford
  University Press, 1942
  My New Order, Reynal & Hitchcock, 1941
  Hitler's Words, American Council on Foreign Affairs, 1944
Alfred Rosenberg, *Selected Writings*, Cape, 1960
  Letzte Aufzeichnungen, Göttingen, 1955
  Der Mythus des 20 Jahrhunderts, Eher, 1934
  Blut und Ehre, Eher, 1939
Baldur von Schirach, *Die Hitlerjugend, Idee und Gestalt*, Berlin, 1934
Gregor Strasser, *Kampf um Deutschland*, Eher, 1932
Otto Strasser, *Ministersessel oder Revolution?*, Kampf Verlag, 1930

Memoirs of Minor Characters
Sefton Delmer, *Trail Sinister*, Secker & Warburg, 1961
Martha Dodd, *My Years in Germany*, Gollancz, 1939
William Dodd, *Ambassador Dodd's Diary, 1933–1938*, Gollancz, 1941
André François-Poncet, *The Fateful Years*, Gollancz, 1949

Neville Henderson, *Failure of a Mission*, Putnam, 1940
Admiral Nicholas Horthy, *Memoirs*, Hutchinson, 1958
Christopher Isherwood, *The Berlin Stories*, New Directions, 1963
Pauline Kohler, *The Woman who lived in Hitler's House*, Sheridan House, 1940
Albert Krebs, *The Infancy of Nazism: The Memoirs of Ex-Gauleiter Albert Krebs 1922–1933*, F Watts, 1976
Ivan Maisky, *Memoirs of a Soviet Ambassador*, Scribners, 1966
Hans Mend, *Adolf Hitler im Felde*, Eher, 1931
Jessica Mitford, *Hons and Rebels*, Orion, 1999
Sir Oswald Mosley, *My Life*, Thomas Nelson, 1970
G Ward Price, *I Know These Dictators*, Harrap, 1937
Hanna Reitsch, *Flying Is My Life*, Putnam, 1954
Kurt von Schuschnigg, *Farewell Austria*, Cassell, 1938
Austrian Requiem, Gollancz, 1947
Im Kampf gegen Hitler, Molden, 1969
William Shirer, *Berlin Diary*, Knopf, 1941
End of a Berlin Diary, Knopf, 1947
Friedelind Wagner, *The Royal Family of Bayreuth*, Eyre & Spottiswoode, 1957
Walter Warlimont, *Inside Hitler's Headquarters*, Praeger, 1964
Ernst von Weizsäcker, *Memoirs*, Gollancz, 1951
Wilhelm Wulff, *Zodiac & Swastika*, Coward, McCann & Geoghegan, 1973

Secondary Sources

Biographies of Hitler
Martin Broszat, *Hitler and the Collapse of Weimar Germany*, Berg, 1987
Alan Bullock, *Hitler: A Study in Tyranny*, Odhams, 1952
Hitler & Stalin: Parallel Lives, Fontana, 1993
Colin Cross, *Hitler*, Hodder, 1973
Eugene Davidson, *The Making of Adolf Hitler*, Macdonald and Janes, 1978
Joachim C Fest, *Hitler*, Weidenfeld, 1974
Konrad Heiden, *Hitler: A Biography*, Constable, 1936
    Der Fuehrer, Gollancz, 1944
Glen Infield, *Eva and Adolf*, New English Library, 1976
William A Jenks, *Vienna & the Young Hitler*, Columbia University, 1972
Franz Jetzinger, *Hitler's Youth*, Hutchinson, 1955
Ian Kershaw, *Hitler 1889–1936: Hubris*, Allen Lane, 1998,
    Hitler 1936–1945: Nemesis, Allen Lane, 2000,
Walter C Langer, *The Mind of Adolf Hitler*, Basic Books, 1972

Werner Maser, *Hitler,* Allen Lane, 1973
J P Stern, *Hitler: The Führer & the People,* Fontana, 1975
Hugh Trevor-Roper, *The Last Days of Hitler,* Pan, 1955

Biographies of Nazi Leaders:
Charles Bewley, *Hermann Goering & the Third Reich,* Devin-Adair, 1962
Gunther Deschner, *Heydrich: The Pursuit of Total Power,* Orbis, 1981
James Douglas-Hamilton, *Motive for a Mission, The story behind Hess's flight to Britain,* Paragon House, 1986
Joachim C Fest, *The Face of the Third Reich,* Penguin, 1972
Willi Frischauer, *Goering,* Odhams, 1951
  Himmler, Odhams, 1962
Erich Gritzbach, *Herman Goering, The Man & His Work,* AMS, 1973,
Helmut Heiber, *Goebbels,* Hawthorn, 1972
Wolf Rüdiger Hess, *My Father, Rudolf Hess,* W H Allen, 1986
Daniel Lerner, *The Nazi Elite,* Oxford University Press, 1951
Roger Manvell and Heinrich Frankel, *Dr Goebbels,* Simon and Schuster, 1960
  Hess, MacGibbon and Kee, 1971
  Himmler, Putnam, 1965
Richard Overy, *Goering The Iron Man,* Routledge, 1984
Peter Padfield, *Himmler: Reichsführer SS,* Macmillan, 1990
  Dönitz, the Last Führer, Gollancz, 1984
Matthias Schmidt, *Albert Speer: The End of a Myth,* Macmillan, 1986
Robert Smelser, *Robert Ley, Hitler's Labour Front Leader,* Berg, 1992
Ronald Smelser and Rainer Zitelman (eds), *The Nazi Elite,* Macmillan, 1993
Bradley Smith, *Heinrich Himmler,* Stanford University, 1971
Peter D Stachura, *Gregor Strasser and the rise of Nazism,* Unwin Hyman, 1983
Jan Weiner, *The assassination of Heydrich,* Grossman, 1969
A Wykes, *Himmler,* Macmillan, 1973

Biographies of Minor Characters:
K H Absagen, *Canaris,* Hutchinson, 1956
Randall L Bytwerk, *Julius Streicher,* Stein and Day, 1983
Wilfried Darre, *Der Mann, der Hitler die Ideen gab* (Lanz), Isar, 1958
Andreas Dorpalen, *Hindenburg and the Weimar Republic,* Princeton University, 1974
Oswald Dutch, *The Errant Diplomat* {Papen), Arnold, 1940
Saul Friedlander, *Pius XII & the Third Reich,* Knopf, 1966
  Kurt Gerstein: The Ambiguity of Good, Knopf, 1969
D J Goodspeed, *Ludendorff,* Rupert Hart-Davies, 1966
Richard Griffiths, *Marshal Pétain,* Constable, 1970

Nerin Gun, *Eva Braun*, Bantam, 1969
George Hills, *Franco*, Macmillan, 1967
H Höhne, *Canaris*, Secker and Warburg, 1979
Douglas M Kelley, *22 Cells in Nuremberg*, Greenberg, 1947
Ivone Kirkpatrick, *Mussolini*, Hawthorn, 1964
Joachim Kramary, *Stauffenberg*, Macmillan, 1967
J A Leopold, *Alfred Hugenberg*, New Haven, 1967
Stan Lauryssens, *The Man who invented the Third Reich*, (Arthur Moeller van den Bruck), Sutton, 1999
Bernard Wasserstein, *The Secret Lives of Trebitsch Lincoln*, Penguin, 1983
J Wheeler-Bennett, *Hindenburg, the Wooden Titan*, Macmillan, 1936

Historical Studies

General
William Sheridan Allen, *The Nazi Seizure of Power*, Quadrangle Books, 1965
Werner Angress, *Stillborn Revolution: The Communist Bid for Power in Germany 1921–1923*, Princeton University, 1963
Hannah Arendt, *The Origins of Totalitarianism*, Harcourt, 2001
Gordon Brook-Shepherd, *The Anschluss*, J B Lippincott, 1963
Thomas Childers and Jane Caplan (eds), *Reevaluations of the Third Reich*, Holmes and Meier, 1990
Winston S Churchill, *The Second World War*, (6 volumes), Cassell, 1960
H W Gatzke, *Stresemann and the Rearmament of Germany*, Norton, 1969
Alex de Jonge, *The Weimar Chronicle: Prelude to Hitler*, Paddington Press, 1978
William L Shirer, *The Rise & Fall of the Third Reich*, Gallery Books, 2003
    The Nightmare Years, 1930–1940, Bantam, 1985
J L Talmon, *The Origins of Totalitarian Democracy*, Sphere, 1970
Fritz Tobias, *The Reichstag Fire*, Secker, 1963
E L Woodward, *British Foreign Policy: The Second World War*, HMSO, 1962

The Nazi Party
Theodore Abel, *The Nazi Movement*, Atherton, 1966
Martin Broszat, *German National Socialism 1919–1945*, Clio, 1966
Rohan Butler, *The Roots of National Socialism*, Faber, 1941
T L Carsten, *The Rise of Fascism*, Batsford, 1980
    Reichswehr and Politics, OUP, 1966
Thomas Childers, *The Formation of the Nazi Constituency*, Routledge, 1986
J M Diehl, *Paramilitary Politics in the Weimar Republic*, Bloomington, 1977
Conan Fischer, *Stormtroopers*, Harper Collins, 1983

The German Communists & the Rise of Nazism, Macmillan, 1991
The Rise of National Socialism and the Working Classes in Weimar Germany, Berghahn, 1996
Donna Harsch, *German Social Democracy & the Rise of Nazism*, University of North Carolina, 1993
Konrad Heiden, *A History of National Socialism*, Methuen, 1934
Michael J Kater, *The Nazi Party: A Social Profile of Members & Leaders, 1919–1945*, Harvard University, 1983
D Mühlberger, *Hitler's Followers*, Routledge, 1991
Jeremy Noakes and Geoffrey Pridham, *Nazism: A Documentary Reader*, David & Charles, 1983
Dietrich Orlow, *The History of the Nazi Party, 1919–1933*, David & Charles, 1971
The History of the Nazi Party, 1933–1945, Pittsburgh University, 1973
Geoffrey Pridham, *Hitler's Rise to Power*, Harper & Row, 1973

The Nazi Economy

Avraham Barkai, *Nazi Economics*, Berg, 1990
Otto Dietrich, *Das Wirtschaftsdenken im Dritten Reich*, Zentralverlag der NSDAP, 1936
Richard Evans and Dick Geary (eds), *The German Unemployed*, Taylor and Francis, 1986
C W Guilleband, *The Economic Recovery of Germany from 1933 to March 1938*, Macmillan, 1939
P Hayes, *Industry and Ideology*, CUP, 1987
Max H Kele, *Nazis and Workers*, North Carolina University, 1972
Burton Klein, *Germany's Economic Preparations for War*, Princeton University Press, 1959
William Manchester, *The Arms of Krupp*, Bantam, 1970
Alan S Milward, *The German Economy at War*, Athlone Press, 1965
W E Mosse, *Jews in the German Economy, 1820–1935*, Clarendon, 1987
Otto Nathan, *The Nazi Economic System*, Duke University, 1944
Franz Neumann, *Behemoth*, Gollancz, 1942
Richard Overy, *The Nazi Economic Recovery, 1932–8*, CUP, 1986
War & Economy in the Third Reich, Clarendon, 1985
James and Suzanne Pool, *Who Financed Hitler?* Macdonald and Janes, 1979
Arthur Schweitzer, *Big Business in the Third Reich*, UCL, 1964
Albert Speer, *The Slave State*, Weidenfeld & Nicolson, 1981
William Teeling, *Why Britain Prospers*, Right Book Club, 1938
Fritz Thyssen, *I Paid Hitler*, Hodder & Stoughton, 1941
H A Turner, *German Big Business & the Rise of Hitler*, OUP, 1985
Alan Whitford, *Unemployment and the Nazi Revolution*, Barnet Unemployed Group, 1986

The Nazi State

K D Bracher, *The German Dictatorship: The Origins, Structure and Consequences of National Socialism*, Weidenfeld, 1971

R A Brady, *The Spirit & Structure of German Fascism*, Gollancz, 1937

Martin Broszat, *The Hitler State*, Longmans, 1981

Jane Caplan, *Government without Administration: State & Civil Service in Weimar & Nazi Germany*, Clarendon, 1989

Ernst Fraenkel, *The Dual State*, Octagon, 1969

Ian Kershaw, *The Nazi Dictatorship*, Hodder, 2003

Paul Seabury, *The Wilhelmstrasse: A Study of German Diplomats under the Nazi Regime*, University of California, 1954

Peter D Stachura (ed.), *The Nazi Machtergreifung*, Allen & Unwin, 1983
The Shaping of the Nazi State, Croom Helm, 1978

Nazi Art & Culture

Richard Barsam, *Filmguide to 'Triumph of the Will,'* Bloomington, 1975

Julien Benda, *The Betrayal of the Intellectuals*, Beacon, 1955

Ursel Berger, *Georg Kolbe, Leben und Werk*, Mann Verlag, 1990

Arno Breker, *Im Strahlungsfeld Der Ereignisse*, K W Schutz, 1972

Hildegard Brenner, *Die Kunstpolitik des Nationalsozialismus*, Rowohlt, 1963

David Hull, *Film in the Third Reich*, California University, 1969

Siegfried Kracauer, *From Caligari to Hitler: A psychological History of the German Film*, Princeton University, 1947

Barbara Miller Lane, *Architecture and politics in Germany 1918–1945*, Harvard University, 1968

Erwin Leiser, *Nazi Cinema*, Macmillan, 1974

Richard D Mandell, *The Nazi Olympics*, Macmillan, 1971

Roger Manvell and Heinrich Fraenkel, *German Cinema*, Dent, 1971

George Mosse, *Nazi Culture*, Grosset & Dunlap, 1966

Emil Nolde, *Mein Leben*, Dumont Literatur und Kunst, 2000

David Roxan and Ken Wanstall, *The Jackdaw of Linz*, Cassell, 1964

Brandon Taylor and Wilfried van der Will, *The Nazification of Art: Art, Design, Architecture, Music and Film in the Third Reich*, Winchester School of Art, 1990

Robert C Williams, *Culture in Exile*, Cornell University, 1972

Life in Nazi Germany

Ralf Dahrendorf, *Society and Democracy in Germany*, Doubleday / Anchor, 1969

Martin Durham, *Women and Fascism*, Routledge, 1999

Richard Grünberger, *A Social History Of the Third Reich*, Weidenfeld, 1971

C Henry and M Hillel, *Lebensborn: Children of the SS*, Hutchinson, 1976

Clifford Kirkpatrick, *Nazi Germany: its Women and Family Life*, AMS Press, 1979

Claudia Koontz, *Mothers in the Fatherland*, St Martin's, 1987
Walter Laqueur, *Young Germany*, Transaction, 1984
Stephen Roberts, *The House That Hitler Built*, Methuen, 1937
David Schoenbaum, *Hitler's Social Revolution: Class and Status in Germany, 1933–1945*, Doubleday, 1967
Hans Siemsen, *Hitler Youth*, Lindsay Drummond, 1940
Evelyn Wrench, *I Loved Germany*, Michael Joseph, 1940

Nazi Ideology
Jay W Baird, *The Mythical World of Nazi Propaganda*, Minnesota University, 1975
Michael Billig, *Psychology, Racism & Fascism*, Searchlight, 1979
Ernest K Bramsted, *Goebbels & National Socialist Propaganda 1925–1945*, Cresset, 1965
Hans Buchheim, *Totalitarian Rule: Its Nature & Characteristics*, Middletown, CT, 1968
Robert Cecil, *The Myth of the Master Race*, Dodd Mead, 1972
Hedwig Conrad-Martius, *Utopien der Menschenzuchtung: Der Socialdarwinismus und seine Folgen*, Kosel Verlag, 1955
Michael FitzGerald, *Storm Troopers of Satan*, Robert Hale, 1990
Daniel Gasman, *Scientific Origins of National Socialism*, Elsevier, 1971
E H Gombrich, *Myth and Reality in German War-Time Broadcasts*, Athlone Press, 1970
Oron J Hale, *The Captive Press in the Third Reich*, Princeton University, 1964
Alistair Hamilton, *The Appeal of Fascism*, Anthony Blond, 1971
Robert Edwin Herzstein, *The War That Hitler Won*, Hamish Hamilton, 1979
Harold D Lassweil, *Propaganda Technique in the World War*, Alfred Knopf, 1948
Daniel Lerner, *Propaganda in War & Crisis*, Ayer, 1972
George Mosse, *The Crisis of German Ideology*, Schocken Books, 1988
Ernst Nolte, *Three Faces of Fascism*, Holt, Rinehart, Winston, 1965
James Parkes, *The Emergence of the Jewish Problem*, OUP, 1946
Leon Poliakov, *The Aryan Myth*, New American Library, 1977
Eva G Reichmann, *Hostages of Civilisation: The Social Sources of National Socialist Anti-Semitism*, Gollancz, 1950
Joshua Trachtenberg, *The Devil and the Jews*, Meridian Books, 1970
Z A B Zeman, *Nazi Propaganda*, OUP, 1964

The Path to War
Max Beloff, *Foreign Policy of Soviet Russia*, OUP, 1947
Peter Calvocoressi and Guy Wint, *Total War: Causes & Courses of the Second World War*, Allen Lane, 1972

William Carr, *Arms, Autarky & Aggression*, Arnold, 1972
Gordon A Craig, *The Politics of the Prussian Army, 1650–1945*, OUP, 1967
David J Dallin, *Soviet Russia's Foreign Policy*, Yale University, 1942
Gerald Freund, *The Unholy Alliance*, Chatto and Windus, 1957
Hans Gatzke (ed), *European Diplomacy Between Two Wars, 1919–1939*, Quadrangle, 1972
Sven Hedin, *Germany & World Peace*, Hutchinson, 1937
Fritz Hesse, *Hitler & the English*, Allan Wingate, 1954
Klaus Hildebrand, *The Foreign policy of the Third Reich*, University of California, 1973
Eberhard Jäckel, *Hitler's Weltanschauung: A Blueprint for Power*, Wesleyan University Press, 1972
James McSherry, *Stalin, Hitler & Europe, 1933–1939*, World, 1968
  Stalin, Hitler & Europe, 1939–1941, World, 1970
Philip Mosley, *The Kremlin & World Politics*, Vintage, 1960
Arnold A Offener, *America & The Origins of World War II*, Houghton Mifflin, 1971
Robert O'Neill, *The German Army & the Nazi Party*, Heinemann, 1966
A J P Taylor, *The Origins of the Second World War*, Penguin, 1965
Otto D Tolischus, *They Wanted War*, Hamish Hamilton, 1940
John Wheeler-Bennett, *Munich: Prologue to Tragedy*, Macmillan, 1956
Elizabeth Wiskemann*: Germany's Eastern Neighbours*, OUP, 1956
  The Rome-Berlin Axis, Collins, 1966

Violence & Mass Murder

A Polish Doctor, (anon), *I Saw Poland Suffer*, Lindsay Drummond, 1941
George J Annas and Michael A Grodin, *The Nazi Doctors and the Nuremberg Code*, OUP, 1992
Hannah Arendt, *Eichmann in Jerusalem: The Banality of Evil*, Viking, 1965
Wolfgang Benz, *The Holocaust: A Short History*, Profile, 2002
P Berben, *Dachau, 1933–1945*, Norfolk Press, 1973
C Bernadac, *L'Holocauste oublié. Le massacre des Tsiganes*, France-Empire, 1979
Elie Cohen, *Human Behaviour in the Concentration Camp*, Greenwood Press, 1984
Norman Cohn, *Warrant for Genocide*, (The 'Protocols of the Learned Elders of Zion'), Serif, 1990
Edward Crankshaw, *Gestapo: Instrument of Tyranny*, Four Square, 1966
Ute Deichmann, *Biologists under Hitler*, Harvard University Press, 1996
Gerald Fleming, *Hitler and the Final Solution*, Hamish Hamilton, 1985
Henry Friedlander, *The Origins of Nazi Genocide*, University of North Carolina Press, 1995
Max Gallo, *The Night of Long Knives*, Harper and Row, 1972
Martin Gilbert, *The Holocaust: The Jewish Tragedy*, Collins, 1986

Robert Harris and Jeremy Paxman, *A Higher Form of Killing*, Chatto & Windus, 1982

Raul Hilberg, *The Destruction of the European Jews*, Quadrangle 1967

Rudolf Hoess, *Commandant of Auschwitz*, Quadrangle, 1967

Edward Homze, *Foreign Labour in Nazi Germany*, Princeton University, 1967

Michael H Kater, *Doctors under Hitler*, University of North Carolina Press, 1989

Donald Kenrick and Grattan Puxon, *The Destiny of Europe's Gypsies*, Chatto/Heinemann, 1972

Robert L Koehl, *RKFDV: German Resettlement Policy*, Harvard University, 1957

Eugen Kogon, *The Theory & Practice of Hell*, Time Warner, 1988

Nora Levin, *The Holocaust*, Schocken, 1973

Guenter Lewy, *The Catholic Church & Nazi Germany*, McGraw-Hill, 1964

Jean-Pierre Liégeois, *Gypsies: An Illustrated History*, Al Saqi, 1986

R J Lifton, *The Nazi Doctors*, Macmillan, 1986

Deborah Lipstadt, *Denying the Holocaust*, Penguin, 1994

Peter H Merkl, *Political Violence under the Swastika*, Princeton University, 1975

Benno Müller-Hill, *Murderous Science; Elimination by Scientific Selection of Jews, Gypsies, & others*, Germany 1933–1945, OUP, 1988

J N Porter (ed), *Genocide & Human Rights: A Global Anthology*, University Press of America, 1982

Louis Rapoport, *Stalin's War Against the Jews*, Free Press, 1990

Gerald Reitlinger, *The Final Solution*, Valentine Mitchell, 1960
  The SS, Alibi of a Nation, Arms and Armour, 1981

Emmanuel Ringelblum, *Notes from the Warsaw Ghetto*, McGraw-Hill, 1958

Lord Russell of Liverpool, *The Scourge of the Swastika*, Greenhill, 2005

Karl A Schleunes, *The Twisted Road to Auschwitz: Nazi Policy toward German Jews, 1933–1939*, University of Illinois, 1970

Friedrich Schlotterbeck, *The Darker the Night, the Brighter the Stars*, Left Book Club, 1947

Gitta Sereny, *Into That Darkness*, Deutsch, 1974

Max Weinreich, *Hitler's Professors*, Yale University, 1999

Simon Wiesenthal, *The Murderers Among Us*, Heinemann, 1967

Resistance to Hitler

Jane Degras (ed), *The Communist International 1919–43*, Frank Cass, 1960–5

Horst Duhnke, *Die KPD von 1933 bis 1945*, Kiepenheuer & Witsch, 1972

Allen Welsh Dulles, *Germany's Underground*, Macmillan, 1947

L J Edinger, *German Exile Politics*, University of California, 1956

Ian Kershaw, *Popular Opinion & Political Dissent in the Third Reich: Bavaria 1933–1945*, Clarendon Press, 1983

Allan Merson, *Communist Resistance in Nazi Germany*, Lawrence & Wishart, 1985

Detlev Peukert, *Die Edelweisspiraten*, Bund Verlag, 1983

Terence Prittie, *Germans Against Hitler*, Hutchinson, 1964

Gerhard Ritter, *The German Resistance, Carl Goerdeler's struggle against tyranny*, Allen & Unwin, 1958

G van Roon, *German Resistance to Hitler: Count von Moltke & the Kreisau Circle*, Van Nost, Reinhold, 1971

Hans Rothfels, *The German Opposition: An assessment*, Oswald Wolff, 1961

Fabian von Schlabrendorff, *The Secret War Against Hitler*, Putnam, 1965

Wilhelm Ritter von Schramm, *Conspiracy Among Generals*, Scribner, 1957

Articles in newspapers & magazines

Dr Edward Bloch, 'My Patient Hitler,' *Colliers Magazine*, March 15 & 22 1941

Heinrich Fraenkel, 'Is Hitler Youth Curable?' *New Republic*, September 18 1944

Erich Goldhagen, 'Albert Speer, Himmler & the Secrecy of the Final Solution,' *Midstream*, October 1971

Oron James Hale, 'Gottfried Feder Calls Hitler to Order,' *Journal of Modern History*, December 1958

Reinhold Hanisch, 'I Was Hitler's Buddy,' *New Republic*, April 5, 12 & 19 1939

Heinz Linge, 'The Hitler I Knew,' *Chicago Daily News*, Oct–Dec 1955

T W Mason, 'Labour in the Third Reich,' *Past and Present*, No 33, April 1966

'Workers' Opposition in Nazi Germany,' *History Workshop Journal*, No 11

Captain Karl Mayr, 'I Was Hitler's Boss,' *Current History*, November 1941

George Mosse, 'The Mystical Origins of National Socialism,' *Journal of the History of Ideas*, January-March 1961

M Novitch, ''Le génocide des Tsiganes sous le régime nazi,'*Revue de l'Association des médecins Israélites de France*,' no 164, March 1968

Reginald Phelps, 'Before Hitler Came: Thule Society & Germanen Orden,' *Journal of Modern History*, March–December 1963

'Hitler and the Deutsche Arbeitspartei,' *American Historical Review*, vol. LXVIII, no 4, July 1963

R Rürup, 'Problems of the German revolution, 1918–1919,' *Journal of Contemporary History*, 3, No 4, 1968

Albert Speer, 'Interview with Eric Norden,' *Playboy*, June 1971

Larry V Thompson, ''Lebensborn & the Eugenics Policy of the Reichsführer SS,' *Central European History*, March 1971

Appendix: Mein Kampf

The following extracts are taken from the first two sections of *Mein Kampf*. They are not all amongst the most well-known quotations from the work but have been chosen as pointers to Hitler's early influences and thinking that relate to some of the themes discussed in this book.

Volume One - A Reckoning
Chapter I: In the House Of My Parents

At school: the ringleader, early reading

When finally, at the age of fifty-six, he [Hitler's father] went into retirement, he could not bear to spend a single day of his leisure in idleness. Near the Upper Austrian market village of Lambach he bought a farm, which he worked himself, and thus, in the circuit of a long and industrious life, returned to the origins of his forefathers.

It was at this time that the first ideals took shape in my breast. All my playing about in the open, the long walk to school, and particularly my association with extremely 'husky' boys, which sometimes caused my mother bitter anguish, made me the very opposite of a stay-at-home. And though at that time I scarcely had any serious ideas as to the profession I should one day pursue, my sympathies were in any case not in the direction of my father's career. I believe that even then my oratorical talent was being developed in the form of more or less violent arguments with my schoolmates. I had become a little ringleader; at school I learned easily and at that time very well, but was otherwise rather hard to handle. Since in my free time I received singing lessons in the cloister at Lambach, I had an excellent opportunity to intoxicate myself with the solemn splendour of the brilliant church festivals. As was only natural, the abbot seemed to me, as the village priest had once seemed to my father, the highest and most desirable ideal. For a time, at least, this was the case. But since my father, for understandable reasons, proved unable to appreciate the oratorical talents of his pugnacious boy, or to draw from them any favourable conclusions regarding the future of his offspring, he was, it goes without saying, dumfounded by such youthful ideas. With concern he observed this conflict of nature.

As it happened, my temporary aspiration for this profession was in any case soon to vanish, making place for hopes more stated to my temperament. Rummaging through my father's library, I had come across various books of a military nature, among them a popular edition of the Franco-German War of 1870-7I. It consisted of two issues of an illustrated periodical from those years, which now became my favourite reading matter It was not long before the great heroic struggle had become my greatest inner experience. From then on I became more and more enthusiastic about everything that was in any way connected with war or, for that matter, with soldiering

But in another respect as well, this was to assume importance for me. For the first time, though as yet in a confused form, the question was forced upon my consciousness: Was there a difference – and if so what difference – between the Germans who fought these battles and other Germans? Why hadn't Austria taken part in this war; why hadn't my father and all the others fought?

Are we not the same as all other Germans?

Do we not all belong together? This problem began to gnaw at my little brain for the first time. I asked cautious questions and with secret envy received the answer that not every German was fortunate enough to belong to Bismarck's Reich.

This was more than I could understand.

Nature

School work was ridiculously easy, leaving me so much free time that the sun saw more of me than my room. When today my political opponents direct their loving attention to the examination of my life, following it back to those childhood days and discover at last to their relief what intolerable pranks this "Hitler" played even in his youth, I thank Heaven that a portion of the memories of those happy days still remains with me. Woods and meadows were then the battlefields on which the 'conflicts' which exist everywhere in life were decided.

The Arts

The habit of historical thinking which I thus learned in school has never left me in the intervening years. To an ever-increasing extent world history became for me an inexhaustible source of understanding for the historical events of the present, in other words, for politics. I do not want to 'learn' it, I want it to instruct me.

Thus, at an early age, I had become a political ' revolutionary,' and I became an artistic revolutionary at an equally early age.

The provincial capital of Upper Austria had at that time a theatre which was, relatively speaking, not bad. Pretty much of everything was produced. At the age of twelve I saw *Wilhelm Tell* for the first time, and a few months later my first opera, *Lohengrin*. I was captivated at once. My youthful enthusiasm for the master of Bayreuth knew no bounds. Again and again I was drawn to his works, and it still seems to me especially fortunate that the modest provincial performance left me open to an intensified experience later on.

Chapter II – Years of Study and Suffering in Vienna

The effects of early poverty

When after the death of my mother I went to Vienna for the third time, to remain for many years, the time which had meanwhile elapsed had restored my calm and determination. My old defiance had come back to me and my goal was now clear and definite before my eyes. I wanted to become an architect, and obstacles do not exist to be surrendered to, but only to be broken. I was determined to overcome these obstacles, keeping before my eyes the image of my father, who had started out as the child of a village shoemaker, and risen by his own efforts to be a government official. I had a better foundation to build on, and hence my possibilities in the struggle were easier, and what then seemed to be the harshness of Fate, I praise today as wisdom and Providence. While the Goddess of Suffering took me in her arms, often threatening to crush me, my will to resistance grew, and in the end this will was victorious.

I owe it to that period that I grew hard and am still capable of being hard. And even more, I exalt it for tearing me away from the hollowness of comfortable life; for drawing the mother's darling out of his soft downy bed and giving him 'Dame Care' for a new mother; for hurling me, despite all resistance, into a world of misery and poverty, thus making me acquainted with those for whom I was later to fight...

...Even today this city [Vienna] can arouse in me nothing but the most dismal thoughts. For me the name of this Phaecian town represents five years of hardship and misery. Five years in which I was forced to earn a living, first as a day laborer, then as a small painter; a truly meagre living which never sufficed to appease even my daily hunger. Hunger was then my faithful bodyguard; he never left me for a moment and partook of all I had, share and share alike. Every book I acquired aroused his interest; a visit to the Opera prompted his attentions for days at a time; my life was a continuous struggle with this pitiless friend. And yet during this time I studied as never before. Aside from my architecture and my rare visits to the Opera, paid-for in hunger, I had but one pleasure: my books.

At that time I read enormously and thoroughly. All the free time my work left me was employed in my studies. In this way I forged in a few years' time the foundations of a knowledge from which I still draw nourishment today.

And even more than this:

In this period there took shape within me a world picture and a philosophy which became the granite foundation of all my acts. In addition to what I then created, I have had to learn little; and I have had to alter nothing.

The power of Youth

Today I am firmly convinced that basically and on the whole all creative ideas appear in our youth, in so far as any such are present. I distinguish between the wisdom of age, consisting solely in greater thoroughness and caution due to the experience of a long life, and the genius of youth, which pours out thoughts and ideas with inexhaustible fertility, but cannot for the moment develop them because of their very abundance. It is this youthful genius which provides the building materials and plans for the future, from which a wiser age takes the stones, carves them and completes the edifice, in so far as the so-called wisdom of age has not stifled the genius of youth.

The Bourgeoisie

I do not know what horrified me most at that time: the economic misery of my companions, their moral and ethical coarseness, or the low level of their intellectual development.

How often does our bourgeoisie rise in high moral indignation when they hear some miserable tramp declare that it is all the same to him whether he is a German or not, that he feels equally happy wherever he is, as long as he has enough to live on!

This lack of 'national pride' is most profoundly deplored, and horror at such an attitude is expressed in no uncertain terms.

How many people have asked themselves what was the real reason for the superiority of their own sentiments?

How many are aware of the infinite number of separate memories of the greatness of our national fatherland in all the fields of cultural and artistic life, whose total result is to inspire them with just pride at being members of a nation so blessed?

How many suspect to how great an extent pride in the fatherland depends on knowledge of its greatness in all these fields?

Do our bourgeois circles ever stop to consider to what an absurdly small extent this prerequisite of pride in the fatherland is transmitted to the 'people'?

Historical knowledge

An orator, for example, who does not...provide his intelligence with the necessary foundation will never be in a position cogently to defend his view in the face of opposition, though it may be a thousand times true or real. In every discussion his memory will treacherously leave him in the lurch; he will find neither grounds for reinforcing his own contentions nor any for confuting those of his adversary. If, as in the case of a speaker, it is only a question of making a fool of himself personally, it may not be so bad, but not so when Fate predestines such a know-it-all incompetent to be the leader of a state.

The Working Class

These [working] men rejected everything: the nation as an invention of the 'capitalistic' (how often was I forced to hear this single word!) classes; the fatherland as an instrument of the bourgeoisie for the exploitation of the working class; the authority of law as a means for oppressing the proletariat; the school as an institution for breeding slaves and slaveholders; religion as a means for stultifying the people and making them easier to exploit; morality as a symptom of stupid, sheeplike patience, etc. There was absolutely nothing which was not drawn through a mud of terrifying depths.

At first I tried to keep silent. But at length it became impossible. I began to take a position and to oppose them. But I was forced to recognize that this was utterly hopeless until I possessed certain definite knowledge of the controversial points. And so I began to examine the sources from which they drew this supposed wisdom. I studied book after book, pamphlet after pamphlet.

From then on our discussions at work were often very heated. I argued back, from day to day better informed than my antagonists concerning their own knowledge, until one day they made use of the weapon which most readily conquers reason: terror and violence. A few of the spokesmen on the opposing side forced me either to leave the building at once or be thrown off the scaffolding. Since I was alone and resistance seemed hopeless, I preferred, richer by one experience, to follow the former counsel.

A revealing metaphor concerning women

The psyche of the great masses is not receptive to anything that is halfhearted and weak.

Like the woman, whose psychic state is determined less by grounds of abstract reason than by an indefinable emotional longing for a force which will complement her nature, and who, consequently, would rather bow to a strong man than dominate a weakling, likewise the masses love a commander more than a petitioner and feel inwardly more satisfied by a doctrine, tolerating no other beside itself, than by the granting of liberalistic freedom with which, as a rule, they can do little, and are prone to feel that they have been abandoned. They are equally unaware of their shameless spiritual terrorization and the hideous abuse of their human freedom, for they absolutely fail to suspect the inner insanity of the whole doctrine. All they see is the ruthless force and brutality of its calculated manifestations, to which they always submit in the end.

If Social Democracy is opposed by a doctrine of greater truth, but equal brutality of methods, the latter will conquer, though this may require the bitterest struggle.

The Jews...

Today it is difficult, if not impossible, for me to say when the word 'Jew' first gave me ground for special thoughts. At home I do not remember having heard the word during my father's lifetime. I believe that the old gentleman would have regarded any special emphasis on this term as cultural backwardness. In the course of his life he had arrived at more or less cosmopolitan views which, despite his pronounced national sentiments, not only remained intact, but also affected me to some extent...

...Once, as I was strolling through the Inner City, I suddenly encountered an apparition in a black caftan and with black hair locks. Is this a Jew? was my first thought.

For, to be sure, they had not looked like that in Linz. I observed the man furtively and cautiously, but the longer I stared at this foreign face, scrutinizing feature for feature, the more my first question assumed a new form:

Is this a German?

As always in such cases, I now began to try to relieve my doubts by books. For a few hellers I bought the first anti-semitic pamphlets of my life. Unfortunately, they all proceeded from the supposition that in principle the reader knew or even understood the Jewish question to a certain degree. Besides, the tone for the most part was such that doubts again arose in me, due in part to the dull and amazingly unscientific arguments favouring the thesis.

I relapsed for weeks at a time, once even for months.

The whole thing seemed to me so monstrous, the accusations so boundless, that, tormented by the fear of doing injustice, I again became anxious and uncertain.

Yet I could no longer very well doubt that the objects of my study were not Germans of a special religion, but a people in themselves; for since I had begun to concern myself with this question and to take cognizance of the Jews, Vienna appeared to me in a different light than before. Wherever I went, I began to see Jews, and the more I saw, the more sharply they became distinguished in my eyes from the rest of humanity. Particularly the Inner City and the districts north of the Danube Canal swarmed with a people which even outwardly had lost all resemblance to Germans…

…What had to be reckoned heavily against the Jews in my eyes was when I became acquainted with their activity in the press, art, literature, and the theatre. All the unctuous reassurances helped little or nothing. It sufficed to look at a billboard, to study the names of the men behind the horrible trash they advertised, to make you hard for a long time to come. This was pestilence, spiritual pestilence, worse than the Black Death of olden times, and the people was being infected with it! It goes without saying that the lower the intellectual level of one of these art manufacturers, the more unlimited his fertility will be, and the scoundrel ends up like a garbage separator, splashing his filth in the face of humanity…

When I recognized the Jew as the leader of the Social Democracy, the scales dropped from my eyes. A long soul struggle had reached its conclusion…

…Gradually I began to hate them

All this had but one good side: that in proportion as the real leaders or at least the disseminators of Social Democracy came within my vision, my love for my people inevitably grew. For who, in view of the diabolical craftiness of these seducers, could damn the luckless victims? How hard it was, even for me, to get the better of this race of dialectical liars! And how futile was such success in dealing with people who twist the truth in your mouth who without so much as a blush disavow the word they have just spoken, and in the very next minute take credit for it after all.

No. The better acquainted I became with the Jew, the more forgiving I inevitably became toward the worker.

...And Marxism

As I critically reviewed the activities of the Jewish people throughout long periods of history I became anxious and asked myself whether for some inscrutable reasons beyond the comprehension of poor mortals such as ourselves, Destiny may not have irrevocably decreed that the final victory must go to this small nation? May it not be that this people which has lived only for the earth has been promised the earth as a recompense? Is our right to struggle for our own self-preservation based on reality, or is it a merely subjective thing?

Fate answered the question for me inasmuch as it led me to make a detached and exhaustive inquiry into the Marxist teaching and the activities of the Jewish people in connection with it.

The Jewish doctrine of Marxism repudiates the aristocratic principle of Nature and substitutes for it the eternal privilege of force and energy, numerical mass and its dead weight. Thus it denies the individual worth of the human personality, impugns the teaching that nationhood and race have a primary significance, and by doing this it takes away the very foundations of human existence and human civilization. If the Marxist teaching were to be accepted as the foundation of the life of the universe, it would lead to the disappearance of all order that is conceivable to the human mind. And thus the adoption of such a law would provoke chaos in the structure of the greatest organism that we know, with the result that the inhabitants of this earthly planet would finally disappear.

Should the Jew, with the aid of his Marxist creed, triumph over the people of this world, his Crown will be the funeral wreath of mankind, and this planet will once again follow its orbit through ether, without any human life on its surface, as it did millions of years ago.

And so I believe to-day that my conduct is in accordance with the will of the Almighty Creator. In standing guard against the Jew I am defending the handiwork of the Lord.

Index